Marketing the Blue and Gray

MARKETING THE BLUE & GRAY

NEWSPAPER ADVERTISING AND THE AMERICAN CIVIL WAR

LAWRENCE A. KREISER, JR.

LOUISIANA STATE UNIVERSITY PRESS
Baton Rouge

Published by Louisiana State University Press

Manufactured in the United States of America
FIRST PRINTING

DESIGNER: *Mandy McDonald Scallan*
TYPEFACE: *Whitman*
PRINTER AND BINDER: *Sheridan Books*

Library of Congress Cataloging-in-Publication Data

Names: Kreiser, Lawrence A., 1969– author.
Title: Marketing the blue and gray : newspaper advertising and the American Civil War / Lawrence A. Kreiser, Jr.
Other titles: Newspaper advertising and the American Civil War
Description: Baton Rouge : Louisiana State University Press, [2019] | Includes bibliographical references and index.
Identifiers: LCCN 2018046178| ISBN 978-0-8071-7082-3 (cloth : alk. paper) | ISBN 978-0-8071-7156-1 (pdf) | ISBN 978-0-8071-7157-8 (epub)
Subjects: LCSH: United States—History—Civil War, 1861–1865—Press coverage. | Advertising, Newspaper—United States—History—19th century. | United States—History—Civil War, 1861–1865—Propaganda. | United States—History—Civil War, 1861–1865—Economic aspects.
Classification: LCC E609 .K74 2019 | DDC 973.7/88—dc23
LC record available at https://lccn.loc.gov/2018046178

The paper in this book meets the guidelines for permanence and durability of the Committee on Production Guidelines for Book Longevity of the Council on Library Resources. ♾

In memory of my mother,
Joan Catherine Kreiser

CONTENTS

ACKNOWLEDGMENTS

Writing this book was enormously enjoyable because, like many people, I like to thumb through old advertisements anyway, but more so, now, because of the opportunity to thank the many individuals who have provided help and encouragement. My colleagues at Stillman College continue to amaze me with their hard work and good cheer. Amid the many classroom demands, Mary Jane Krotzer and Mark McCormick reminded me to find the time to research and write. When that balance sometimes seemed difficult to achieve, Linda Beito offered a needed perspective. Even though busy with her own work, Kathy Brewer Strayer always took the time to ask how the writing was coming. Dabney Gray inspires me as a professor and, more important, a person.

George Rable encouraged this project from the outset, when I first mentioned that newspaper advertisements made frequent reference to the Civil War. His advice as the idea turned into a manuscript was invaluable, as was his feedback on earlier versions. Beyond the academic world, however, I appreciate the friendship of George and Kay, his wife. The Rables have provided welcome conversation about travels and family, as well as, in the fall, the humor and optimism necessary to cheer for the Cleveland Browns. I also thank Paul Wright for his comments on earlier versions of the manuscript. His deep knowledge about newspapers helped to guide me through the business aspects of advertising. Over the years, Larry Kohl has encouraged me to become a better professor and mentor, and I am fortunate for his example.

At LSU Press, Rand Dotson guided the manuscript through the publication process. His sound editorial advice made the difference as I worked through the revisions, and his patience and support were welcome throughout. Susan Murray is a superb copyeditor, and her sharp eye saved me from any number of stylistic and grammatical mistakes. I also thank Lee Sioles and Catherine Kadair for their help in readying the manuscript for publication.

Not surprisingly, many mid-nineteenth-century newspapers are, today, in extremely fragile condition. The staff at the Library of Congress graciously allowed me access to the titles that have yet to be digitalized for the Chronicling America online collection. At the Western Reserve Historical Society in Cleveland, Ohio, Ann Sindelar, the reference supervisor, patiently answered my questions about their extensive newspaper holdings and directed me to titles that I otherwise would have missed.

The awarding of a faculty residency through UNCF/Mellon in fall 2016 was a wonderful professional opportunity that allowed me the time to research and write and, at the annual conference, to meet with faculty and students at other HBCUs. I am deeply grateful to Cynthia Neal Spence, the program director. That semester, the Summersell Center for the Study of the South at the University of Alabama was my host institution. I thank Kari Frederickson, then-chair of the Department of History, and Joshua Rothman, former director of the Summersell Center, for supporting the project and sharing their vast knowledge of American history.

After reading so many advertising pitches and gimmicks it might be easy to become a bit jaded, but I am fortunate that Alicia, my wife, is as genuine a person as they come. Her love keeps us centered and reminds us, as a family, of what is most important. While I worked on this project, Julia and Anna, my daughters, have gone on to, respectively, college and high school. They are smart and kind, and I am—and always will be—enormously proud of them. Sadly, while I finished the manuscript, my mom died from breast cancer. My dad and my brothers and sister, and their spouses, have shown a strength and faith that I find truly humbling. Mom had a passion for life and inspired everyone around her. The time with her was a gift, and I dedicate this book to her.

Marketing the Blue and Gray

Introduction

In an era when Americans are bombarded by sales pitches on television, radio, and social media, they might be surprised to learn that newspapers were the primary means of advertising during the mid-nineteenth century. Changes in printing technology had dramatically reduced the time and cost to print a paper, causing readership to boom. By the early 1860s, several million Americans subscribed to daily and weekly papers. Advertisers took full advantage of this fast-growing readership and spent more money than ever before to market their goods and services. According to one contemporary observer, the advertising columns had become "among the most important" reading matter in the newspaper. "No man really becomes acquainted even with the news of the day until he has thoroughly perused the advertisements," he explained. "They are the pulse and commerce of universal activity." Another writer agreed, declaring that the notices "are to the reflecting reader the most suggestive and interesting portion of a daily newspaper."[1]

The rapid growth in advertising drew a mixed reaction. Frederic Hudson, the managing editor of the *New York Herald*, delighted in the notices. To his way of thinking, the words and images revealed "the hopes, the thoughts, the joys, the plans, the shames, the losses, the mishaps, the fortunes, the pleasures, the misery, the politics of the people." Henry Sampson saw only the "shames" and the "misery." A former English journalist, Sampson was shocked by the "blasphemy" and "indecency" in American advertisements. He fumed about patent medicines and personal columns that would have been "rejected by the gutter journals" of his native country. Whatever a newspaper reader thought about advertisements, they had eclipsed much else in American culture. George Wakeman, a journalist and writer, marveled that the "names of successful advertisers have become household words, where great poets, politicians, philosophers and warriors of the land are as yet unheard of." Even the "humblest individual" seemingly had taken to writing a sales pitch, in the hope of turning a profit. "To advertise," Wakeman declared, "is the monomania of the time."[2]

According to one British traveler, the obsession with advertising was a distinctly American characteristic. While thumbing through a daily paper in New York during the early 1860s, George Augustus Sala was struck by the sheer number of notices. "Everybody advertises in the States," he observed, "from the Government downwards." There were announcements for, among other items, war bonds, patent medicines, food and drink, and boots and shoes. A boarding notice for a "few respectable single gentlemen . . . mechanics preferred" especially caught his attention. "There you have an epitome of Democracy," he explained. "Every man a gentleman and every woman a lady." In another announcement, an "accomplished young" pianist was enrolling students for his music school. Sala wondered if, when the teacher paid for the advertising space, the clerk looked "at him over the top of the desk to see if he is young, and if he looks accomplished." Probably not, but such salesmanship matched the brashness of the young republic. For better and worse, Sala believed, the "advertising and puffing system" was "as much a part of American civilization as the cocktail, the spittoon, the illusion waist, and the bay rum for the hair."[3]

Despite their prevalence, advertisements from the 1860s have received only a passing mention from scholars. Advertising and cultural historians focus on national campaigns that began with the rise of a consumer culture in the late nineteenth and early twentieth centuries. They recount how advertisers used slick images and words to sell an image of wealth, beauty, and youth, as much as an outfit, a cigarette, or an automobile. Prior to the 1890s, advertisements were "dark and staid" and "deadly dull."[4] Civil War historians, in turn, have long cited newspapers but have ignored the advertisements. William C. Davis reminds readers that newspapers "are the surest windows on the attitudes of the time." All of the "daily affairs of the common people play out in the pages of newspapers, only perhaps in smaller type than the antics of the great and powerful." Studies now exist on the press and popular reactions to military campaigns and political events. Amid a swirl of important-sounding headlines and editorials, advertisements attract little notice. No full-length study of Union and Confederate newspaper notices has been published.[5]

This project analyzes how advertisers marketed the Civil War to sell everything from biographies on Abraham Lincoln to "secession cloaks" and other politically themed fashions; from patent medicines that promised to cure almost any battlefield wound to dioramas on the fighting at Gettysburg. Merchants rarely ran their notices in anything beyond a small typeface, but they drew attention by connecting their wares to national issues. "The Union Forever" headlined an announcement for women's shoes and boots. "Support Southern Industry" led a notice for lamp oil. The goods themselves were not going to determine whether the Union or the Confederacy ultimately won the Civil War, but advertisers offered their readers a sense of turning an everyday purchase into a political activity. A customer might strike a blow for the war effort without ever leaving the storefront. Shopping had become its own form of patriotism, one of the more enduring legacies of the fighting that raged between 1861 and 1865.[6]

Advertisers recognized the war's high stakes and marketed their goods with an eye toward the historical record. Their notices provide insight into the items that contemporary Americans believed important, from their daily lives to national affairs. Publishers offered their histories of the "Union War" and the "Second American Revolution" as a way to record the conflict's vast sweep. As important, the books offered a "permanent record of the fighting" and an "honor roll of participants" for future generations. Other salesmen touted the material quality—and hence durability—of their goods. A political pamphlet that sold at ten cents for fifty copies was meant to last only through an upcoming election. An image of Abraham Lincoln that was "handsomely designed" and printed "on quality stock" was a family keepsake. A set of blank muster rolls was meant for immediate use; a soldier's "diploma," listing dates and locations of service, was meant for the scrapbook. A *carte de visite*—a wallet photograph of today—that an artist had hand-colored was expensive, but it was an heirloom that might pass from generation to generation.

An adage from the rise of the United States as a global power during the late nineteenth century was, "Commerce follows the flag," but advertisers living during the early and mid-1860s would have recognized the sentiment. The war opened to them new and unanticipated markets. Tactical manuals for soldiers and military dictionaries for civilians flooded the "To Sell" columns. In the aftermath of Fort Sumter, dealers in military uniforms and equipment, including muskets and cannons, shopped their goods. Once the fighting began in earnest, embalming services, artificial limbs, and "air tight" caskets all took up advertising space. With financial costs soaring by late 1861 and early 1862, the Union and Confederate governments sold war bonds. Foreshadowing the government-led borrowing campaigns that helped the United States to finance World War I and World War II, the Union and Confederacy touted "patriotic loans" and "investment opportunities." Rebel businessmen pitched shares in blockade-runners, with profits distributed once a ship had slipped into a southern port. That was not always a given, and northern newspapers advertised auctions of cotton, foodstuffs, and other items seized from captured blockade-runners.

• •

The immediacy of advertising to Americans and their daily life was relatively new at the start of the Civil War. In the early nineteenth century, newspapers covered much of their operating expenses through printing contracts and special postage rates offered by the federal government and political parties. Commercial notices ran infrequently because they generated little revenue. Editors still watched these spaces carefully, to avoid "quacks" and "swindlers" who might hurt their reputation. In the *Yazoo City Whig and Political Register,* James Stevens declared that he kept the "For Sale" columns to a minimum. The notices that did run in the Mississippi paper included only those that would be "welcome to the elder members of every family." Another editor admitted that although he accepted a "few advertisements," none would run for more than three or four lines. The emphasis upon the news and the arts kept his paper "highly spoken of throughout the country."[7]

The relatively few advertisements followed the so-called agate rule. Named after the 5½-point type used (about the size of today's baseball box scores), the agate rule attempted to impose a general sense of fairness on the advertising page. A product sold according to what the advertisement said rather than how the advertisement looked. No illustrations were allowed beyond generic images—such as a ship for a steamboat line or a train for a railroad company—because any detail gave merchants who were able to afford a larger space an "unfair" advantage over those who purchased a smaller space. The uniform appearance allowed editors to line up their commercial sections "neatly and systematically," which gave newspapers a "dignified" look.[8]

Helping to maintain a crisp appearance, advertisers purchased newspaper space by the "square." The term originated from the columns used to display the content of a page. Generally, a nineteenth-century newspaper ran from four to eight columns per page, from top to bottom and left to right. The lead story might run several columns, followed immediately by the next story. An advertiser purchased space in one of the columns, including, in many papers, on the front page. Editors grouped these notices together so that an insertion from a merchant or a lawyer would not be sandwiched between articles about a battle and an election. In the daily papers, editors attempted to place advertisements under a general heading for easier access by readers, such as "Dry Goods," "Political," and "Clothing." By contrast, weekly papers ran an eclectic mix of notices (perhaps reflecting the whims of the editor or the order received). An announcement for a political meeting might run alongside those for hoopskirts, books, and foodstuffs. Whether in a daily paper or a weekly paper, the advertising squares ran down a column and were separated by either a thin white space or a black line.[9]

Advertisements became much more numerous during the mid-nineteenth century due to the increasing commercialization of the news. Political funding became less important as the nation expanded. Booming economic, population, and territorial growth encouraged editors to promote community pride as much as political beliefs. By the early 1860s, newspapers relied increasingly upon advertising revenue. Some subscribers grumbled that the "For Sale" columns had grown too long, at the expense of news and other reading matter. Hearing such complaints, one editor replied that it "is in consequence of advertising patronage, more than from any other fact, that newspapers are so numerous, and so freely and widely diffused." The "craving" for more news reminded him of children gathered around a butcher and all calling for the beef's liver. One boy, when "seeing he was not likely to get a slice, says, 'Mr. can't you kill an ox next time that's all liver?'" The analogy became only more relevant as the nineteenth century progressed. By the 1890s, advertisements had replaced subscriptions as the primary source of newspapers' revenue.[10]

Advertisements broke from the agate rule as they jostled for attention, and illustrations began to appear. Photography was a relatively new art during the 1860s, and professionally taken pictures would not appear in newspapers for many decades. Instead, advertisers made images from either engraved wood blocks or wax-marked limestone slabs, a cumbersome and expensive process.

The newspaper sheet was rolled onto the block or slab, transferring the image. The pictures often were rough- and lifeless-looking and the source of some derision. An Indiana editor later described an image of Confederate president Jefferson Davis that had run in a rival newspaper as "absolutely frightful" and hoped "it might not be seen by the ladies." Still, as newspaper editors and advertisers increasingly learned, images have more power to capture the eye than text. By the late nineteenth century, and as the technology became more advanced, images became standard features in newspapers and magazines.[11]

Rather than engravings, advertisers used images formed from combinations of words and letters to attract a reader's notice. In the *Navarro Express,* published in Corsicana, Texas, merchants used several versions of diagonal lines to draw attention to their wares. H. C. Moss ran a dropping diagonal line across an entire column to announce that in men's clothing he had:

Coats,
Pants,
Vests,
Shirts,
Hats,
Boots

Moss went to greater creative lengths to highlight his ladies' dress goods. In the shape of an X that again spaced across the entire column, Moss listed that he had, among other items, robes, linens, trimmings, and silks. Another merchant used a " > " shape running down one-half of a column to announce a stock of clothing to his "old customers, and the community generally."[12]

In the Illinois *Freeport Weekly Journal,* advertisers displayed an especially imaginative use of images and shapes created from words. R. Little, a new merchant, formed his lines in the shape of a step pyramid:

Q
Q
UALI
UALI
TY, STYLE,
TY, STYLE,

AND PRICE. I
AND PRICE. I
HAVE JUST OPEN
HAVE JUST OPEN
ED, UNDER THE BREW
ED, UNDER THE BREW
STER HOUSE, A LARGE AND
STER HOUSE, A LARGE AND
SPLENDID STOCK OF CLOTHES
SPLENDID STOCK OF CLOTHES

The advertisement ran down one-half of a column, so the use of white space made as much of a visual impression as the shape of Little's words. In the same issue, F. E. Dankin, a druggist, formed his words in the shape of a physician's mortar. The shape had the added benefit of reinforcing to the reader that a "Gilt Mortar" hung in front of the store.[13]

Other advertisers used different visual techniques. A merchant in New York City offered a sale of six men's shirts for fifteen dollars. Rather than use text that could perhaps become lost in the shuffle, he used rows of the actual numbers to form the numerals in "6 shirts for 15 dollars." In Brooklyn, a Mrs. Sherman had hoopskirts on sale. To draw readers' attention to that fact, she formed the letters of her announcement in the shape of a hoopskirt. A Rhode Island merchant ran a promotion that printed sideways, the only one on the page to not run from top to bottom. In the *Pittsburgh Daily Gazette and Advertiser,* a clothing store announced "Thompson's Celebrated Skirts." Other advertisements on the same page ran for greater lengths, but the Thompson's notice drew focus because it printed in white letters on a black background.[14]

All of these announcements brought attention and business to newspapers, prompting editors essentially to advertise to get their readers to advertise. They touted the benefits of their circulation and location to merchants. The *Indianapolis Daily Journal* declared, "It's Just the Paper to Advertise In!" because its circulation was "already very large and is increasing very rapidly." In Philadelphia, the *North American and United States Gazette* judged that because it circulated among "so large a portion of the commercial community," it was "perfect" for advertisements from the "business community." The *Daily Rocky Mountain News* gave its subscription numbers at 542 people. The reach was much greater for advertisers, however, because the Denver paper circulated in "every shop and home through the various regions of these valleys and those 'great mountains.'" In New Orleans, the *Black Republican* placed its weekly circulation at 5,000 copies. "Advertisers please notice!" requested the editor.[15]

The key to advertising was persistence, especially in crowded markets. By the summer of 1860, a Missourian found that more and more merchants seemed open for business. Rather than bemoan the competition, existing store owners who wanted to attract business should advertise "Not grudgingly, but extensively and continuously." A Massachusetts paper reminded readers that "What You Sell—'Keep before the People.'" Anyone with an item to sell should "apply to business the cheapest development of intellectual power known, viz: Printer's ink. No investment pays better than JUDICIOUS ADVERTISING." A New York paper declared that advertisements are the "Life of Trade! If you have new goods to sell, let the people know it. Advertise!" Those businessmen who felt too financially stretched to advertise should reconsider. "Many men from small beginnings, through judicious advertisements," one California editor reminded, "have acquired great wealth and influence."[16]

Isaac Singer, who helped to invent and widely distribute the sewing machine in the United States, served as an example of how newspaper advertising might transform, in the words of one newspaperman, "an extremely poor young man into a millionaire." Singer spent large sums of money on advertising his machine, but the expenditure had more than repaid itself. For every ten dollars spent, Singer had "received back one hundred dollars in profits." An anonymous grocer in Colorado might have even beaten Singer's return on advertising. The *Tri-Weekly Miner's Register* reported that the man had spent five dollars on newspaper advertisements and "cleared $100 in business." All of the success stories might have seemed a bit over-the-top to the editor of the *South-Jersey Republican*. Relating a story of a local man who had placed a notice for his lost reading glasses and "went home to find them just where he had left them," he told readers, tongue in cheek, to "See the advantage of advertising!"[17]

Editors constantly reminded readers to browse the advertisements. Like today's, they highlighted the savings gained. One newspaper asked readers to look through its "large number" of advertisements: "A careful perusal would probably pay for your trouble." Another paper cautioned its patrons that if they neglected a close reading of the notices from merchants and grocers, "you may often miss chances for good bargains." The more customers who shopped at a store after a promotion ran, the more important the need to advertise. An Iowa paper offered some "good advice" to its readers. Before going shopping they should always read through the sale notices. They would learn where to go first, because the "man who advertises liberally is a dealer; he sells more goods than old fogies who hide their light under a bushel and is therefore able to sell cheaper." A paper in the Dakota Territory called attention to its listing of goods and services before pointedly declaring, "There are many others whose ads should appear." Crowded stores only prompted the advertising cycle to begin all over again, to the delight of the *Tolland County Herald*. The Connecticut paper thanked its advertisers, who have kept "up the healthy growth of the journal."[18]

By the start of the Civil War, newspapers dominated the advertising business. Editors acknowledged that merchants had other ways to promote their sale goods, including handbills and posters. Yet these printed materials had only a limited circulation and, if distributed on the street, very often ended up trampled underfoot. Notices appearing in a newspaper faced none of these obstacles. They circulated throughout a community, and on a regular basis. "A thousand doors are open to welcome it," one editor declared, "a thousand messengers are daily and weekly seeking the post office to receive it, a thousand people look for its coming, and a thousand read it when it comes." Those last few words were perhaps the most welcome information for any shopkeeper: "Sooner or later every advertisement will be read by every subscriber, who will be interested or influenced by its contents." With a sizeable readership eagerly scanning the newspaper, the rest was up to the individual merchant. "It is true some advertisements are read more than others," the same editor cautioned, "but this is on account of the tact of the advertiser, and not the fault of the newspaper in which they appear."[19]

The federal government also recognized how newspapers dominated the advertising business and saw in them a financial resource to help fight and win the Civil War. In early 1862, the House Ways and Means Committee introduced a bill to tax newspapers at 3 percent on their advertising revenue. This would be one of the few direct taxes on knowledge since the ill-fated Stamp Act, showing the extraordinary federal efforts to raise money for the war effort. Some congressmen protested that smaller papers would suffer from the excise, however, because they relied almost exclusively upon advertisers for their operating budgets. The American people would be the ultimate losers because fewer papers meant less freedom of the press. The committee revised the legislation to exempt smaller, and less financially profitable, newspapers. The amended bill became law that summer and, over the next three years, raised $400,000. For a nation engaged in the most expensive war in its history to that time, the advertisements had made an important financial contribution.[20]

Editors believed that their readers were influenced by the notices, but the corroborating evidence is more elusive. Unlike today, when reams of data exist on consumer behavior, marketing surveys and polls were not conducted during the 1860s. Professional advertising organizations were established only in the early twentieth century; before that, the handfuls of advertising agents worked to negotiate better rates for their clients (rather than to write copy).[21] Comments from American shoppers on their purchases are also thin, even amid the massive outpouring of letters and diaries during the Civil War. A wife might mention that she bought a particular book or medicine, a soldier might record the amount of money he spent for a loaf of bread or pair of socks. Unremarked was whether an advertising notice had initially drawn their attention to these items. Given the spate of recent studies on marketing and the subconscious, consumers might even have been unaware that the notices had influenced their purchasing decisions. To mid-nineteenth-century Americans, the "art of advertising" meant merchants and their creativity rather than customers and their motivations.[22]

Yet, references to advertisements permeated the popular culture during the Civil War years, a reflection of their importance to everyday life. Much like today's readers thumbing through old editions of *Time* and *National Geographic*, mid-nineteenth-century Americans were fascinated by antique newspapers. While on a summer vacation, one journalist read through a weekly from the early 1790s. The pages were "quaint and yellow with age," but he imagined his grandparents reading the same stories. "A newspaper of the last century seizes on the imagination more closely than a book of the same period," he declared. "The newspaper is the mirror of the hour and the day." There were only a handful of notices, but one especially caught his eye. A reward ran for the apprehension of a gang of roughs who had broken into a local store. The thieves had carried off everything they could, including men's and women's clothing, coins, a Bible and other books, and almost 150 ostrich feathers, "some of them large and elegant." The journalist believed this one notice, even though briefly written, had told him more about the past "than whole commentaries of modern moralists."[23]

More Americans spent their time reading novels and serialized stories, and these often made reference to newspaper advertisements. The tragic fate of the fictional Philip Nolan was told in "The Man without a Country," by Edward Everett Hale. Convicted of treason in the early 1800s, the young army officer cries out, "D—n the United States! I wish I may never hear of the United States again!" The judge takes this request literally and banishes Nolan to sail aboard American ships for the remainder of his life, never to hear or read again the name of his former homeland. The sailors censor the few foreign newspapers they allow their prisoner to read, by tearing out any advertisements and political speeches that "alluded to America." In the middle of reading about a battle fought or a speech made during the Napoleonic wars, "poor Nolan would find a great hole, because on the back of the page of that paper there had been an advertisement for a packet for New York, or a scrap from the President's message." That Hale believed it necessary to specifically address the notices or risk the story seeming less credible indicates his presumption of their centrality to his readers.[24]

Other authors used the advertisements as a plot device. Women made up much of the reading public for the "sentimental" literature of the day, and, in the stories, the heroines found new opportunities through the notices. In "Out of Nazareth," a small-town schoolteacher has grown disenchanted with her daily routine after refusing a neighbor's marriage proposal. Seeking a way out of the doldrums, she "chanced upon an advertisement for a governess which seemed to promise something." Appealingly, all the "wisdom of Solomon was not, for a wonder, required of the applicant. She was not expected to sing like Pattl, play like Gottschalk, and dance like Mademoiselle Cubas." She applies for, and receives, the job. After two years in New York, she returns to Nazareth, recognizing that her heart, and her true love, always had resided there. In another short story, a Miss Yuler has just been released from her job as a music instructor at a private academy. The now unemployed teacher finds herself paging through an evening paper, when she comes across "WANTED—A MUSIC GOVERNESS." She had been "merely glancing at the list of new publications when this advertisement met her eye." Deciding to pursue the notice, she finds new employment and adventures.[25]

Joseph Mount, a deaf and mute school teacher, used the advertisements to draw a moral lesson. In an essay that ran in the *Ladies' Repository*, Mount recalled how one of his students, also named Joe, had frantically used sign language to read through the newspaper announcements for his classmates. In one, a "Capt. Joe——" announced his candidacy for sheriff. Joe exclaimed, "There is something wrong here. I 'an't no captain no how'—if I am, I did not know it before, not yet having seen the commission." Below that, another notice announced the marriage of "Joe—— to Miss Sarah White." The young student "uplifted his arms, his face aglow with a blush, and said, 'O, goodness me! I am not married now. Who is Sarah White?'" A third announcement informed the readers that the governor had recently appointed a militia colonel. That was the Joe the boy really wanted to be. "No mute born on American soil, he remarked, had ever been thus titled." That ambition led Mount to remind his readers that such earthy successes were fleeting. He asked them, "Knowest thou that earthly honors are all vanity and vexation of spirit?"[26]

For readers needing a laugh, the advertisements provided rich material. Humor served as an important form of stress release during the Civil War, and the sale columns provided a shared cultural reference. In *Harper's New Monthly Magazine*, James Belcher wrote an essay on typographical errors. The advertisements especially drew his attention because of their "many strange mistakes." Especially worthy of a guffaw was a Philadelphia newspaper that ran a notice for a local politician who would address "the masses." By the accidental misplacement of "merely a 'space' the public was informed that the address would be delivered to 'them asses at National Hall.'" In an article on "Verbal Anomalies," another author also found plenty of examples in the announcements. He reprinted several, including:

> LOST—a leathern lady's portmanteau.
>
> FOR SALE—a piano by a lady about to visit Europe with carved legs in an oak case.
>
> WANTED—a horse for a lady of a dark color, a good trotter and of stylish action. Must be young and have a long tail about fifteen hands high.

Such awkwardly phrased notices helped to show that, although the point of language was not to conceal a person's thoughts, "we must acknowledge that it is very well adapted for that purpose."[27]

One contemporary observer believed that, ultimately, Americans needed the hype found in the newspaper advertisements. Writing under the pen name Molly O'Malley in 1862, she recounted the story of a friend reading through "advertisement after advertisement" to find a finishing school for her daughter. The mother finally settled upon a female seminary that promised to look after the "health, manner, and morals" of the students and provide them with "all the Comforts of home." A few weeks into the term, the daughter wrote to Molly. She revealed that the notice and the reality of the school "do not exactly tally." Discipline was ferocious, food was poor, and living conditions were squalid. "It seems hardly consistent with my regard for the 'dear reader,' to add any thing by the way of a remark on this true school-girl letter," wrote Molly. "But it is so suggestive." She observed that few advertisements actually squared with the facts. Even in notices for the elite schools that might have stood on their reputations, "there is a little humbug." The fault was less with the advertisers than with their readers. Molly argued that Americans "will hardly look at a plain advertisement. The truth is, we love to be humbugged. Among the 'wants of the age' may be classed *humbug*." Even amid the carnage of the Civil War—and, perhaps, because of it—Americans sought, and found, a magic in the advertising pages.[28]

• •

Highly visible and by many individuals eagerly anticipated, the advertisements helped to expand American democracy by offering their readership access to almost every aspect of the Civil War. Even while Union and Confederate armies battled mightily over the nation's future, the sales columns pitched secession badges and military-themed board games. In the Confederacy, fighting to maintain a white man's republic, notices for the sale of slaves ran even while the guns fell silent around Appomattox Court House. In her study of the popular literature during the war, historian Alice Fahs argues that poems, songs, and novels shaped new ways of "imagining" individuals' relationships to the American nation.[29] The sale columns allowed advertisers to engage these evolving concepts of citizenship. They marketed images of Frederick Douglass and biographies of John Brown in abolitionist newspapers, and extended offers to Union and Confederate widows to collect their husband's back pay. By appealing to a diverse readership, the advertising pages reflected a broadening involvement in the war effort.

Participation in the public life came with a cost, and salesmen attempted to manipulate their readers' emotions. Union and Confederate officials certainly did the same, from military recruiters to clergy, politicians to newspaper editors. But advertisers hit the theme from almost every angle. Purchasing a pricey military map to display in the family parlor demonstrated that the buyer had good taste and refinement; a bottle of medicine allowed anxious soldiers to (supposedly) survive virtually any illness and wound. Shopping at a particular store showed a reader's support for the war effort simply because the owner had headed his notice with an appeal to the Union or the Confederacy. Pride, duty, fear, and guilt all combined to sell products during the largest and bloodiest war yet fought in North America.

The advertising men were aggressive, but they did allow their readers choices. In his book on popular culture and the Union home front, historian Matthew Gallman argues that civilians found the guidance necessary to win the war in advice manuals and other printed materials.[30] Newspaper announcements offered a less clear-cut path. In the presidential elections of 1860 and 1864, the parties ran notices touting vastly different visions of the nation's future. Merchants hawked partisan wares for each of the candidates, with campaign biographies and politically themed badges and pins. On the same pages, military recruiters appealed to white men and, in the Union after 1863, black men to volunteer for military service. For the more hesitant patriots, entrepreneurs offered "draft insurance" after the Union and Confederate governments had resorted to conscription to help fill the ranks. Through their sometimes messy choices, the advertising pages offered readers the opportunity to participate—or not—in the war effort.[31]

The sheer scope of advertising during the Civil War is impressive. Because of the difficulty in counting titles—some ran as daily, weekly, biweekly, and even triweekly—the total number of newspapers published during the mid-nineteenth century is still uncertain. Many scholars place the number as high as 3,700 titles, in all forms, by 1861. About 10 percent of these papers appeared daily.[32] I have chosen to examine newspapers that attempted to appeal most widely in readership and advertising. The 550 newspapers researched in this study come from across the Union and the Confederacy. The titles represent a mix of political affiliation, urban and rural readership, and white and African American presses.

My study also draws upon illustrated newspapers, magazines, trade journals, and other contemporary publications because they often talked about the newspaper advertisements. The tone differed depending on the writer's perspective. George Bagby, the editor of the *Southern Literary Messenger*, saw the daily and weekly papers as rivals for advertising revenue. He cautioned merchants that where a "magazine lasts, newspapers are torn up, thrown away, burnt." By contrast, in 1861, the compiler of a newspaper directory declared that readers had no reason to look elsewhere for their needs. From fashions to railroad and shipping schedules, the advertising columns provided a "universal directory to minister to all of our wants." By providing a perspective from outside of the newspaper columns, these writings offer an important context for the meanings and influences of the notices.[33]

Advertisers certainly believed that they reached a wide audience. Scholars sometimes claim that newspapers from the nineteenth century had a narrowly elite appeal. The readership often came from the more prosperous members of a community, who might be able to afford the subscription price; and the white men, who could actively participate in the political life of their city and town. The concern might be valid for the headlines and editorials but not for the advertising pages. Newspapers often were read aloud in taverns, meeting halls, and other public places. Even an illiterate person might garner considerable information from the so-called daily rag.[34] As much as any other printed material, the advertising pages reflect the diversity of American life. Men and women, blacks and whites, rich and poor, foreign and native born, civilians and soldiers, all commingled in the advertisements of the 1860s.

Marketing the Blue and Gray focuses on two themes. The first is how the Civil War influenced the practice of advertising. Chapter 1 analyzes the use of wartime headlines to sell goods. Appeals to ideology and identity promoted everything from clothing to soap. These leads indicate a commitment to the Union and Confederate war efforts, even as the casualty toll mounted. Chapter 2 explores the attempts by advertisers to sell their goods nationally—to the extent that was possible during the early and mid-1860s—especially with war-related images, books, and medicines. Publishing companies exploited the demand among civilians for knowledge on the maneuvers and battles of the armies by listing their war-themed books and maps as family heirlooms and works of art. Recognizing the grim reality of army life, patent medicine dealers exploited fears of death from disease. By buying a bottle of stomach bitters, parents and wives might support the war effort and keep their sons and husbands safe.

The second theme, covered in the last four chapters, is how advertising influenced a particular aspect of the Civil War. Chapter 3 traces the use of political notices to rally support during the presidential elections of 1860 and 1864. Advertisers recognized the deep public interest in who occupied White House and offered everything from partisan trinkets to candidates' biographies and images. The focus then shifts in chapter 4 to how the advertising columns helped raise the largest armies yet seen in North America. That was not always a given, and announcements also ran for the purchase of substitutes and the capture of deserters. Chapter 5 examines the marketing of slavery and perceptions of race. In Confederate newspapers, the phrasing of slave announcements remained slick and self-assured, even while the slaveholders' republic crumbled. Notices in the Union offered sharply different takes on the role of slavery in the coming of the war, and, later, the transition of the freedpeople into American society, depending on whether they ran in a white- or a black-owned newspaper. Chapter 6 analyzes the blurring of the war between the battlefield and home front. Merchants sold uniforms and weapons, while the national governments pitched war bonds. The human cost of the war was never sanitized, with announcements for artificial limbs and embalming services running underneath the front-page headlines that trumpeted "glorious victories."

Although we live in a commercialized age, my study avoids using the nineteenth century to anticipate the twenty-first century. There are parallels between sales notices then and now, especially with lofty appeals mixed with low gimmickry; and a better life balanced against greater appetites. But throughout the manuscript, my primary focus remains on how advertisements provide an understanding of mid-nineteenth-century Americans as a people and a nation modernizing even while they passed through a period of great peril and suffering. To view these notices as an idle curiosity would mean missing a window into how advertisers influenced their readers' lives and society during the most turbulent domestic event in the nation's history.

CHAPTER 1

The War as the Lead

Created in the 1840s, the telegraph helped to transform the American newspaper business by offering readers almost instant access to the news. Editors could now claim to have the scoop on stories that otherwise might have taken weeks to arrive and, when they had, been already out of date. "By Telegraph! Important!! Read!!!" screamed more than one front-page headline. There was some grumbling that perhaps too much news came over the wire. One editor complained that recent dispatches informed the nation that a man had broken his arm while crossing the street and that a grocery store had been "robbed of four wooden hams." The public, however, was hooked on the breaking news. Writing in the autumn of 1861, Oliver Wendell Holmes Sr. described the almost irresistible pull of the newspaper. "If we must go out at unusual hours to get it, we shall go," he wrote. "If it finds us in company, it will not stand on ceremony, but cuts short the compliment and the story by the divine right of its telegraphic dispatches." Holmes believed that Americans might sacrifice much, but "We must have something to eat, and the papers to read."[1]

Over the next four years, advertisers exploited the public's demand for news. In part, they created war-themed headlines that had little, if anything, to do with their products and services. In 1860, "Lincoln Elected! War Anticipated!!" helped to sell dry goods. The next year, "75,000 Soldiers in the Field" and "South Carolina in Arms" led into pitches for groceries and tinware. Beneath the large type, salesmen clamored for customer loyalty. They explained why shopping at their store allowed an individual to strike a blow for the war effort. The layout of the newspaper only helped these merchants because the news and the advertisements often mixed on the same page. As one scholar has recently noted of mid-nineteenth-century public reading materials, the juxtaposition of items "tended to deny (or at least to suppress) their differences." Merchants often blurred the commercial and the political, and their notices provide insights into Union and Confederate perceptions about nationalism, identity, and the war.[2]

THROUGH THE EARLY WAR

White southerners believed that they must accomplish any number of things to gain their independence, but George Fitzhugh argued that winning the advertising war was among the most important. Writing for *De Bow's Review* in late 1860, the southern-born intellectual believed that his "countrymen" had too often fallen victim to northern marketers. With the rise of inexpensively published newspapers in New York, Boston, and other northeastern cities, Yankees had taken to hawking "cheap and worthless literary and manufactured wares." Wanting to stay current with the latest fashions—be they in habit, literature, or clothing—southern readers were "continually deceived, duped, and cheated." Fitzhugh believed that the solution was to begin "fighting the devil with fire." Southerners must "advertise and puff, and drum, too." They must no longer stand on their "excessive Southern dignity, but learn, like Northerners, 'to stoop to conquer.'" This did not mean writing half-truths and flatteries. Rather, "in this jostling, struggling, pushing world, all men of business must push themselves and their trade into notice, or they will be overlooked and downtrodden by their eager and unmannerly competitors." The stakes were high. Should northerners continue to dominate the advertising pages, they "would impoverish equally our minds and purses, and gradually reduce us to the savage state." By Fitzhugh's way of thinking, southern advertisers were in the vanguard of the effort to establish a Confederate nation.[3]

Southern merchants found motivation in the same logic during the winter of 1860–61, when they embraced the secession movement. The commercial incentives were great, with tremendous public enthusiasm among white southerners for the so-called Confederate States. Only weeks after Louisiana had seceded in late January 1861, a distributor of a "coal oil lamp" in New Orleans had recognized the changed political climate. His business was "by far the largest and most complete in the CONFEDERATE STATES OF AMERICA." That spring, the maker of a horse tonic in Richmond was uncertain whether Virginia might secede. Until the politicians reached a decision, he assured readers that his ointment was sold by all "Druggists in the late United States and in the Southern Confederacy." Other store owners wanted their wares associated with the new nation and marketed "Southern Confederacy" cigars, "Southern Star" cotton gins, and "Southern Confederate" boot polish.[4]

When they attempted to explain why a customer should shop for southern-made products, merchants were eager and ready. Many reminded their readers that they were native to the region. A dry goods dealer in Montgomery advertised "Southern Trade from a Southern Market Purchased by a Southern Man." A Louisiana merchant believed the time he previously had spent working in the North should not be held against him. "I am a southern man by birth and education," he assured his customers. Other salesmen claimed to understand the home market better because they were southerners. A hardware merchant in Tallahassee, Florida, sold tools shipped from Charleston. These items were the best suited for the "southern life" because they were made "expressly for the southern trade." Thomas Smith sold "southern boots and shoes" in Thomasville, North Carolina. He knew that he could meet the needs of his customers because his footwear was "particular adapted to the southern market." The claim was short on specifics, but Smith's goal was to bring customers into the store through a shared sense of identity.[5]

Store owners also played upon their readers' perception that northerners were out to gouge them. That Yankees placed profit above almost anything else had deep roots in the South by the mid-nineteenth century. One merchant announced that he had a "wonderful discovery" for catching fish that literally had the bass and carp biting at the hook. To assure readers he was not telling a long tale, he declared, "This is no Yankee humbug or catch penny." Based in Atlanta, the Southern Life Insurance Company provided a specific for what they saw as the "humbug." They sold family policies with "no extra premiums charged as northern companies do." A carriage maker in Houston combined worry over northern greed with pride in southern workmanship. He asked why his neighbors and friends continued to buy "northern shams." Saddles and harness made in the North were "half made" and "come to pieces in the first shower." His items were reliable because they came from "good, honest home made work." Southern merchants stopped short of full-out libel, however, not wanting to alienate any potential customers. Newspaper editors shared no such concerns. During the secession winter, many of them castigated Yankees as abolitionists, infidels, and with any number of other seemingly extreme epithets.[6]

Whether southern-made goods were of a higher quality than a comparable "imported" item depended upon the advertiser. A Mr. Philbricks offered a qualified response for his book and gift store in Charleston, South Carolina. At the "Home Institution," shoppers would find his products "equal, if not superior, to those ordered from northern houses." More merchants responded in the affirmative. One salesman asserted that his soap was "better" than that offered by the Yankees, while another declared his jeans "superior to any northern goods." At the Mississippi Foundry in Port Gibson, Samuel Gilman sold sawmills, gristmills, and other machinery. He reminded potential customers that his equipment was "of Southern invention and manufacture" and possessed a "style and quality unequaled by any Northern importations."[7]

Where Rebel merchants again found agreement was in challenging their readers to put action behind their talk of Confederate independence. The people at home who encouraged their young men to rush to the colors might also strike a blow in defense of the fledgling nation through their pocketbooks. Customers who supported "Equality and Protection" and "No Compromise with Anti-Slavery" should shop for their clothing at stores in Alabama and Florida. Families who believed it necessary to "protect southern rights" should purchase a sewing machine in New Orleans. In Dallas, "Southern Rights and Good Bargains" headlined a promotion for fall and winter goods. Another merchant turned to verse:

> Ho! *Southern* men, who raise your voice,
> And loudly shout for *Southern* rights,
> Yet send your *money north*, from *choice,*
> And thereby strengthen *northern* might!

These blowhards might demonstrate their support of the Confederacy by shopping for, among other items, a "coat, hat, and boots!" According to a craftsman in Georgia, the time had come for men and women who talked about buying southern goods to "prove it."[8]

That any white southerner might help to build the Confederate nation through their shopping decisions offered a broader understanding of citizenship than many politicians and newspaper editors could imagine, or at least express. These officials made clear that they envisioned a white man's republic by casting the southern independence movement as the realm of husbands and fathers. To them, talk of "the people" in building a slaveholding republic was tightly circumscribed by gender. Merchants adopted a more inclusive tone and often appealed directly to women. Notices for ladies' shoes and fashions declared support for "Southern Enterprise and Industry!" and "Southern Goods" that the "South should encourage." In Texas, Mrs. A. M. Kinnen made sure her store was in the forefront of the independence movement. By offering only bonnets made in the South, she was "Ready to do her part in the way of self protection." Female readers were, too, and they supported their fledgling nation by wearing the "Home Manufacture," especially a "secession bonnet." According to one newspaper, the "latest fashion" was made of white and black cotton and ornamented by streamers "with palmetto trees and lone stars, embroidered in gold thread."[9]

Shopping as a political activity carried some risk, and advertisers warned that buying northern-made products only empowered the "black Republicans" to incite racially based violence in the South. A carriage maker in Lynchburg, Virginia, claimed that orders placed with his Yankee competitors went to "enrich and enable the Abolitionists to make Sharpe's Rifles and Spears to send our negroes to kill us." The reference to Sharpe's rifles and spears carried especial significance in the Shenandoah Valley, where John Brown had hoped to use these weapons in his failed attempt to incite a slave rebellion at Harpers Ferry. Yet, merchants never exploited the image of black sexual violence that often streamed forth from the political halls and editorial pages. Rooted in the patriarchal mind-set of the secession movement, politicians and newspaper editors raised the fear that abolitionists would incite the slaves to rape and plunder should the South remain in the Union. From their perspective, secession was a conservative movement because it protected white women from black slaves.[10]

Even amid the talk of civil war and racial violence, southerners should continue to shop, but, according to two Tennessee druggists, just with the right merchants. They ran a notice in the *Memphis Morning Enquirer* cautioning readers to avoid patronizing any of their northern-born rivals. Money spent among these men might as well be sent to "Yankee Emigrant Aid Societies" to buy weapons. At their store, however, potential customers would find only medicines made from the "simple plants that grow in our woodlands, on our river banks, bayous and lakes." Reinforcing the determiner "our," the druggists reminded their readers that they "were born, reared and educated under the benign influences of SOUTHERN INSTITUTIONS."[11]

By early 1861, southern merchants offered their readers a commercialized version of a Confederate identity. Like many other white southerners, they had moved with a remarkable suddenness to embrace their newly formed nation. But, as many recent studies have suggested, Confederate public officials offered historical, social, and even religious rationalizations for secession. Merchants touched upon few of those justifications. Instead, they used the breakup of the American nation to argue that their goods were at least the equal of, if not superior to, those of their northern competitors. They asserted that because they were southerners, they knew the demands of the "home" market and sold at fair price. By that way of thinking, advertisers also pitched that readers might do their part in striking a blow for the new nation simply by shopping.[12]

Robert Barnwell Rhett Jr., the editor of the *Charleston Mercury,* believed the points had gained traction. Writing in the summer of 1861, he claimed that the disposition of southerners to "bestow upon the newborn enterprises a sustaining patronage and all legitimate encouragement, is unmistakable." Merchants, however, needed to continue the fight. He reminded them that they "must seek success where the shrewd Yankees, whom they wish to supplant, have found it—in extensive and judicious advertising." While touring the Confederate States that June, William Howard Russell, a journalist for the London *Times,* was struck by the number of notices run by southern manufacturers. These merchants announced everything from railway cars to "all the smaller articles for which even Southern households find a necessity." To Russell, the promotions indicated the viability of the new nation because they demonstrated the "creation of new branches of workmanship, mechanical science, and manufacturing skill."[13]

••••••••••••••••••••••••••••••

While many southern advertisers readily promoted the Confederate States, the response among northern merchants to the secession crisis was more measured. They referenced national affairs but mostly as a gimmick. A Mr. Smith in Wisconsin trumpeted the "Dissolution of the Union" in promoting his store. In this case, Smith was about to "secede" from his brother's store and open a new business. J. Holmes declared, "Secession in Holmes County." The northern Ohio county was not actually about to leave the Union; Holmes just wanted residents to know that he had received a new stock of fall and winter goods. The owner of a grain mill in Marion, Massachusetts, wondered, "What is to be done with the southern secessionists?" He was uncertain, but customers might ponder the point while they filled their grain bags. In California, William Backman declared, "The Country is Safe." This was because the town of "Red Bluff will not secede" from the Union, and he had lumber for sale.[14]

A few northern merchants went even further and proclaimed the nation at war. Headlines read, "War! War!!," "War Prices," and "Another Battle Fought!!" Two merchants in Indiana and Michigan at least gave some specifics. Edward Malley had "War! In Fort Wayne for 10 Days Longer." Malley was fighting a war against high prices and, to help win the victory, had put his clothing on sale. Lazare's Clothing Store in Marshall declared a "War with Mexico!" The conflict notwithstanding, customers might come browse the merchandise and find considerable bargains. In February, a "bloodless victory!" was announced in Cleveland. This triumph was from men's boots on sale.[15]

Rather than attention-grabbing words, George Taylor, a Philadelphia merchant, believed that moral persuasion sold goods. In the *National Anti-Slavery Standard*, the weekly newspaper of the American Anti-Slavery Society, Taylor promoted his store to customers "WHO ARE UNWILLING TO SUPPORT SLAVERY." Too often, he believed, northerners unwittingly bought goods that benefited plantation owners, such as a shirt made from southern cotton. Taylor, however, stocked only goods produced by "free labor." He acknowledged that buying a shirt or a tablecloth made from someone working on his or her own time might seem a small blow against slavery. Yet even buying a handkerchief made by a free person "is a good testimony against slavery." He hoped that northerners who were willing to support temperance and other reform movements might "lend their influence in a like manner against slavery."[16]

The issues seemed less clear to advertisers in the Border States. Delaware, Maryland, Kentucky, and Missouri were all slaveholding states, but they had more diverse economies than those in the Deep South and close commercial connections to the northern states. Some salesmen echoed calls to buy southern but to their own advantage. A boot and shoemaker in Missouri asked his customers to "Encourage Home Work." The man worked from his own home, so the phrase was more literal than political. Another Missourian declared that "If Every Man Will Do His Duty the Country is Safe." In this case, duty meant customers with outstanding debt paying off their bills. A store owner in Louisville, Kentucky, attempted to please everyone, selling envelopes that hailed "Union Now and Forever" and "The South Now and Forever." He ran the notice well into the spring, an indication that the market in divided loyalties remained brisk.[17]

The ambivalence of northern merchants toward the secession movement continued even as the political crisis deepened. When President Lincoln rejected the idea of a peaceful disunion during his inaugural address in early March, advertisers again pulled from the headlines. "Secession or No Secession!" trumpeted T. Gould in Boston, he had a new spring hat for sale. The owner of a men's clothing store announced, "FORT SUMTER RELIEVED!" By his count, the "10,000 men" of the relief force had declared his outfits the best available. A restaurant owner declared:

AID FOR THE SOUTH
End!

He had a lunch special that residents of the neighborhood would find tasty. To these advertisers, the possibility of a civil war provided another way to market their goods and services.[18]

• •

Following the start of hostilities, southern merchants continued their calls to support "home industry." Summons to boycott Yankee wares became, if anything, even more strident. "Southern Goods Found in Abundance," headed one advertisement for a dry goods store. Shoppers might find anything from cloaks, to shoes, to linens. "I want it distinctly understood," the store owner declared, "that I have No Yankee goods. Nor do I want them, for none but Black Yankees will keep them." A toilet soap company in Richmond proudly boasted that it used raw materials from the South, making its product "Equal to any in the North." Should a reader wonder about the comparison, the company hastened to add: "This establishment has no connection with any house in the North." Other notices sounded the now familiar theme that through the purchase of southern-made products, customers avoided "Yankee humbug" and encouraged "Southern Manufacturers."[19]

Fort Sumter, the opening battle of the war, offered a new and hopefully golden opportunity for Confederate advertisers. The Union-held fort at the entrance to Charleston harbor surrendered after a two-day bombardment. Within days, advertisers used the Confederate victory to help sell their goods. In late April, an Arkansas grocer announced:

FORT PICKENS AND FORT SUMPTER SURRENDERED
ARKANSAS LEAVES THE UNION

The headline perhaps reflected some wishful thinking. Arkansas had yet to secede and would not until early May, and Fort Pickens, off the coast from Pensacola, Florida, remained in Union hands throughout the war. Another advertiser announced his goods by proclaiming, "Great Victory! Fort Sumter Taken!" According to a Texas grocer, the capture of the Federal stronghold marked the "Revolution at the South! The First Great Battle!"[20]

Other Confederate triumphs soon followed. A Mississippi grocer used the rout of the Union army during the Battle of Bull Run to announce a sale at his store. The next spring, a Virginia merchant drew upon the battlefield successes of General Thomas "Stonewall" Jackson in the Shenandoah Valley. Considerably outnumbered, Jackson used fast marching and quick thinking to stymie several Federal armies. "Old Stone-Wall Jackson," the merchant gloated, "Gave the Yanks the Devil at Winchester and took six thousand prisoners. The ball is now open and our cause is crowned by glory." Customers might discuss the "latest intelligence" regarding Jackson while shopping at the store. In June, another merchant announced the "Repulse of the gunboats *Naugatuck* and *Galena* within seven miles of Richmond." The Rebel victory prompted him to "offer my customers the best in spring and summer fashions."[21]

Echoing the statements of politicians and newspaper editors, Confederate advertisers treated the ever-tightening Union blockade with a great deal of contempt. An Atlanta merchant wrote that he had goods "Direct from Europe. Blockade, Stone Fleet, and the Rail Splitter to the Contrary Notwithstanding." The headline played upon Abraham Lincoln's reputation as a "rail splitter" in the 1860 presidential election, as well as unsuccessful Federal attempts to close off Charleston harbor by sinking ships filled with stones in the entrance channels. A grocer in Pine Bluff, Arkansas, poked fun at Union efforts to blockade the Mississippi River. He had plenty of "provisions and produce" despite the order of "Uncle Abe's Cabinet" to close off the waterway to southern commerce.[22]

Southern merchants used military-themed headlines to draw attention, but their notices also helped to create patriotic commercial literature. In her study of Confederate nationalism, historian Anne Sarah Rubin argues that southerners sought to establish an intellectual independence from the North. "For Confederates," she writes, "literary independence seemed to function as a symbolic, and frankly, a more attainable, stand-in for political independence." Magazine editors especially picked up the theme, claiming that southerners "need Southern pens to record their fame." They called for their readers to show support by purchasing the works of southern authors. By linking battlefield successes and material wares, Confederate merchants carried a similar message to perhaps an even wider audience. In the phrasing of one newspaper editor, the press, more than any other print material, was the "great medium of communication between the producer and the consumer." The calls to "shop" the Confederacy into its independence found any number of takers. Newspapers reported citizens as "busy shopping" for fashions and accessories that were "most in keeping with the times."[23]

While Confederate salesmen touted military exploits, Union advertisers emphasized patriotism. Almost immediately after the start of the war, they trumpeted the American nation. That was not an obvious decision in times of national crisis through the mid-nineteenth century, when local and family ties ran deeply. In a recent study on nationalism in the Union, Melinda Lawson reminds readers that other than at the ballot box and post office, "most Americans had almost no connection with their national government." To help promote a sense of national community, many merchants drew upon the past. A literary-minded store owner in Vermont found a common touchpoint in Aesop's Fables: "In Union There Is Strength." More merchants found a recent and useable past in the nullification crisis. During the early 1830s, President Andrew Jackson had vowed to use federal force to keep dissatisfied South Carolinians from acting upon their threats of disunion. Playing upon a toast that Jackson had made at a state dinner, advertisers in 1861 proclaimed, "The Government Must Be Sustained!" and "Our Union Must Be Preserved!" A Pennsylvania clothier quoted directly from the former president, declaring, "The Union Must and Shall Be Preserved."[24]

In the *St. Louis Missouri Democrat,* William Kevill referenced the American flag as a symbol of a national unity. The hat salesman reminded his readers that despite political differences before the war:

DO
NOT
DENY
YOUR COUNTRY'S FLAG!

The banner had been won not only by the blood of the Revolutionary generation but by the generations of Americans who had followed. "Is our beautiful ensign a mere rag," he thundered, to be "tired of in so brief a period of our existence as a United Nation? It cannot be!" As long as he had breath, only the "Star Spangled Banner . . . shall ever wave" from his store. Other merchants announced sales with "UNION FLAG AFLOAT!!," "One Country! One Flag!," and "Our Flag Is Hoisted!"[25]

In appealing to a national identity, advertisers emphasized a patriotism through consumption. Potential customers might shop for a bargain while also helping to preserve the Union. A New England merchant explained that in "this great struggle of aggression and injustice against Liberty and Freedom, it is not only a man's duty to defend his Country and Flag, but money should flow as free as water." Any citizen might help in that process by shopping his assortment of "ready made clothing." Families especially might shop for "cool and comfortable" summer clothing for their father or husband in the military in case he was still "'hot' with excitement at the wrongs we suffer at present from a forced civil war." The maker of a "suspension waist and skirt supporter" appealed to the "LADIES' 'HOME GUARDS.'" The garment was a "perfect 'Union' institution" because it united the "Corset, Shoulder-Brace, Anti-Lacer and Skirt Supporter" in one piece. The "Constitution must be Preserved," and every woman might do her part by "wearing these Waists." Other merchants informed readers that they might "Save the Country" by "building yourselves homes" and "maintain our rights" by buying "Wallace's Bread, Cake, and Crackers."[26]

Other northerners—especially the organizers of sanitary fairs—turned to patriotic symbols. These men and women held bazaars in cities across the Union to aid wounded soldiers. To sell tickets, they featured exhibit halls that showcased a combination of new technologies and period pieces. Set alongside the latest harvesters and other pieces of agricultural equipment, clothing, furniture, and knickknacks from an earlier time helped to create a sense of the nation's past and future. The arc from the Founding Fathers to the present generation and beyond appealed to a "selfless patriotism." Whatever their perspective on the war and its progress, northerners were Americans who might come together to help the sick and wounded soldiers. "Open your heart, hand, and purse," requested one editor before a sanitary fair in Pennsylvania. The tightfisted literally were taking medical supplies away from the "poor soldier" and "ought to be ashamed of themselves."[27]

That merchants were not directly aiding the war effort when they sold corsets, cakes, and crackers distinguished their commercial patriotism from the selfless patriotism of the sanitary fares. To them, the connection between patronizing local stores and preserving the Union was an important selling point. That did not seem crass to their readers because shopkeepers did the same thing. One woman wrote that in Washington during the spring of 1861, the flag "floats from every public building and nearly every shop displays some patriotic emblem." Only a few days earlier her sister had gone shopping and "amused herself by saying to everyone: 'You have no flag out yet! Are you getting one ready?' etc. Shopkeepers said in every instance: 'No—well—we mean to have one, we are having one prepared' etc." That summer, a visitor to Chicago wrote that the streets were a sea of flags: "Shops were decorated with them, Ice Cream saloons sported them, and every Indian at the Tobacconists who formerly presented cigars to a weedless public, now waved triumphantly '*Our Flag.*'" She quipped that with the run on the nation's emblem, "patriotism became expensive."[28]

In addition to national pride, battlefield events dominated the headlines in northern advertisements. The Union had suffered defeats at Fort Sumter and Bull Run, yet advertisers turned the reverses to their advantage by emphasizing resolve. The owners of a clothing store in Massachusetts acknowledged that Fort Sumter had surrendered. But "Barnard, Sumner & Co. have not; they continue to sell silks at 37½ cents—a better investment than Southern Confederate bonds!" Turning to verse, Isaac Isaacs in Ohio explained the relationship between the fighting at Bull Run and his clothing store. The story supposedly came from a veteran of the battle who now worked at the store: "As from his mouth he gave it us / At ISAAC'S UNION HALL." After several hours of desperate fighting, a "panic struck our army / And caused it to retreat." The Confederates held the battlefield, but that was all:

> No victory gained the rebels,
> Dearly did they have to pay.
> For the flower of their army
> On the battle-field did lay.

The veteran no longer wished to dwell upon the "horrors" of the battle. Instead, he closed with:

> But ask our friends to UNION HALL
> Where we do good CLOTHING sell.[29]

Fortunately, more promising military news followed for the remainder of 1861 and into 1862. In October, the owner of a clothing store took advantage of the Confederate retreat from the high ground south of the Potomac River and overlooking Washington. "The Stars and Stripes have taken the place of the Secession rag on Munson's Hill," he gloated; "its ramparts have been deserted by the ragged rebels." The "stout hearted and loyal men" now defending the hill looked especially sharp because they were "dressed in substantial and elegant uniforms" available at his store. Another merchant trumpeted that in South Carolina: "A Great Battle Fought at Beaufort. The victory is gained." While the Union army was victorious in the field, customers might enjoy their own triumph by shopping a sale at his business. That spring, an Ohio merchant crowed that New Orleans, a major Confederate port, was about to fall to the Union navy: "While we are waiting to hear the Glorious News, I would call attention to the . . . Large Stock of Boots and Shoes" he had available. The battlefield successes at Beaufort and New Orleans caused another shop owner to announce that the "backbone of the 'secesh' is broken!" While customers looked forward to the "prospect of the speedy downfall of the Rebel army," they should not forget to look over a "wide range" of goods at "inexpensive" prices. During 1862, other advertisers boasted: "Enemy Totally Routed" and the "Rebellion Ended!"[30]

In Boston, a Mr. Jackman adopted an edgier strategy to market men's clothing. Two days after Confederate general John Floyd had abandoned his military command prior to the surrender of Fort Donelson in Tennessee, Jackman created his own headline and announced that the Rebel officer had fled to Canada. He had reportedly hidden in New York before learning that federal authorities were closing in. How had an "Arch Traitor" eluded capture? He was dressed in the "Garb of an 'Honest Man'!" These and other fashions might be found at Jackman's store. As for Floyd, "he may elude justice this time but a day of retribution is coming. Honesty, notwithstanding little practiced, would have been the best policy."[31]

Military headlines presumably helped sell goods, and northern advertisers especially took advantage of the Battle of Antietam. Fought in western Maryland on September 17, 1862, Antietam was the bloodiest single-day battle in American history.[32] Advertisers emphasized the Union victory, with the Confederate army retreating back into Virginia. The horrors of the battle went unmentioned. A merchant in Pennsylvania declared that the fighting is "attracting the attention and awakening the liveliest sensation of delight throughout all of the loyal states and sending dismay in the ranks of the rebels." A store owner in Maine declared "GLORIOUS NEWS! The Rebels have abandoned their position in Maryland but Berry still maintains his Union Crockery store." A shoe and boot maker in Des Moines announced that the Union victory at Antietam made possible his opening a new store. With Confederate general Stonewall Jackson "having recrossed the Potomac with his battered army," there was "no likelihood of his coming to disturb the peaceful citizens of Iowa." General Robert E. Lee had commanded the Confederate army during the Maryland Campaign, but Jackson, with his stunning triumphs in the Shenandoah Valley, had seemingly spooked this advertiser.[33]

Advertisers did not directly address the bloodshed of Antietam and other battles, but some of them played upon popular sentiment for the Union to wage a hard war. Into early 1862, Union armies generally respected property rights in the South, including the ownership of slaves. The federal government made clear that the war was fought to preserve the nation rather than to revolutionize southern society. Many northerners, however, believed that rebels should be punished, an impatience increasingly picked up by advertisers. Their phrasing often veered into the ludicrous, a crudity missing in the announcements that referenced battles. A furniture store in Missouri called for "War to the Knife"—in this case to kill "old credit"—while a dentist in Connecticut declared a "War of Extermination," but against tooth decay. The connections between the war and the items for sale were often tenuous at best. A merchant in Pittsburgh selling wallpaper headlined his notice with, "The Enemy Driven into the Entrenchments. We Shall Show No Quarter." In the meantime, the store will "Take All the Quarters We Can Get." In Milwaukee, a store owner declared that "The Horrid Barbarity of the South" was equaled only by the "Lightening Fly Killer" that he was selling. The distinction likely reflected how a vigorous prosecution of the war would inflict the pain primarily upon southerners, while a battle had already brought grief to many northern families. Whatever the case, advertisers boasted that a hard war would result in a "Great Slaughter" in the price of their goods.[34]

The loose use of words by northern merchants in these and other newspaper notices drew criticism from Louis Stephens, the editor of *Vanity Fair.* He blasted advertisers for their poorly phrased announcements. In an editorial entitled "Reform Needed," he fumed that the "newspaper public are every day outraged by the development of some new species of torture to which the English language is subjected." He was especially critical of an announcement that ran: "Wanted—For the Navy Department, Some Good Propellers." To him, this meant that any person with a bundle of sticks might sell them "to a company which intends adapting them to the back of the Navy Department, as 'propellers.'" Such "imbecility" led him, in 1862, to advertise for a new dictionary. Two of the proposed entries read:

Quack, See Advertisement.
Zany, See Daily Paper.

He promised that subscribers to the tome would experience a sensation "of turning and turning and turning again, until his head will become suddenly and severely turned."[35]

Stephens recognized the power of the notices to draw attention, however, when he ran war news as fake advertisements. Following the arrests of Confederate ambassadors James Mason and John Slidell while sailing for England in late 1861, he had "John Bull" place a notice for a "PEREMPTORY SALE." The Englishman had drawn "lately, in a Raffle, the BIGGEST KIND of an ELEPHANT named THE REBEL AMBASSADORS" and hoped to get rid of it immediately. "If anybody on earth can find anything for it to do," he pleaded, "any room for it, or any good of any sort in any way connected with it, now is the time to secure it at a BARGAIN." That spring, he ran "INFORMATION WANTED" on John Frémont. The Union general had sent no news since assuming command of a military department in Virginia: "Fearing that he has been foully dealt with, or that he has been dealing foully with somebody, the undersigned will gladly receive any information that might be addressed to UNCLE SAM." Stephens had turned the tables on advertisers and their use of fake news, and, in doing so, implicitly acknowledged the wide readership of the notices.[36]

THROUGH THE END OF THE WAR

The tenor of Confederate advertisements changed by mid- and late 1863, with references to specific battles and campaigns virtually disappearing. There were fewer clear-cut triumphs to announce, with the war increasingly turning into a contest of attrition and maneuver. Yet the absence of some of the war's fiercest fighting from the shopping headlines more likely reflects the troubles of southern newspapers. The buying and selling of civilian goods had slowed to a trickle due to a combination of Confederate war production and the Union blockade. By the spring of 1864, a daily newspaper in North Carolina ran only two new advertising squares, one of them for a lost pair of glasses. In a late war edition, Richmond's *Daily Dispatch,* one of the more highly circulated newspapers in the Confederacy, ran only 3½ of 14 columns with advertisements. Many of these notices dealt with auction sales of property and items "lost, strayed, &c."[37]

Paper shortages further shrunk the newspapers and their advertising. By early 1862, white paper made from a mix of wood pulp and rag pulp had all but disappeared. Lacking quality, some editors had to reduce their run from four pages to two pages and to print on a brown paper that strained readers' eyes. Two years later, the price of even this poor paper had risen to almost fifty cents a sheet. "Such prices are ruinous," bemoaned one editor. Wartime disruptions to newspapers' print schedules created other operating woes. Newspapers in the Shenandoah Valley published only sporadically, for example, as Union and Confederate armies swept back and forth. One editor promised that whenever the front lines stabilized, "we expect to make a decided and determined stand." Richmond's *Sentinel* suspended publication for three days in 1863, when a Union cavalry raid threatened the Confederate capital. The paper regretted the "irregularity" in the print schedule but praised the "patriotic men of our office" for helping to man the city's defensive works.[38]

Despite shrinking newspapers and a shrinking nation, merchants continued to identify their goods with the Confederacy. The owners of a women's hat store touted "Confederate bonnets." They offered the "latest and most approved styles" but did not want a reader to think he or she might see goods from London or Paris. Theirs was a "Southern Enterprise." A railroad car manufacturer made clear that his was a "Southern Car Factory." Continuing to link shopping to support of the war effort, the operator of a lumber mill announced "GLORIOUS NEWS!" Customers repairing a fence or building a house benefited the Confederacy, through purchasing his wood. "Now is the time to strike for freedom in the manufacturing line," he explained. A grocer sold more than the sugar and soap that lined his shelves. He offered "Sundries and Southern Rights." And readers of these notices should still not worry that they were being duped by "Yankee Humbug."[39]

Some merchants moved beyond the almost incessant need to declare their products as superior to northern-made items and, instead, competed against their fellow southerners. They sought to reinforce a sense of a distinct identity because shoppers favored Confederate-manufactured products. The owner of a coal mine in North Carolina recognized that readers might have a more ready access to the fuel from local dealers. They should not accept cheaper prices for an inferior product, however. His coal was "undoubtedly the best in the Confederate States." George Brandt made the same claim for his cotton yarn. "The thread is of a superior quality," he declared, "not surpassed by any in the Confederacy." Only slightly more modest was the owner of an iron foundry. Household goods and farm equipment made from his cast iron were at least "equal to any in the Confederacy." Other merchants judged their products as the "BEST IN THE SOUTH" and the "very finest and best . . . in the Confederacy."[40]

Auctions for blockade goods might have cast some doubt on the quality of Confederate-made goods because they often included a large number of "Yankee" and European items. Foodstuffs, clothing, and notepaper, among other items, smuggled from the North and overseas, received frequent mention from "Wholesale Dealers." These goods were not necessarily better than those made in the South; they simply offered shoppers a wider selection. Auction houses claimed that the amount of wares they had for sale was "unsurpassed" and the "largest and most desirable." R. A. Paingle had an "Important Arrival!" of men's and women's clothing in Mobile, Alabama. Shirts, dresses, coats, ribbons, and fabrics all were on sale. These goods, along with the southern-made materials he always had on hand, offered a "larger stock than was brought to this city from the Emporium of our Yankee oppressors." The emphasis on goods from outside of the South brought a Richmond merchant full circle. Under the heading "Blockade Goods," he announced, perhaps tongue in cheek, that he sold only "Goods of Every description manufactured in the Confederacy."[41]

The reference to Yankees as "oppressors" drew attention to the quantity of goods at the Alabama auction, but such jibes became relatively infrequent as the war progressed. Merchants continued to talk about northern "humbug" as a way to establish their own trustworthiness. They more often ignored the Yankees and suggested instead that purchasing a locally made item helped sustain the Confederacy. Aside from military-aged men, potential customers were not likely to pick up a musket to defend their homes. Advertisers rallied readers to shop rather than to fight. By contrast, as the war increasingly turned against the Rebel armies, many other southerners increasingly demonized their Union opponents. In speeches, editorials, and letters, Yankees were vandals, heathens, and a whole range of other disreputable things. Such denunciations braced the Confederates to continue fighting because, to them, military defeat offered an almost unimaginably worse alternative.[42]

Southern merchants were perhaps too successful in their calls to shop, and there were criticisms that the home front had become overly fond of fashions and trinkets. In late 1863, the editor of the *Augusta Chronicle* fumed that while many Confederate soldiers were hungry and poorly clothed, even more civilians were comfortable. "Ladies must eschew fashions and gentlemen their expensive habits," he encouraged. "We must all economise, if we would win our freedom." Early the next year, the *Southern Literary Messenger* reprinted a letter from a "lady correspondent" in Alabama. She lectured that even with the Confederacy in the "throes of mighty agony," women "bow to fashion's shrine, and burn the most costly incense." She urged them to sacrifice rather than spend, "lest sinful levity should lead to thy destruction." Such criticisms do not necessarily indicate a weakening of national morale because more editorials and letters praised the patriotism shown on the home front. But the comments do indicate that merchants and their notices had contributed to public worries over decadence and corruption that their own appeals to a Confederate identity were attempting to surmount.[43]

• •

Upbeat messages characterized Union advertisements as well, but here the attempt was to gloss over internal divisions. On New Year's Day 1863, Abraham Lincoln's Emancipation Proclamation had declared free the slaves in all states still in rebellion against the federal government. The expansion of Union war aims was politically controversial and became a point of contention for the rest of the war (and beyond). Advertisers, though, stuck with what worked and ran headlines featuring the preservation of the Union. Although ideological, sales pitches that emphasized the nation rose above the partisan politics of the day. Republicans and Democrats bitterly disagreed over the destruction of slavery but not over maintaining the American Union. Notices that ran "The Union Must Be Saved," "The Union Forever," and "Hurrah for the Union" drew wide agreement.[44]

Only a few advertisers made reference to the destruction of slavery. An Ohio clothier declared that he had "Good News." That included "The Union, The Constitution, and The Rights of Man," as well as a sale at his store. In April 1864, a Michigan bookseller announced he had "Contraband of War." The term was used by many white northerners to refer to freed slaves as "prizes" rightfully seized from the South. Not by the bookseller, however. He literally had contraband and was selling books seized from a Confederate blockade-runner. A rare direct mention of the Emancipation Proclamation occurred in the *Sunbury American*, a weekly newspaper published in central Pennsylvania. The advertisement for a clothing store ran:

> THE PRESIDENT'S PROCLAMATION—The President's proclamation upon the subject of slavery is now the great theme of conversation. There are more kinds of slavery than one. There is human slavery, slavery to fashion, slavery to appetite, and slavery to bad habits. Among the latter description of slavery may be mentioned the neglect of good taste and Comfort involved in the wearing of inferior garments, when such elegant and economical wearing apparel can be procured at the Brown Stone Clothing Hall of Rockhill & Wilson, Nos. 603 and 605

> Chestnut street, above Sixth. Every man's own sense of good taste and propriety should enter a proclamation of emancipation from all bad and graceless habits.

Even in a society often rife with racism, this merchant had crassly turned a struggle against slavery into a crusade for better fashions.[45]

Advertisers had much more to say about an equally controversial policy: the Union military draft. By 1863, the federal government was threatening to force some men into the ranks if not enough of them volunteered. Merchants made frequent references to conscription because the topic so captured public attention. Whatever they thought about the war effort, northerners understood that their sons and brothers, if not themselves, were potentially subject to the forced enlistment. "The Draft," ran one notice from Joseph Lomard. He wanted readers to know he had the "best material" available for a custom-made coat. Similarly, M. S. Adams declared, "Conscription!" He had just received a new stock of dry goods. In New Hampshire, E. R. Locke screamed: "DRAFT ORDERED! 300,000 MEN CALLED OUT!" Locke was ready with a "large stock" of boots and shoes for sale.[46]

A Mr. Common in upstate New York was one of the few advertisers to address the civil unrest that followed the draft. This took its deadliest form in New York City, where rioters especially focused their anger on the free black population, leaving scores of men, women, and children killed. The summer after the 1863 violence, Common promoted his shoe store with "Another Draft on New York City." For other merchants, the violence at home made the riots off-limits in their advertising. Possibly they worried that a reference to the bloodshed might scare off readers. Fear of alienating potential customers did not come into play, with Democrats generally opposing the draft and its expansion of federal power. By contrast, Union soldiers were scathing in denouncing the rioters as miscreants who encouraged the Rebels and prolonged the war. They would meet violence with violence and desired to cut the troublemakers "down in heaps" and watch them "weltering in their own gore."[47]

Other than the draft riots, however, few topics were too unsettling to commercialize. Some creative merchants wrote their own war news. They ran notices declaring "A Glorious Victory" with the "Surrender of the Whole Garrison of High Prices," and "Another Victory" with the capture of a "heavy stock of family groceries and provisions." Increasingly, they simply fabricated

Union battlefield victories. In late 1862, one merchant declared "Vicksburg Is Ours! The Mississippi Open." Another store owner announced two years later: "Hurray! Fort Sumter Battered Down!" With the "big brick pile removed from our front," he was able to offer low prices. The two Confederate strongholds would eventually fall, but not until much later and after considerable hard fighting. Perhaps most heart-stopping to many northern readers, another merchant declared nearly two months after the surrender of the Confederate army in April 1865, "THE END IS NOT YET!" He, however, meant his sale on clothing continued.[48]

The use of fictitious war news did not always distinguish merchants from journalists. Because reporters were attempting to beat one another into print, they often filed incomplete, and inaccurate, stories. In his study on how contemporary Americans wrote about the Battle of the Wilderness in May 1864, Stephen Cushman demonstrates that editors often published rumors and speculations as truths. They did so less because they failed to understand the significance of the fighting than because its enormity "swallowed up certainty and made a shambles of both promptness and adequacy." Editors were often as "confused and bewildered" about the events at the front as their readers. The fluidness of the war-related news created an uncertainty that advertisers also struggled with and, sometimes, blatantly exploited.[49]

As the war continued, Union generals often found themselves at the center of the sales pitches. Advertisers had used the names of high-ranking military officers to promote their goods earlier in the war, but the risk was high. A military defeat might diminish a general's fame and no longer draw the type of notice an advertiser desired. Messrs. Schapker and Bessing found out as much in the summer of 1862. The two Indiana merchants purchased a yearlong advertisement in the *Evansville Weekly Gazette* for their mercantile store in June. The notice declared Union major general John Pope the "Hero of the Day." There was grounds for the claim, with Pope having won some success in the western theater. Transferred to the East, however, Pope suffered a smashing defeat during the Second Bull Run Campaign that August. For a number of months more, Schapker and Bessing had to smart under the claim that "It is an undisputed fact that General Pope is entitled to any position in the gift of the Government for his untiring energy." Schapker and Bessing had hoped to draw attention to their clothing on sale, but the point was lost amid the ebb and flow of Union military fortunes in northern Virginia.[50]

By early 1864, advertisers had found a seemingly safe bet in Union lieutenant general Ulysses Grant. Newly appointed as general-in-chief of the Union army, Grant had won major victories in Tennessee and Mississippi. He had achieved such a level of national prominence that one newspaper reprinted an advertisement purchased by Grant while working as a store clerk in Illinois during the late 1850s. The editor explained that the advertisement had no financial value, its interest consisting simply in seeing something related to Grant before he had become a Union military hero.[51] Grant made his headquarters with the Army of the Potomac, and the headlines flowed. Even before a spring campaign started, a merchant in West Virginia proclaimed, "Good News from Grant!" He provided no more detail from the front lines but added that customers might also find good news in lower prices at his store. In late May, after the Army of the Potomac had launched a new campaign to capture the Richmond, the Confederate capital, and win the war, two Pennsylvania store owners declared that Grant "is the man to thrash the Rebels." While the general did so, readers should remember that the "store of Steacy and Bauers is the place to buy your goods."[52]

High Union and Confederate casualties followed as Grant ultimately fought his way into Richmond, but the advertising headlines remained upbeat. Grant had seemed stalemated by the late summer of 1864, a lack of progress that caused President Lincoln to despair of being reelected. Individuals with goods to sell, however, continued to see Grant as a way to promote the retail trade. One businessman in late July announced: "General Grant! Richmond invested and Reinforcements arriving!!" The reinforcements were new items that lined the shelves in his dry goods store. The next month, a clothier described Grant as the "hero of many battles" whose "successes are well known." Almost as victorious as the Union general was his store "in selecting the best and most fashionable goods for its customers." These goods included "Silks, Shawls, etc." That winter, after several important fall campaigns and with Lincoln safely elected, R. W. Ludewig blared, "Grant has taken" Richmond, or "expects to soon." Ludewig "HAS ALSO taken possession of his New Store." The site was "well fortified" and bids "Defiance to any Attack in the line of COMPETITION from any prices North, South, East or West."[53]

By the time Grant actually had led the Union army to the capture of Richmond, the use of war-themed news in the advertising headlines had caught the attention of the humorist Robert Newell. Writing under the pen name Orpheus Kerr, Newell satirized much of the Union war effort in fictitious letters to a nephew. In this case, he described a "thoughtful Boston chap, with one of those enlarged business ideas which will yet enable that section to betrade the whole world." The man manufactured "burglar-proof safes" and was an avid reader of the war news. He soon moved to Washington, "read the war-news once more," and ran a notice:

Buy the Celebrated
WASHINGTON SAFE!

Northerners thought "it was the safe they'd read so much about in the papers, my boy, and several hundred were sold." Amid the good military news that ran in the advertising columns by early 1865, northerners might also share a chuckle.[54]

••••••••••••••••••••••••••••

The military defeat of the Confederacy is reflected in many of the advertising columns that appeared in the war's immediate aftermath. Large stretches of southern cities and farms had suffered devastation, and northern-made goods again seemed everywhere. The presence of so much "Yankee Humbug" was, of course, exactly what many southerners had hoped to avoid prior to the war. Yet, in May 1865, with the Confederate surrender at Appomattox Court House only one month earlier, the *Arkansas State Gazette* advertised a hoop-skirt shipped from New York. Customers might find this item in towns and stores "throughout the United States." In New Berne, North Carolina, which was captured by Union forces early in the war, John Conk also sold goods imported from New York, including "Sugars, Butter, Pipes, Candies, etc." The presence of northern-made products in Little Rock and New Berne was hardly exceptional. In the *Charleston Daily News*, founded in the summer of 1865, one-third of the advertising space that ran later the same year came under the heading of "N. York Advertisements." In Tennessee, the *Clarksville Chronicle*, which had urged secession in early 1861, listed goods from Louisville and Cincinnati in four of the thirteen advertising columns in the autumn of 1865.[55]

Although Rebel armies had surrendered, merchants still prized a southern identity. They urged shoppers to spend on local products, to help rebuild from the war. A grocer in Jackson, Mississippi, encouraged residents to "Keep Your Money Home." He had stocks that came from local farmers, a pointed jab at the advertisements from New York that ran heavily in the same paper. Three days before Christmas, an ale maker in Fredericksburg even more emphatically urged shoppers to "KEEP YOUR MONEY IN VIRGINIA!" Consumers received a better draught—the brewer declared "no other American Ale" surpassed his make—and, more important, benefited a city heavily damaged by the Union army. Underneath notices for hay and wheat imported from the North, a mill owner in Georgia advertised his flour. Possibly he could not match the price and quality of his national competitors. He urged, however, the "importance of home industry. Every barrel of Flour made in Savannah gives employment and furnishes livelihood to some Savannah family."[56]

Other advertisers took pride in being a southern business, an appeal to a distinct regional identity used since the secession crisis. The influx of northern-made goods and services following the end of the war triggered a new round of declarations. C. T. Ames promoted his "New Orleans Menagerie Circus" across the Southeast. Among other acts, the traveling exhibition featured "performing horses, trick ponies, educated mules, acting monkeys, sagacious dogs, etc." Ames acknowledged that other circus companies traveled across the region, including one operated by P. T. Barnum. He asked readers to "BEAR IT IN YOUR MIND" that "this is strictly a southern enterprise." The fact alone that he was not a Yankee presumably made the circus more appealing. Unlike the competition, Ames and his associates kept every promise made "to the letter." A life insurance company made equally clear its connection to the former Confederate States: "THIS IS EXCLUSIVELY A SOUTHERN COMPANY, AND AS SUCH should commend itself to the favor and confidence of our people." The company boasted Nathan Bedford Forrest, Wade Hampton, John B. Gordon, and several other former Confederate officers among its directors. Should a reader miss the regional emphasis, another notice added that the company conducted its business "with the southern states, and to them it appeals for patronage."[57]

In Georgia, the co-owners of a boot and shoe store turned to Confederate sheet music to pitch their wares. In a nearly one-half-column notice, Messrs. Pike and Robinson reprinted "Come! For the War, Love, Is Over." Composed in 1864, the song recounted the experiences of a Confederate soldier waiting until "Sweet Peace will once more bless our land" to marry his sweetheart. Pike and Robinson added two more verses:

Now, three cheers let us give for our bright sunny South.
Let the echo resound from each heart and each mouth;
And with it the good news has reached us of late.
Of the New Boot and Shoe Store at One Thirty-Eight

Let the sound of rejoicing be borne on the breeze.
To each village and hamlet, o'er rivers and seas,
Why? Because Boots and Shoes so cheap are for sale
By Pike & Robinson, Wholesale and Retail.

The two merchants closed by promising that they "are always on hand" to fit any customers with "shoes that will stand."[58]

The appeal to a Confederate identity in the newspaper advertisements lacked the ambivalence sometimes voiced in other venues. Merchants recognized that money spent in their stores remained in the region. They appealed to white southerners, or, as described in a notice by E. B. Spence, a tailor, the "Citizens of the Late Confederacy." Business, however, was business. A Federal soldier on occupation duty or a northern schoolteacher might just as easily spend his or her money in the shop. Southern politicians and editors claimed to value more than dollars and often fumed that money spent on a product advertised from New York or any other northern city benefited their one-time enemies. Yet they also recognized they sometimes needed access to that same material wealth. H. Rives Pollard, the editor of the *Richmond Examiner*, attempted to explain the dilemma. He acknowledged that the paper ran a number of notices from northern businesses. However, since the end of the war, "trade has revived between the North and the South." With commerce on the increase, Pollard and his editorial staff "can recommend our Northern advertisers as first-class, reliable, and responsible business gentlemen." Some Yankees were apparently acceptable, if they were spending their money in a southern store or advertising page.[59]

More northern "business gentlemen" spent their money at home rather than in the South, and they made frequent reference to the war. A midwestern merchant declared in the autumn of 1865 that he had "STARTLING NEWS! BOSTON TAKEN!" The surprise attack was "Not by the Rebels" but by his store. Readers who stopped by might find the latest fashions at "very low cash prices." J. P. Biles owned an iron foundry in Wellsboro, Pennsylvania. He played off the reputation of the Iron Brigade, one of the more hard-fighting units in the Union army, in the *Tioga County Agitator*, announcing:

> General Order No. 1
> Headquarters of the Iron Brigade
> All persons whether liable to draft or not, wanting any articles made wholly or in part of cast iron
> Are hereby notified that the headquarters of this Iron Brigade is presently located at the
> Biles Foundry.

He promised to fill any order upon presentation of "The Greenbacks."[60]

Other advertising headlines celebrated the Union triumph. By the end of the fighting, 360,000 Union soldiers had died from battle and disease. Advertisers helped to explain why these men had sacrificed their lives. In Denver, T. H. Kastor trumpeted: "OUR COUNTRY IS SAFE! Lee has surrendered! Richmond taken!" In like fashion, Kastor had defeated "General Price." High prices had gone into full retreat, and Kastor offered men's clothing at the "lowest cost." J. Mocre advertised his clothing store in Centralia, Illinois, with: "JEFF. DAVIS HAS FAILED! AND WHY? HE WAS IN A BAD CAUSE!" Merchants often failed as badly as the former Confederate president because they were careless "in buying goods." Not so Mocre, who enjoyed "Small Profits and Quick Sales!" A grocer in New York equated the destruction of the Confederacy with the defeat of the wayward in the Bible. Referring to the Book of Revelation, where God ushers in the Millennium, he declared "Richmond Is Ours! Babylon Is Fallen!"[61]

A druggist in upstate New York and a merchant in Massachusetts looked to the future of the nation in their advertising headlines. Thomas Harks declared in the *Buffalo Morning Express:* "ONE FLAG, ONE DESTINY! This is the motto of our Government." He had on hand a full range of treatments for almost any medical ills that ailed his customers. In the *Worcester Palladium*, P. W. Hall announced: "Gold Is Down! Cotton Is Falling!! The Nation Still Lives!" The People's Store also still survived. "With our facilities for doing business," he said, "we can and will sell at the lowest prices in the region!"[62]

As the advertising headlines began to look toward the future, their use of the Civil War to help market their goods drew mixed reactions from contemporary observers. A northern magazine editor argued that the transition from the war-related news to a sales pitch was too jarring for the reader. "Critical persons, indeed," he asserted, "might set forth that the sudden transition from a battle field to a Broadway Concert Saloon might be compared to a short but rapid trip from the sublime to the ridiculous." An anonymous author in the *Round Table*, an arts and culture journal published in Chicago, included merchants' use of fake news as one of several "Advertising Nuisances." He fumed that the "advertisers' use of the reading columns" was a "reprehensible abuse." The unscrupulous editors who accepted such "paid puff" should recognize that the "evil" practice would, ultimately, hurt their business. The advertising men thought differently. By the late nineteenth century, the use of "reading notices" had become a widely used gimmick. Explained one trade journal, these announcements were "insidious, attractive and interesting. Appearing as it does in a semi-news way, it will be read and thoroughly considered, because it carries the endorsement of the medium in which it is published." Editors also saw opportunity, and, by the 1890s, charged more for the advertising news that ran on the front page than the inside pages.[63]

Yet, the advertising news had revealed as much about the war as the products for sale. Whether a powerful Confederate identity existed is a point of scholarly debate, but advertisers had acted upon the assumption that white southerners perceived themselves as a distinct people. Their calls for "self protection" through the purchase of southern-made wares were addressed to white men and women, reflecting a broader vision of citizenship than offered by the original architects of the Confederate republic. The campaign to win the "advertising war" continued even after the last of the Rebel armies had surrendered, with postwar appeals to support regional merchants. Northern advertisers likewise emphasized a consumer patriotism. Whatever a potential customer thought about the conduct of the war, he or she might help to preserve the Union through a visit to the local store. Some merchants went a step further and ran an onslaught of sensationalized war-related headlines. Ultimately, Union and Confederate advertisers had attempted to link together purchasing decisions and national affairs. That the technique continued well after 1865 suggests that, amid the momentous events of the Civil War, they had succeeded.

CHAPTER 2

The Millions

The increased circulation of American newspapers allowed merchants to promote their goods across much of the nation by the mid-nineteenth century. Writing in 1850, one businessman acknowledged that, for many shopkeepers, a notice run in the local paper was sufficient. They already had a loyal customer base that just needed an occasional reminder. But for those individuals hoping to achieve a wider visibility, a notice placed in even five or six newspapers might "challenge the attention of half a million persons." To ignore advertising widely was "like resolving never to travel by steam nor communicate by telegraph." He encouraged merchants to "be like the time" and take notices in several newspapers, or risk losing business to their "wiser rivals." That opportunity only increased during the Civil War, with the enormous public demand for news. An advertiser who took notices in multiple newspapers might reach readers who numbered, gushed one observer, in "the millions."[1]

Publishing companies and patent medicine makers were the most prolific in advertising across the Union and Confederacy because they appealed to different consumer needs. Publishers claimed to offer a deeper understanding of the war and encouraged readers to follow the progress of the armies on military-themed books and maps and, with visual images, to "see" the war-related headlines. The medicine men peddled a mix of fear and hope, announcing supposedly curative powers to help soldiers survive almost any illness and wound. The war became so common in marketing pitches that advertisers had to find additional ways to distinguish their wares. They touted a wartime history as a family heirloom; a map of the "seat of the war" as a work of art. A pill helped to rejuvenate a veteran; a bottle of stomach bitters showed support for the war effort. The "confidence men" who had so plagued antebellum Americans by taking advantage of their trust had, by 1861, moved to the advertising columns.[2]

PUBLISHING THE WAR

With the bombardment of Fort Sumter, the American print culture turned almost exclusively to national affairs. The war-related titles appeared so quickly that publishers moved beyond earlier marketing announcements such as "New Books" and "Books!" They now trumpeted "Great Books," "Thrilling Incidents," and "Books for the Times." War titles were in such demand that some printers added other historical topics. In May 1861, readers might buy a book on the Spanish army during the Peninsular War. According to one reviewer, that military force was distinguished more by its "inordinate pride and arrogance" than its fighting prowess. "This presentiment is so astonishing," he wrote, "that we can hardly persuade ourselves that the Confederate army did not stand for the photographic picture." The *National Intelligencer* in Washington offered a book on the British capture of the city during the War of 1812. Rather than dredge up past defeats, the analysis of the American battlefield effort "will be particularly interesting to military men at the present crisis."[3]

Histories dominated the war-related titles and claimed to be impartial compilations of facts. To many mid-nineteenth-century Americans, enough information gathered together helped to make sense of the massive undertaking of the Civil War. The first attempts to record the fighting began almost immediately. In early May 1861, less than three weeks after the first shots had arced into the air and toward Fort Sumter, *The Rebellion Record* by Frank Moore was advertised. Published by G. P. Putnam in New York, the book offered "Carefully edited" and "Verified FACTS." Nowhere on the pages would a reader find "RUMORS, GUESSES OR PREJUDICES."[4] That summer, Frank Leslie marketed his *Pictorial History of the War.* An illustrated magazine published twice monthly, Leslie's work "embodies many valuable statistics, and an amount of historical facts that make it an important periodical." The attempt to write an objective history of the conflict continued even after the fighting had ended. In late 1865, Porter Alexander placed a card in a Richmond paper announcing his plan to write a "history of the late war." A high-ranking officer in the former Confederate Army of Northern Virginia, Alexander solicited military reports, political speeches, and other written materials. Individuals who sent such items "would confer a great favor, besides contributing somewhat to the vindication of the truth of history."[5]

Histories of the war were numerous enough to spark fierce competition. Publishers recognized the momentous issues of the war and pitched their works as historical keepsakes. By early 1864, Frank Moore had expanded the *Rebellion Record* to six volumes. That required a significant investment in shelf space, but customers would then own a "permanent DIGEST for future reference." H. C. Clarke of Vicksburg, Mississippi, published the *Diary of the War for Separation* in early May 1862. The title contained "full and minute statements of all the battles, skirmishes, and engagements" through the fighting at Shiloh only one month earlier. The work would remain the "most popular history of the war yet published." Henry Bill, a publisher in New York, appealed to family to help sell John Abbott's two-volume *History of the Civil War in America.* The book offered "impartial and graphic descriptions of the campaigns." No parent should worry about too much graphic description of battlefield gore because the history was an "excellent family work." In fact, they should hurry to purchase their copy. "No American," Bill cautioned, "can deprive himself or his children of the benefits of reading a complete and consecutive history of this great conflict."[6]

Quality, price, and the occasional gimmick also became part of the sales pitch for war histories. Horace Greeley, the editor of the *New-York Tribune,* wrote a study of the fighting into 1864. The length and price of *The American Conflict* were hefty, at 648 pages and, for a cloth cover, $3.50 (an "embossed leather, marble edge" cover ran fifty cents more). The publisher meant for the book to last: "In quality of paper, printing and style of engravings, it is believed to be unequaled by any other history of the war." Henry Howe printed his *Illustrated History of the Rebellion* in English and German. As many as two hundred thousand German American soldiers served in the Union army, so the immigrant market was sizeable. Howe's work included a description of the recent Union triumph at Vicksburg during the summer of 1863. The book was "beautifully illustrated" and "what every family wants." That same year, Ann Stephens published her *Pictorial History of the War for the Union.* Perhaps sensing an opportunity in marketing a history authored by a woman, John Wells, the publisher, sought "Female agents" to sell the book. Their job would be relatively easy, because Stephens's book had two hundred "first-class engravings" and a relatively inexpensive cover price. "It is just the work for the people," Wells declared, "and will sooner or later find its way into every family." For young women still nervous about selling the book, Wells offered a simple incentive: "Now is the Time to Make Money. . . . Agents are meeting with extraordinary success."[7]

The push for customers had publishers downplay the sometimes overtly political message of their histories. In his memoir, Greeley admitted that he decided to write his history only after the issuing of the Emancipation Proclamation. Only then had the conflict become a true "struggle for liberation." He made a similar point in the introduction, claiming that *The American Conflict* was the first to show the influence of "Slavery in molding the opinions of our people, as well as in shaping the destinies of our country." That claim was often lost in the detail of the advertisements. A prepublication announcement declared the work offered a "deeper, broader, more exhaustive exhibit of the long train of CAUSES which impelled to this bloody collision—the conflicting IDEAS which rendered it inevitable." By the time the reader had digested what causes and ideas, the notice had moved to describing the material quality of the work, as well as its abundant "maps, diagrams of battle-fields, sieges, naval actions, views of places of historical interest, etc." Even the year after the book was published, when political battles over the reconstruction of the South already were brewing, advertisers declared that the work would please everyone. "This history," one salesman claimed, "has received the highest commendations from men of all parties and from the Press of every political shade and religious denomination."[8]

Henry Bill took a similarly neutral approach in marketing *The History of the Civil War in America*. In the opening chapter, John Abbott declared that the war was a battle between slavery and freedom, with its origins going back to the beginnings of human civilization. "This fierce fight," he wrote, "which has arrayed more than a million of men in arms, and which made our ship of state reel and stagger, as if smitten by thunderbolts and dashing upon rocks, was but one, though a sublime act, in the drama of that great conflict, between patrician arrogance and plebian resistance." In publicity announcements, however, Bill declared the book a "full and impartial account of the origin, and progress of the Rebellion." This included the "various Naval, and Military engagements" and the "Heroic Deeds Performed by Armies and Individuals." Another announcement emphasized that, "bound in leather" and heavily illustrated, "This will be THE History."[9]

That encomium might more properly have gone to Moore's *Rebellion Record* because readers appreciated its versatility of use. When the first volume appeared in the spring of 1861, there was some dismay that the publisher intended to provide updates. One magazine editor quipped that he wished no harm to "Mr. Putnam and Mr. Frank Moore." However, "with profound faith in the justice of our cause," he hoped that the "necessity of publishing any record may speedily cease." That was not the case, and, by late that year, defense lawyers had reportedly used the most recent volume as evidence in the federal trial of a Confederate sailor for piracy. The attorneys argued that some of the documents in Moore's work had demonstrated the "reality of secession" and that their client had engaged in a legitimate act of war. One reporter declared that "It was the first time, in legal and literary history, that a book not yet completed has been so stamped with authenticity as to be admitted as evidence in a Court of Law." Two years later, a reviewer praised the work for helping to personalize the war for readers. Amid the vast sweep of the armies, they might find information on where their loved ones had fought. "The battle in which a brother, father, husband, or son, perhaps fell," he explained, "must always possess the deepest interest of the family."[10]

Controversy drew readers' attention to Moore's history. William Howard Russell, a British journalist, had witnessed the Battle of Bull Run and later published a disparaging account of the Union army in the London press. That fall, the editor of the *Christian Review* praised Moore's first volume for setting the record straight. "Nothing known or written of this battle," he declared, "of any value whatever, whether from Federal, Confederate, or English sources, seems here to be wanting." That included materials that contradicted Russell's account and "must prove very damaging to that gentleman's reputation." Writing for the "Society for the Diffusion of Political Knowledge," an anonymous author claimed that Moore's volume on the dismissal of Union general George McClellan in late 1862 had put the "illustrious commander" in a bad light. Moore had not included several paragraphs from an official report in which McClellan had defended his conduct of the war. The writer believed the "omission was doubtless unintentional," with the relevant information likely having "fallen from a compositor's desk." He encouraged readers to buy a complete copy of McClellan's report from a different publisher, to gain a fuller understanding of the episode.[11]

Other war-themed books focused on military heroes. To many contemporaries, biographies helped to give a deeper understanding of the fighting. Northern publishers focused on successful generals to draw attention to the war's progress. That was a gamble since success sometimes proved fleeting. Works appeared on General Winfield Scott, Lincoln's top military advisor before battlefield defeats in the summer and fall of 1861 forced his retirement, and General Benjamin Butler, the military governor of Louisiana removed from command under a cloud of controversy and scandal. By 1864, publishers had found staying power in Ulysses Grant. Biographies on the Federal general billed him as "THE HERO OF Donelson, Vicksburg, and Chattanooga!" and "THE CAPTOR OF 100,000 Rebels, 500 Cannon and 200,000 Small Arms!" Even while he led the Union Army of the Potomac through bloody fighting during 1864, customers might read about the "principal battles fought by Grant and his generals." Younger readers might browse P. C. Headley's volumes on Generals Philip Sheridan and William T. Sherman, two of Grant's top subordinates, and "Captain" John Ericsson, the "Inventor of the Monitor." Written "expressly for Boys and Young Men," the biographies made for the "most interesting library of the season."[12]

Confederate officers gained the most literary fame through a battlefield death, highlighting for readers the courage and sacrifice required to form the new nation. Turner Ashby, a cavalry officer, was the first Rebel martyr. Killed during the Shenandoah Valley Campaign in 1862, he was within weeks the subject of a proposed biography. A publisher in Richmond hoped to gain information on the fallen colonel from "friends and families and soldiers." With the materials, he would keep alive the "dashing and gallant Ashby" in the public memory. The next year, General Thomas "Stonewall" Jackson suffered a mortal wound. Biographers quickly set to work. Charles Halleck published a study with a "full and accurate account" of Jackson's "dying moments" because the "public feel a deep interest in everything connected with the illustrious hero." A Richmond-based publisher authorized a biography that focused more on the military career of the "great hero." Based in official papers and "personal acquaintance," the book "contains many anecdotes of the illustrious soldier that have never before been published." By contrast, Robert E. Lee, the commander of the Confederate Army of Northern Virginia, was the subject of no wartime biographies. Only in death did Confederate military leaders transcend from heroes to martyrs and become symbols of the ultimate devotion to their cause.[13]

In addition to the generals, publishers touted books on the men in the ranks. James Hosmer focused on the heroism of the Union soldier. A military chaplain, he recorded scenes in camp and battle that had a "more than ordinary interest." The result was a tale of "daring and suffering" that would "furnish materials for the novelist, the poet, the painter, as well as the historian." F. G. DeFontaine hoped to do the same for the Confederate army. A correspondent for the *Charleston Courier,* he ran a notice asking for soldiers to send him their stories of military life "in every phase." If a tale "has enlivened a camp fire, or a deed of daring had marked a battle field, . . . let it be recorded." In *Thirteen Months in the Rebel Army,* William Stevenson recounted his unusual wartime experience. A New Yorker, he was visiting Tennessee when he was impressed into the Confederate army in the spring of 1861. Prior to escaping, he claimed to have traveled widely across the South as an infantry sergeant, cavalry courier, and hospital steward. The book's publisher declared that Stevenson "saw all and tells what he saw" with "unusual graphic power." The resulting adventures were "more startling than the wildest fiction."[14]

Advertisers marketed fewer titles on women and their wartime contributions. A memoir by Sarah Edmonds received considerable attention because, disguised as a man, she had enlisted in the Union army. Under the alias "Franklin Thompson," Edmonds had served for nearly two years before illness forced her to desert rather than risk discovery. W. S. Williams, the publisher, embellished what Edmonds had witnessed, wary that her cross-dressing might dissuade some potential customers. Rather than calling her a soldier and allowing for a clear dislodging of gender identities, he used "Nurse, Scout, and Spy." From that vantage point, Edmonds witnessed "BATTLES, SEIGES [*sic*], EXPLOITS, CHARGES, SKIRMISHES, SACRIFICES, SUFFERING and achievements" of "our gallant and heroic soldiers." The result was a "vivid picture of the great American War." Otherwise, in the advertising columns, the memoirs and works of nonfiction were the domain of white male soldiers. By contrast, in other print materials, women assumed an increasingly visible presence. In her book on popular literature during the war, Alice Fahs argues that poems, novels, and newspaper stories focused on women's wartime contributions and sufferings. This "feminized war" was not intended to overshadow the significance of soldiers and politicians but to bring recognition for the many sacrifices women made.[15]

For the more visually inclined, publishing companies printed maps to allow readers to trace the maneuvers of the armies. Merchants had sold maps during the Mexican War, but these usually focused on the entire region. Few Americans were familiar with the seemingly far-off place-names in the nation's first foreign war. One printer sold a map of "Mexico, Texas, and part of the United States." By "part," he meant "California and Santa Fe." Another map displayed all of Mexico and was advertised as the "largest and most correct map of this Republic ever published."[16] During the Civil War, maps appeared in newspapers and usually focused on a particular battle. These representations often were poorly done—and inaccurate—because of time pressures and the fine level of detail involved. Maps issued by a publishing house appealed to a more permanent market by offering a general overview of the war's progress. The *Republican Banner* in Nashville sold a map depicting the "Seat of the War" in 1861. The "Bird's eye view" included Virginia, Maryland, and Delaware. The *Southern Banner* in Athens, Georgia, also sold a map of the "Seat of War," but in Mississippi: "All of the important places are plainly listed, enabling one to understand the positions and movements of the contending armies." In Vermont, the *Burlington Free Press* sold H. H. Lloyd's "Southern States Map." The map was the "best way" for civilians to trace the route of recent Union offensives along the coast of North Carolina and "other Southern Expeditions."[17]

In a crowded market, Willis Hazard proved remarkably adept at marketing his war map. Based in Philadelphia, he had his "Railroad and Military Map of the Southern States" for sale by early 1862. Hazard claimed that Secretary of War Edwin Stanton was so impressed he had "distributed 1,000 copies among the Generals and Colonels of the Army." Stanton's interest was enough for Hazard to proclaim his "The Official War Map!" The size of the map—32 by 55 inches—"shows at a glance the principal places, and all the strategic points" across the seceded states. Union general George McClellan has "acknowledged the great importance of it to his movements." Others also found the map useful. Hazard claimed that he was constantly "told by those who already have several of the maps rushed upon the public that they have laid them aside and used only this one." With such glowing endorsements, Hazard was certain that "every intelligent man" wanted "The Best and Only Official Map."[18]

With Hazard claiming his as the "official" map of the war, other cartographers used different strategies to market their works. H. H. Lloyd and Company, a publishing house in New York, sold a "military campaign chart" in addition to the "Southern States Map." With sixteen maps on a single sheet, the campaign chart also listed the "Population and Military Force of the Free, Secession, and Other States." Trying to create demand by advertising demand, Lloyd declared that it would require "600,000 Agents" to sell the map across the Union, or almost as many men as the Federal army had under arms at any particular time. In late 1861, a bookstore in Kansas advertised a "new war map." The publisher was unlisted, but the map received billing as "indispensable to a proper understanding of military movement." Better yet for the cost-conscious, the map sold "as cheap as dirt!" Publishing in Columbia, South Carolina, Evans and Cogswell created a map showing the "eastern portions" of Virginia and North Carolina. They drew a series of concentric rings around Richmond so that a viewer might more easily determine distances from the Confederate capital. For more ready access to customers on the go—as many southerners were as the tide of the war increasingly turned against them—Evans and Cogswell offered to bind their work as a pocket map.[19]

Following the maneuvers of the armies involved more than pointing to places, and publishers marketed their creations as works of art and keepsakes. Hazard intended his "Railroad and Military" map for prominent display in northern homes. The map was "beautifully colored" and inexpensively priced to compete with "inferior" imitations. He offered a copy mounted on muslin cloth, "with rollers and varnished." The "military campaign chart" sold by H. H. Lloyd was "elegant" looking. He claimed that "No pains are spared to make the coloring and finish nearly as perfect as possible." It should "be hung up by every fireside." Another publisher had a map showing the western theater of the war. The map itself was small—only several inches on either side—but was topped by a "large, splendid Head-piece." The illustration showed Union soldiers "protecting the *Stars and Stripes* with Muskets and Rifled Cannon." In the foreground "are Zouaves tramping on the Rebel Flag, and a serpent underneath." The map and "head-piece" made for an image that was "Bold, Spirited and Attractive."[20]

Some contemporary observers criticized the war maps for including too many details and confusing the reader. Writing for *Vanity Fair*, a "Bothered Contributor" found a number of issues in the various maps showing the "Seat of the War." Among these were "Dotted lines running every direction. Big blots to represent forts. Little blots to represent camps. Spider trenches—intoxicated spiders, too, to represent roads. . . . It's all a muddle." It might take a reader several hours to find a particular river, and "as for Court-Houses, there are about ten thousand in Virginia alone." Another magazine writer criticized the newspapers for selling maps that had nothing to do with the war. In this case, he was upset by a New York paper offering a chart for a nearby yacht course.[21]

Customers, however, reportedly praised the war maps for being as good as promised. A Union corporal referred to "Lloyd's military map" to help his family pinpoint his regiment's location in Louisiana. His outfit was encamped at a bayou above a "sudden bend in the river above Baton Rouge." Rather than trying to describe the location in more detail, he told them to look at their copy of the map, where the "bend and the bayou are both plain." A sailor wrote his sister that she might "trace" his routes along the Ohio and Tennessee Rivers by looking at her war map. In Virginia, a commercially printed map hung from a wall in a Union military hospital. A nurse wrote that during spare moments, "We sit there and read the papers and study it." A Georgia newspaper editor declared that an image of southern railroad lines was the "most complete map of the kind ever issued." Readers wishing to see why Atlanta was such an important Confederate transportation hub might take a look. And just as important, claimed one Confederate official, the Evans and Cogswell pocket map of the Atlantic seaboard was a pleasure to the eye. He enthused that the work was "beautifully printed and bound." Valued for their content and appearance, maps helped northerners and southerners to visualize the sweep of the war and the role of their loved ones in that effort.[22]

In addition to books and maps, artists and printmakers allowed readers to keep current with the names and places they read about in the newspaper. They most often produced images of high-ranking military officers because these men dominated the war-related headlines. Northerners might purchase pictures of, among other officers, Major Robert Anderson, the Union commander at Fort Sumter and a "heroic soldier," and Lieutenant General Ulysses Grant, the general-in-chief of the Union army and the "Greatest military leader of all times." Southerners might buy prints of General Robert E. Lee, the commander of the Army of Northern Virginia, and Thomas "Stonewall" Jackson, one of Lee's top subordinates and, after the triumph at Chancellorsville, the "Great Flanking General"—as well as of P. G. T. Beauregard, the "hero of Manassas." A book dealer in Ohio sold images of Union and Confederate officers, although he made clear his loyalties. He had on stock lithographs of Anderson and "other heroes in the War for the Union!" Pictures of Jefferson Davis and other Rebel leaders "hanged" from his store window, where they shared the "fate of all Traitors!"[23]

Which Union generals would earn a positive press remained a guessing game during the early war, when many northern advertisers wasted space on officers of great military promise but little battlefield success. An engraving of Major General Winfield Scott, the commander of the Union army, and many of his subordinate officers was widely announced soon after the start of the war. *Scott and His Generals* included John Wool, John Dix, and Nathanial Banks. The "splendid Engraving" was "suitable for parlor or office." For a little extra cost, the buyer might have the image "framed and preserved for a number of years." A customer might soon have second-guessed that decision. Scott resigned from the army under pressure in late 1861, and few of the other officers in the picture went on to achieve notable military careers. H. A. Brown, the owner of a picture gallery in Boston, placed his faith in Union major general George McClellan, the new army commander. He offered an "elegant" engraving of "our GLORIOUS GENERAL," whose "plan is now developing in the triumphant march of the Union forces." Brown had sent the image to Abraham Lincoln and published the reply. "The engraving is beautifully executed," wrote the president, "and the likeness is perfect." Regardless of the quality of this likeness, McClellan moved slowly in the field, and Lincoln removed him from command the next year. Merchants were touting other Union generals who dominated the headlines by that time, and lithographs and engravings of the two former army commanders all but disappeared from the advertising columns.[24]

Reflecting the diverse range of people who appeared in its pages, the antislavery press offered a wide mix of images. In late 1863, readers might purchase a collage featuring the "friends of freedom." Union general John Frémont, who had unilaterally declared slaves free in Missouri; former president John Quincy Adams; and John Brown, described in the notice as a "martyr," were among the highlighted ministers, politicians, and generals. Abraham Lincoln was noticeably absent, even almost a year after he had issued the Emancipation Proclamation. Another newspaper offered a similar group picture, although this one featured only "Colored American Patriots." Women had taken an active role in the abolitionist movement, and some readers wanted to see their pictures. A New York photography studio offered a collage of "Representative Women." The members included Harriet Beecher Stowe, Lucretia Mott, and Lydia Maria Child. The publisher was pleased to provide the image to those "friends who have so long been desiring copies."[25]

The war was more than generals and other well-known figures, and merchants also encouraged soldiers and their families to carry pictures of one another. That was not always easy for a husband or father to do when the army was in the field. Advertisers offered "Army" and "Soldier" photographic albums as a solution. The leather cases were small, with space for only a dozen or so card-sized images, and slipped easily into a uniform pocket. The compactness allowed a soldier to have "relatives and friends always by him." Parents, wives, and children might return the favor. Turner's Photographic Gallery in Philadelphia urged anyone with a likeness of a "father, brother, son, lover, or friend in the Union Army" to have made a "Carte de Visite." The small photograph, mounted on a thicker paper stock, was "suitable for Framing, or placing in a Breast-pin, Locket, Ring, or Photographic Album." A photographer in Indiana recognized the uncertainties of life by the summer of 1864, whether in the army or at home. He encouraged soldiers and civilians to have images of family members made "before their dear faces are hidden from your view by the grave." No one would deny the value of such a picture. "Then delay not a day," the photographer urged, "lest the substance fade ere you secure the shadow."[26]

Readers did not delay, and *cartes de visite* allowed soldiers and their families to record their own war histories. By the end of the fighting, perhaps as many as several million of the small photographs were produced. One Massachusetts editor claimed that the man who "has not had struck off by the immaterial types of the sun at least one edition of his counterfeit presentment" would soon be "as uncommon and exceptional as one who has never sat before the camera at all, or who has never ridden in a train car." In 1862, one Union soldier mailed his parents an image of his commanding officer. "It does not do him justice," he admitted, "yet it is, of course, a likeness. Place it in my album, if you please." In a letter to his wife, Hallock Armstrong enclosed a photograph of one of his regimental officers. "He is rather rough," the Pennsylvania chaplain wrote, "but brave to a fault. . . . Now consider yourself introduced!" The images became so popular that the federal government eventually levied a tax on their sale, at a few cents for each picture.[27]

By helping to personalize the war, *cartes de visite* contributed to a growing emphasis among northerners and southerners on the human side of the struggle. In her study on the popular literature of the war, Fahs argues that poems and songs increasingly emphasized the "individuality of the ordinary soldier." The emphasis served as a counterpoint to earlier writings that had highlighted the individual as subordinate to the state. Personal images reminded readers that the otherwise nameless soldiers in the newspapers were also husbands, fathers, and sons. Easily found in the advertising columns, the photographs were, in the words of one contemporary observer, the "sentimental 'green-backs'" of the war.[28]

That sentimentality carried into images of battle, and merchants offered only a highly romanticized depiction. They described Union and Confederate soldiers as "brave and noble hearted," "magnificent," and "splendid!" The battles they fought were "thrilling" and "glorious." Walter Smith turned the fighting at Gettysburg, the bloodiest battle of the war, into something for family and friends to enjoy. He offered a "beautiful picture of the battle" that was sure to be a "Great attraction." Better yet, from his perspective, the image sold at "New York and Philadelphia prices." Another art seller offered pictures of the fighting that had occurred in Virginia and Mississippi during the spring of 1862. The Battle of Shiloh that April had been especially shocking because of the high casualties. Not to the art merchant: "What views!," he gushed. Two years later, southern readers might buy an image of the successful Confederate defense of Charleston harbor against a Union naval assault. The oil painting did not emphasize iron and gore but rather a panoramic view of the fighting that was "beautiful" and a "treasure."[29]

In marketing an orderly and relatively bloodless portrayal of battle, advertisers offered a much different impression than photographers. Matthew Brady, Timothy O'Sullivan, Alexander Gardner, and other northern photographers captured some of the grim aftermath of Civil War combat. Most famously at the time, in his New York studio, Brady ran a display showing Confederate dead from the fighting at Antietam in 1862. Images of bloated corpses from the Sunken Road and the West Woods, scenes of particularly bloody combat, were on view. The *New York Times* concluded that if Brady "has not brought bodies and laid them in our dooryard and along streets, he has done something very like it." Still reflecting on the photographs the next year, a writer for the *Atlantic Monthly* was haunted that these "wrecks of manhood thrown together in careless heaps or ranged in ghastly rows for burial were alive but yesterday." The images confronted viewers with the inescapable fact that war was a "repulsive, brutal, sickening, hideous thing." Unlike national advertisers, however, Brady might rely upon the shock value of his images. The photographs of the dead at Antietam were meant to convey the human cost of the war rather than to hang in the family parlor.[30]

By 1865, publishing companies and visual artists had pitched their wares as offering a better understanding of the war and its participants. In the desire to sell their war histories, they marketed the books as neutral collections of facts. That worked well for Moore's *Rebellion Record* but led to downplaying of the political overtones in Greeley's and Abbott's histories. In other war-related titles, publishers announced memoirs that reflected the contributions of white soldiers. Readers perusing these sales pitches would not find a "feminized" war, unlike in the popular literature. In their announcements, engravers and printmakers touted stylized depictions of battle. Photographs showing the aftermath of the fighting at Antietam, Gettysburg, and other battles demonstrated, however, that combat was not "beautiful" and "thrilling" as these merchants had claimed. Yet, many publishers marketed images that helped their readers to personalize the war. Amid the newspaper headlines that often touted Union and Confederate generals, they announced *cartes de visite* so that soldiers and their families might gaze at one another across great distances. Those miles might seem fewer when northerners and southerners looked at commercially printed maps and found the wartime location of their fathers, husbands, and sons. For these readers, advertisers had helped to make the otherwise vast scale of the Civil War a more knowable experience.

IN SICKNESS AND HEALTH

Any number of goods and services were announced in Union and Confederate newspapers but none as frequently as patent medicines. Well before any government regulation, medicine makers sold pills, potions, and ointments that promised to cure everything from bad breath to cancer. Like advertisers in the early days of the internet, makers of patent medicines recognized the opportunity offered by the increased circulation of newspapers. By the 1850s, the printed page offered promoters of supposed "medical miracles" access to the American family at home. The reach and visibility proved invaluable. "I can advertise *dish water*, and sell it, just as well as an article of merit," boasted one nostrum seller and newspaper regular. "It is all in the advertising." Revenues and name recognition soared. Some medicine makers earned profits that reached into the six figures, in an era when a farm laborer earned only tens of dollars per month. By 1870, Thomas Holloway, a maker of "universal pills," was perhaps the most recognized name in the world. His advertisements ran in Asia, North Africa, Europe, and the Americas. In a mix of bewilderment and admiration, one advertising agent later dubbed Holloway the "Napoleon of Advertising."[31]

Patent medicines put newspapers in a dilemma. Some editors refused the money, arguing that publishing notices for potions and pills that promised much and delivered little was dishonest. An Illinois paper refused to take any more advertisements from "quack doctors" after one too many promised to cure, among other illnesses, "Inflammation of the Abdominal Regions, Ager Fits, Shakinquaker, and all kinds of Anniversaries." An abolitionist press dismissed patent medicines and other "specific remedies" as "neither solicited nor published." More editors, however, accepted the advertisements for patent medicines as a valuable source of revenue. These notices often ran several columns and across multiple issues, a financial windfall for the paper publishing them. Asked why he accepted advertisements from accused hucksters, one hard-nosed editor responded, "Business is business—money is money."[32]

Following the bombardment of Fort Sumter, makers of patent medicines exploited soldiers as potential customers. They did not have to know much about history to recognize that diseases often ran rampant during wartime. With poor sanitation and often inadequate rations, far more American soldiers had died from disease than battle during the Mexican War. In Europe, the losses from disease among the Russian and Allied combatants of the Crimean War (1853–56) had caused an international outcry. The situation had changed little by the start of the Civil War. The lack of medical understanding of germs and bacteria meant that dysentery, measles, and typhoid swept through the volunteers of 1861 and 1862. Antiseptics were not yet known, and wounded men faced surgeons with unclean hands and instruments. Almost as many Union and Confederate soldiers were in the hospital battling disease, infections, and a host of other medical ailments as were on the firing line. Many men never returned to the ranks. By the end of the war, three soldiers had died from disease for every soldier killed in battle.[33]

Thomas Holloway exploited this hard reality and played upon soldiers' fears of dying from disease and wounds to market his pills and ointment. The so-called Professor ramped up his marketing almost as fast as the Union army mobilized. By the summer of 1861, he cautioned soldiers to "see to your health—do not trust to army supplies." Disease and illness will "follow your slightest indiscretion." The only way to avoid a hospital stay and possible death: "Holloway's pills should be in your knapsack." After the Battle of Bull Run in northern Virginia that July, Holloway judged that "Many soldiers died from lack of medical treatment." His medicines "would have prevented this." The next year, Holloway again cautioned that "small pox has already sacrificed some of our best and bravest troops. Soldiers! Listen to the voice of reason, and supply yourself with Holloway's Pills and Ointments." The tablets "purify the blood and strengthen the stomach," while the lotion "removes all pain and prevents pit marks." Smallpox was not the only silent killer. "To Arms! To Arms!," Holloway declared in 1863. "The citizen soldier will find a more deadly foe in the brackish muddy water and damp night air than in the most determined enemy." Only his pills strengthened the blood against these natural hardships and helped Union volunteers to "remain healthy."[34]

Worries over soldiers' well-being extended to wives, mothers, and families, all of whom Holloway targeted. "Friends and Relatives of the Brave Soldiers and Sailors, HOLLOWAY'S PILLS AND OINTMENT," ran the headline to one notice. Another promotion ran, "Wives, Mothers, Sisters Whose Husbands, Sons, and Brothers Are Serving in the Army, HOLLOWAY'S PILLS AND OINTMENT." The message was the same, regardless of the headline used. Soldiers sometimes forgot to look after themselves amid the many demands of military life. Families at home could not afford the same luxury. They could not put into the "Knapsacks of your Husbands and Brothers a more valuable or more necessary gift" than a supply of Holloway's medicines. The "Soldier's never-failing friend" cured headaches, coughs, lack of appetite, and sore feet, among other ailments. Holloway sold his pills at twenty-five cents for one box, and ointment at thirty cents a pot.[35]

Competitors were never far behind, although they lacked Holloway's advertising budget. Edwin Baker, a druggist in Richmond, sold his stomach bitters to Confederate soldiers serving in Virginia and North Carolina. Baker promised that one bottle of his drink would cure "BILIOUSNESS, NERVOUSNESS, COUGHS and COLDS." Inexpensively priced, a better cure "cannot be found." Stephen Sweet sold his liniment to Union soldiers. A "famous bone setter" in Connecticut, Sweet claimed that his rub "never fails" to work when applied to everything from wounds and cuts, to stiff necks and sore feet. Dixon's Blackberry Carminative and Strickland's Anti-Cholera Mixture promised to cure the dysentery that often swept through army encampments. One bottle of the medicines had cured patients "after being pronounced incurable by their physicians." Even when not sick, a soldier might want to drink a bottle of Schenck's Seaweed Tonic after a meal. The drink "will dissolve your food and prevent dyspeptic feelings." Soldiers might order a range of other medical products, from Leonard's itch ointment that also doubled as a "destroyer of camp vermin," to abdominal supporters that helped to "regulate the bowels."[36]

Few advertisers recognized the physical and mental costs of the war to otherwise seemingly able-bodied men. Although the numbers are uncertain, many veterans returned home in precarious health. These men drew relatively little attention, with the public gaze focused squarely on the war and its aftermath. George Bulpin called the attention of "Invalid Soldiers Returning from the War" to Laurie's Life Pills in 1862. The tablets are "of inestimable value to their shattered constitutions." Sold by the box, the pills and "THEIR SURPRISING EFFICACY IN CASES OF FEVER AND AGUE, and its consequences, have been admitted as unparalleled." Three years later, Dr. S. O. Richardson of Connecticut advertised to "OUR RETURNING SOLDIERS." If suffering from "chronic diarrhea," veterans should take his "Blood Root Elixir." A mouthful of the elixir taken every day corrected "Consumption of the Blood, which proves fatal to so many of our brave soldiers, after their return to their homes and friends."[37]

The New York Electrical Institute advertised its "Hashish Candy" for "THE 'HORRORS,' THE 'BLUES,' MELANCHOLY from loss of friends in battle." The candy transformed "nervous, weakness, and ennui" into a "'World of Beautiful Dreams." Beyond making a user temporarily forget the war's human cost, the candy gave a "finer" intoxication than strong drink and opium "without their bad after effects." The Electrical Institute boasted that it was selling one thousand dollars' worth of the candy every day. That was some total, since the hashish sold for twenty-five cents for a small box, and one dollar for a large box.[38]

In their marketing to soldiers and their families, medicine makers employed a variety of gimmicks. They increasingly pandered to a fear of dying from disease. Thomas Holloway had used the high rates of illness in the Union army to market his pills, but he rarely phrased his pitches as a literal matter of life or death. In a crowded market, other charlatans showed no such restraint. The maker of a tonic in Ohio headlined his notice by screaming:

DIARRHOEA
LIFE OR DEATH!
SOLDIERS,
DON'T GO BACK TO THE WAR,
For many have died from Diarrhoea and Dysentery in your regiment,
Now take warning and do not return without supplying your knapsacks
With a bottle of Dr. Strickland's Anti-Cholera Mixture.

Another huckster declared his drink was "THE SOLDIERS SAFE GUARD" because it offered "Safety Against Death." Using logic to back the claim, he correctly noted that more deaths "in all wars" occur from disease than battle. That made his drink "as useful as the musket." A few swigs and "no sickness will break out or pestilence prevail." For mere pennies, soldiers and their families might have the peace of mind brought by his "New Weapon of Defense."[39]

Running testimonials was another attention-grabber that patent medicine makers employed. Enough customers survived an illness to attribute remarkable curative powers to the pills and potions they had been using. The firsthand accounts—whether genuine or manufactured—only added to the promise of restored health from the self-described doctors and professors, and they were featured prominently in the notices. Dr. C. M. Jackson printed a letter from a Union major praising his stomach bitters. Isaac Malone had fallen so ill that he was unable to consume any food or drink without vomiting. Literally wasting away, Malone chanced upon a supply of the bitters. Two bottles later, Malone had gained ten pounds and was looking forward to visiting his wife and family. Jackson's medicine had saved his life: "There is no mistake in this." Testimonials headlined the advertisement for Dr. Hostetter's stomach bitters. "Hear the Witnesses," he encouraged his readers. Private Samuel Ryan wrote from a "convalescent camp" in northern Virginia. He suffered from "dyspepsia" and had spent several hundred dollars seeking a cure in other medicines. A bottle of Hostetter's bitters achieved the "greatest success imaginable" by offering a permanent cure rather than a temporary relief. Ryan was ready to return to duty and thanked Hostetter for his "invaluable" help.[40]

Putting a twist on the use of testimonials, a New York–based medicine man ran an endorsement from a Confederate newspaper for his "Plantation Bitters." P. H. Drake claimed that the *Richmond Whig* regretted the war had cut off the supply of his medicine, "formerly found in most Southern homes." Exposure and poor diet were now incapacitating as many Rebel soldiers as were northern bullets. According to this editor, since no local substitute for the bitters might be found, "our government has opened negotiations with Dr. Drake through a secret agent." Drake puffed that he was "exceedingly obliged" to the Virginia paper for "its remembrance of 'Auld Lang Syne.'" However, he could assure "Our Government" that his medicine was "not for sale to any secret agents." Besides, he crowed, there were "probably several other things 'Our Government' will want."[41]

Other hucksters attempted to associate their medicines with the Union medical establishment. The maker of Hostetter's stomach bitter claimed that the federal government authenticated every bottle of his medicine. That was a massive task, especially during wartime, but the service was done to "guard against dangerous impositions." Potential customers should remember that his brand had such official approval. In 1863, a Dr. Brandreth commended the Union military for banning the use of calomel as an emetic. The harsh treatment had drained, as often as it had restored, the physical stamina of soldiers. Still, they sometimes had stomach ailments. Brandreth called upon the army to adopt his "vegetable pills." A few doses cured "all fevers and afflictions of the Bowels." There were no harsh aftereffects because the pills "are as innocent as bread." Brandreth promised a "'new era' in the practice of medicine, which would then become emphatically THE HEALING ART."[42]

Using current headlines was another gimmick, and nostrum dealers found ample material to work with in the Civil War. "GREAT BATTLE," thundered the headline for Farnsworth's Liniment in mid-April 1861. Unlike the fighting around Fort Sumter, this battle was between Farnsworth's rub and "pain caused by a strain." After a few applications, "the pain retreated." The liniment was good for more than strains and also "defeated" headaches and bruises. During the presidential election of 1860, Heimstreet's Hair Restorative asked if perhaps a few politicians had turned prematurely gray from the "excitement attending that subject." If so, the hair tonic "will remove all traces of the battle." Five years later, after the last Confederate armies had surrendered, Christadoro's Hair Dye declared "No Recognition." The southern people had given up hope of being recognized, and "it is equally difficult to recognize northerners whose heads of gray, yellow, white, brown, or red hair have surrendered their colors." A few uses of Christadoro's dye, however, would turn "such blacks and browns as nature might mistake for her own."[43]

A Dr. Radway attempted to explain "What the Federal Troops Are Fighting to Sustain" in a notice for his stomach medicines. He believed that many northern families did not understand why their husbands and sons were fighting because they had not studied the American Constitution. The fault was not theirs because even teachers no longer required their students to read the "sacred" document. He would send a copy of the Constitution free of charge to anyone who ordered his bitters. Once customers had read the nation's founding words, they "will become convinced of the holiness of our cause and of the wickedness of those who are striving to overthrow this grand palladium of freedom." Potential customers did not even need to live in the United States. He would ship to all who can "read the English language." This would convince recipients that "Our People" were "Not Only Right" in "WIPING OUT THIS FOUL BLOT OF SECESSION . . . BUT ARE ESTABLISING ON A SOUND BASIS THE FREEDOM OF THE PEOPLE THROUGHOUT THE WORLD." Courtesy of Dr. Radway, readers might gain both a better digestion and appreciation of the Union war effort.[44]

Southern medicine makers turned the headlines to their advantage by appealing to a Confederate identity. An opportunity presented itself with the start of the Civil War and the disappearance of northern-produced medicines. J. L Eagon declared in the *Staunton Spectator* that his "Southern Liver and Antibillious Pills" were perfect for Confederate families. Eagon acknowledged that "purgative medicines" were "scarce" across the South. Every family should keep on hand a box of his pills because they cured almost any stomach ailment. Equally important, the pills were made in Virginia. The southern origins made them superior "in point of virtue and efficiency over Northern pills," with a "double claim on the patronage of our people." Made in Richmond, Leonard's Pills were perfect to cure headaches, upset stomachs, and "all diseases arising from the derangement of the liver." Sold by the box, the pills were a "Southern medicine for Southern people." Other medicines claimed that they were "carefully placed to cure the southern diseases."

After trying them, "Every southerner will be satisfied"; this was "No Yankee Hype!"[45]

William Jenson even appealed to a Confederate identity to sell his teething medicine for infants. A druggist in Charleston, Jenson hoped to capture a market otherwise dominated by northern-made elixirs. To calm infants to sleep, Jenson offered to mothers and nurses his "Southern Soothing Syrup." The formula was emphatically not the northern medicines bottled and sold under a different name but rather the recipe of an "old and experienced" nurse in England. Every mother should make the syrup a "household acquisition." If they did, a spoonful will "bring rest to yourselves and give relief and strength to your infants." Confederate mothers thought otherwise, perhaps confused by how much "southern" was in a recipe from England, and by early 1863, advertisements for Jenson's syrup disappeared, but not before the editor of the *Cincinnati Daily Press* had some fun. After summarizing several recent Union military successes, he advised all Confederates who happened upon his column "to use freely their *Southern* soothing sirup"[46]

In all of these pitches, the advertising men had to work against two trends in Civil War medicine. First, soldiers were learning to better protect their physical and mental well-being. In her study on health and the "environment of war," historian Kathryn Shively Meier argues that Yankees and Rebels, when in camp, quickly learned the value of eradicating pests, eating fruits and vegetables, and taking exercise. This self-care helped the armies to remain effective military forces. Second, the medicine practiced in Union military hospitals was increasingly becoming a healing art. Looking back at the start of the war, Union surgeon Charles Tripler admitted that "all sorts of doctors—steam, eclectic, and even advertising quacks—were sometimes commissioned as medical officers." Drawing upon actual field experience, however, Union surgeons instituted reforms that improved treatment of the wounded. By 1865, the creation of an ambulance corps and field hospitals close to the front lines had helped to transform American medicine from a hodgepodge of ideas into a science.[47]

How well, then, did the "advertising quacks" market their wares? The answer is found, in part, through the strong reaction against patent medicines expressed by many northerners and southerners. A columnist for the *Southern Literary Messenger* joked that a "quack doctor" had, late in life, donated his money to an insane asylum. When asked about his generosity, the charlatan supposedly replied that he was happy to wish his fortune to the "liberal class who patronized him." Tongue firmly in cheek, another magazine writer declared that patent medicine makers had every reason to tout the successes of their pills and potions because "as many folks lived by 'em as what died by 'em." In a book on supposed "humbugs," an anonymous author claimed that the United States had become the "Paradise of Quacks." He apologized if "readers who are wedded to their favorite 'pills' and 'syrups'" might not agree with him. Yet, of all the "pure, unalloyed impositions" that his countrymen cherished, "none is more wide-spread and prominent than the *Patent Medicine Humbug.*" In reacting so clearly against patent medicines, these writers indicate that many people were responding to the sales pitches.[48]

The success of the medicine men reflected their wartime opportunism. In city directories published during the war, any number of residents listed their occupation as "patent medicine agt. [agent]." If living in Pennsylvania, these salesmen had to purchase a state-issued license. By late 1862, the auditor general reported that the license fee had earned the state more in revenue than the "sale of public property." Eventually, perhaps too many Yankee and Rebel entrepreneurs went into the business. Published in 1864, a business-advice manual cautioned young men to avoid going into the trade because so many others had preceded them. "The business of making patent medicines is much overdone," he warned, "even to an extent beyond almost any other." That advice might have been lost upon readers of *Round the Block: An American Adventure.* Published during the late war, the novel featured a wife who planned to invest heavily in advertising her tutoring business. When the husband questions the amount she intended to spend, she counters that she "had personally known three quacks who made half a million apiece out of patent medicines." Like the wife, many Americans might claim the same well into the postwar era.[49]

• •

In 1862, the *Western Sentinel* in North Carolina ran a humorous essay on a militia officer readying for the war. The captain was practicing "military maneuvers" in the family garden, when he accidentally flipped himself into a ditch. When his wife rushed to check if he was okay, he fussed, "What do you know about war?"[50] By 1865, advertisers had offered their readers a number of answers. They sold *cartes de visite* that allowed families to record a visual history of the war and the role of their husbands and sons. Through maps depicting the "Seat of the War," potential customers might follow the maneuvers of the armies. Yet, advertisers also touted a great deal of misinformation. Their depictions of battle were highly stylized. Worse, because of the false hope offered, their pills and potions promised restored health amid the very real ravages of disease and wounds. That they continued to sell these medical shams to "The Millions" showed that their gimmicks had tapped a market that even actual advances in military care could not dispel. Union and Confederate advertisers had hyped a humbug as much as a product, one of the more unwanted and unintended legacies of the nation's largest and bloodiest war.

CHAPTER 3

The Vote

Having spent a decade in the United States following the conclusion of the Mexican War, David Mitchell took a dim view of the nation's democracy. In his travel memoir, the British author reported that Americans were too often swayed by their momentary passions. He recounted a story from the early nineteenth century, when one congressman, angry at a loose pig rooting through his garden, killed the animal. When the man ran for reelection, the pig's owner voted against him. That one ballot swung the election, and, in 1812, the new representative cast the decisive vote to declare war against England. "But for this pig," Mitchell quipped, "we should have been probably saved from that war." He believed that Americans were no better informed of the political issues by the late 1850s and that newspapers bore the blame. In the weeks before an election, the parties ran announcements telling their readers how to vote. Often, the people were unfamiliar with the proposed candidate and "equally ignorant" of his "character and principles." After some rallies, and, often, copious amounts of drink, they went to the polls. "Their wishes were never consulted," Mitchell wrote of the political sham, "and they vote for [their candidate], by secret ballot, blindly."[1]

Modern-day readers might discount such grumblings as those of a European observer more comfortable in a world of aristocracy and privilege, and with some merit. A greater percentage of eligible voters cast their ballot in the presidential election of 1860 than in any other in the nation's history, to that time. Yet, despite these impressive-sounding numbers, some scholars have recently argued that Mitchell had a point. In their deeply researched study, Glenn Altschuler and Stuart Blumin assert that the high voter turnout "did not necessarily indicate a widespread and deep engagement in politics on the part of the American people." Paying particular attention to newspaper stories and editorials, they claim that party stalwarts were remarkably successful in using gimmicks and stunts to mobilize their supporters. The two social scientists mention the advertisements that had become so pervasive. In these notices, however, the parties employed shorthand appeals and marketed political memorabilia to help engage the vote. Additionally, as the war drew to a close, the notices commercialized the assassination of Abraham Lincoln. A political weapon as much as a sales pitch, the advertisements often were at center of the public's reaction to the nation's most turbulent domestic crisis.[2]

THE PRESIDENTIAL ELECTION OF 1860

Mid-nineteenth-century newspapers were themselves a form of political advertisement because they often were openly partisan. Although no longer entirely dependent on the political parties for operating expenses as they had been even three and four decades earlier, many editors still received lucrative printing contracts. In addition to payment for campaign-related broadsides and handbills, newspapermen often accepted a range of material perks from politicians. One straight-laced editor fumed that his colleagues received "free paper, pens and ink, free drinks and chewing tobacco, free board at the hotel, free travel by railroad." In turn, the papers ran favorable editorials for the candidates. The publicity became especially intense during the critical presidential election of 1860. The very future of the nation seemed at risk over the question of slavery expansion and the response if the new Republican Party captured the White House. The combination of political patronage and sectional passions fueled editors to report on the contest with, according to historian Harold Holzer, "a biased fury unimaginable in previous or subsequent generations."[3]

Amid the election-year rhetoric, editors discovered the business opportunities. They touted circulation figures to potential office seekers, as they did to merchants, lawyers, and other advertisers. The *Winona Republican* reminded readers that it was the "only daily paper" in Minnesota outside of St. Paul. For access to rural voters and their political wants, it was the "best advertising medium." The editor of the *National Republican* turned the abundance of newspapers published in the nation's capital to his advantage. "As ours is the only Republican paper published in the city," he explained, "it is fair to presume that advertisers, through its columns, may reach a class of readers who cannot be reached through any of the other city papers." A few editors believed high circulation allowed them to charge more for political announcements. The *Oxford Intelligencer* in Mississippi billed "candidates for office" nearly twice as much as the regular rate. That was a bargain by comparison to an Indiana paper, where political candidates had to pay five times the usual. No explanation was offered, although this editor insisted that payment was "invariably in advance."[4]

Attempting to get their money's worth, the political parties went right to the heart of their selling points by reducing long speeches and editorials to just a few words: the individual votes mattered. Whether slavery should expand into the western territories dominated much of the public's attention and often involved parsing the words of America's founding documents. Rather than rehash the details, political advertisements invoked a general patriotism. Supporters of John Bell and the Constitutional Union Party mentioned the "Union" five times in a notice that ran in the *Arkansas State Gazette.* "Let every Union man work for the Union," they encouraged, "as if its preservation depended upon his work; and let every Union man vote for the Union, as if its preservation depended upon his vote; and the Union will be preserved." Southern Democrats announced a campaign rally by borrowing from a party song penned earlier during the nineteenth century. Men interested in attending should:

> Come as the winds come, when forests are rended
> Come as the waves come, when navies are stranded
> Come as true Democrats, with strong hearts and brave,
> Come as freemen come, when there's a Union to save.

More directly, a Republican advertisement reminded readers that a vote cast for Abraham Lincoln was a vote cast for "THE UNION."[5]

The parties were equally succinct in portraying themselves as the saviors of the American nation, and the others as representing narrow sectional interests. A notice for Bell accused the Democrats and Republicans of attempting to distract the public for their own purposes. Those two parties were heading the nation into civil war through their politicking on slavery and the western territories. Instead, the "question to be decided is whether this UNION shall remain unimpaired in its glory, or whether it shall be destroyed, and UNIVERSAL RUIN usurp the place of peace, harmony, and brotherly love. Union men, do your duty!" Northern Democrats argued that only they stood for "Liberty," by calling for the western settlers to decide whether to ultimately join the Union as free or slave states. A ballot cast for any of the other parties would continue to agitate the issue and ultimately result in the "dissolution of the Union." Republicans countered that they were the true party of "Freedom." Distilling the party's platform down to among its most important words, notices for Lincoln declared that he was the candidate best capable of maintaining the "peace and harmony of the country."[6]

Editors recognized the visibility of the advertisements and used them to facilitate their own partisan message. Under the headline "Whitewashing Ministers," James Gordon Bennett, the editor of the *New York Herald*, reprinted a notice run by a local minister seeking work as a "wall painter." He was not the only reverend pulling some extra hours, charged Bennett. Other northern ministers were "industriously engaged whitewashing republican doctrines, irrepressible conflict sentiments, [and] impending crises false statements." Even worse, some men of the cloth "have been caught trying to whitewash Southern niggers in order that they might escape detection while *en route* for Canada on the underground railroad." At least the local minister was "honest and legitimate." Too many others were "revolutionary and illegal." In Memphis, the *Daily Appeal* dug up a notice run by William Seward, a Republican stalwart, in a Georgia newspaper in 1819. Seward had briefly served as a teacher at a private academy and was recruiting for students. The editor scoffed that the "'head and front' of the Black-Republican party," had been pandering for work since he was a teenager.[7]

Other newspapermen attempted to gauge the political atmosphere through the advertising columns. In early 1860, a New York editor observed that the "proprietors of Southern watering places are preparing for a good season" by running an unusually large number of notices. This was a "significant sign of the times" because it suggested that southerners no longer felt comfortable traveling in the free states. Should the loss of tourism continue, the "people will fix the responsibility where it belongs—on the party of Seward, Sherman, Helper, Greeley and John Brown." As a Republican victory loomed increasingly likely that fall, Robert Barnwell Rhett Jr. worried that the number of announcements for slave sales had increased in the Deep South. In an editorial in the *Charleston Mercury*, he argued that these transactions were not conducted to turn a profit but "for the simple object of getting rid of" an owner's property. Such hastiness indicated that some timid hearts already were in despair over the future of slavery as an institution. Should the election go against the slaveholding states and they were to meekly submit to the "rule of Abolitionists," the fortunes already invested would be irrevocably lost. To his mind, the "terrors of submission . . . are ten-fold greater even than the supposed terrors of disunion."[8]

In addition to rallying support, newspaper announcements helped to facilitate the political gatherings. Barbeques, choirs, and rallies had bolstered earlier presidential campaigns, and they continued into 1860. Pole raisings also were widely promoted. In a ceremony that dated to the colonial era, participants hoisted a tree trunk capped by a political symbol and banner. In eastern North Carolina, Democrats sponsored a pole raising in Lenoir County on one weekend and another in New Hanover County the following weekend. Food and "eminent speakers" would follow at each of the ceremonies. In Dayton, Ohio, the Young Hickory Club proudly advertised that the pole they intended to raise "is to be 190 feet high." A pole raising for John Bell included music and speakers. The organizers promised readers of the *Cincinnati Daily Press* that "if a good political time can be had, they will have it upon this occasion."[9]

The Republicans mobilized their supporters through the Wide Awakes. A marching organization for young men first organized in 1856, the Wide Awakes numbered perhaps as many as five hundred thousand members four years later. The camaraderie and purpose helped to mobilize the vote, but so did the opportunity to mingle with the young women also invited to the festivities. In Illinois, the Freeport Wide Awakes were to report in "full uniform" of black coat and pants "for the purpose of a street parade." The men might be excused from cutting their eyes to the side because the "ladies are ESPECIALLY INVITED to attend" the celebration. In Newport, Rhode Island, the Wide Awakes traveled by steamboat to Providence for a parade and fireworks display. The men were invited to bring their wives and sweethearts. They need not worry about a rough-and-tumble atmosphere aboard the steamer *Perry*, despite the late evening. The organizers promised that the "arrangements for the accommodation of ladies and preservation of order on the boat are of the most perfect description."[10]

According to the northerners and southerners who attended these activities, the notices had struck the right balance between the political and social. A pole raising in Warrenton, Missouri, included speakers and barbeque and reportedly drew two thousand people. A sympathetic editor back East reminded his readers that those numbers were "an immense gathering in that remote region." A participant at a political rally in Petersburg, Virginia, described a crowd perhaps too enthusiastic for the evening's speaker. After the man was introduced, the crowd broke into "shouts, yells, bell ringing, fire crackers, rockets, roman candles, &c." The noise might be excused because the "people could not repress their joy that night." A Massachusetts editor breathlessly reported that a torchlight parade held by the Wide Awakes in Boston was, "without doubt, the most brilliant spectacle of the kind ever witnessed in the New England States." The thousands of marchers formed a "living line of light" that was a "scene of beauty." More important than the pageantry, the parade had demonstrated the "immense popular support" the Republicans enjoyed in the region.[11]

For readers attending the rallies and parades, merchants offered the opportunity to display their political sympathies. Women might wear a bonnet or use a fan embossed with the name of their favorite presidential hopeful. Men might wear a "bosom pin" displaying an image of any of the political candidates. According to this notice, the fashion accessory was a "neat article for gents' wear during the coming campaign, and more desirable than any thing yet offered the public." Partisans of any political stripe might wear the badges and medals sold by an Indiana merchant. He advertised his wares with "Republicans!! Democrats!! Americans!!" A Mr. Hanna was equally inclusive. He sold "those nice little medals containing [the] correct likenesses of the different candidates for President and Vice President." About the size of a large gold coin, the medals made a "beautiful campaign charm or badge."[12]

Medals and pins might be discounted by modern-day readers as some of the gimmickry used to rouse a temporary political enthusiasm, but a range of evidence suggests that voters prized these mementos. A maker of campaign badges reported that he was producing thousands of them per day and barely meeting the demand. A group of "True Republicans" informed the party nominee that they wore a small badge with his image "as tokens of our devotedness to you." In the late nineteenth century, W. S. Hutchinson wrote a short story that involved the partisan badges as a plot device.[13] These are historically significant insights, but the notices provide the strongest evidence of a home market for political merchandise because they emphasized the breadth and quality of their wares.

Campaign-themed literature received much notice. As in past elections, there was an abundance of cheaply produced pamphlets to circulate a speech or a public letter. Yet notices for books were marketed toward the home and a sense of historical import. *A Political Text-Book for 1860* offered a brief history of all previous presidential elections, as well as the "most famous" speeches and letters of "all the statesmen now prominently before the public." Published by the New York Tribune Association, the 250-page book was "handsomely printed" and "should be in the hands of everyone." A political textbook by M. W. Cluskey weighed in at a staggering 800 pages and sold for three dollars. Readers should not be put off by the length or the cost because the book had "*permanent value.*" Between the covers was the "only complete work on the politics of the United States to the present time." The publisher claimed that fourteen thousand copies of the book already had sold and that "no intelligent man should be without a copy of it." Other books on the presidential election included maps that were "beautifully colored" and printed on "heavy paper," as well as "accurate portraits" of each of the four candidates.[14]

Biographies of Abraham Lincoln sold briskly. The Republican candidate was a relatively unknown figure to many northerners, and publishers rushed to fill the gap. They labeled some of the titles as "campaign tracts" but, more often, highlighted the quality of the work for home consumption. Follett and Fosters announced that their biography "IS AUTHORIZED BY MR. LINCOLN" and "gathered from the lips of his intimate friends." With steel-cut images, the book is "altogether superior to any other edition announced." They encouraged readers to "GET THE BEST!" Derby and Jackson used the same line—"GET THE BEST"—to promote its *Life and Speeches of Abraham Lincoln.* The book is "authorized, authentic and reliable" and "contains more matter than any other." A "pamphlet edition" was available, without the speeches, for Republican clubs. Yet it was the home edition that could not "fail to give satisfaction." A "Fine Steel Plate of 'Honest Old Abe'" and "attractive binding" helped to make the book "large and Beautiful."[15]

If not reading about Lincoln and the campaign, a family might purchase an image of one of the candidates. The quality and size of the pictures indicates they were for home use. In New York, J. C. Buttre sold "engravings on steel" of each of the four presidential and vice-presidential candidates. Included in the picture were images of the party platform and the Constitution. The engravings were large enough (11″ × 15″) to see the detail from across a room. Buttre also sold a small (4″ × 6″) image of Lincoln, done on the "the finest enamel." Suitable for a table or a desk, the picture was "a little gem." A merchant in Richmond, Virginia, had "beautiful miniatures" of John Bell and John Breckinridge. These might go in a scrapbook, to mark the election. He promised that "elegant steel plate engravings"—that might be placed on a mantle—"will soon be for sale."[16]

The images of Lincoln drew a sharp reaction in the South, an indication of the political passions aroused by material goods. In a story reprinted in several southern newspapers, a correspondent for the *Charleston Mercury* traveled with a friend to a New York springs. While there, the dinner table conversation turned to Jean Lafitte, the "notorious buccaneer and freebooter" who had aided the American cause during the War of 1812. One of the two southern men asked another guest, a loudly self-proclaimed Republican, if he would comment on a picture in his possession of, supposedly, Lafitte's son. The man looked long at the image before he exclaimed, "with indignant feelings, that all men could see in the lineaments of that face low cunning, deep and damnable treachery and piracy, most distinctly marked." The reporter's friend then revealed that the picture actually was of Lincoln and not a caricature but a photograph that was "admitted to be a correct likeness of the Republican candidate for the Presidency." The blood drained from the guest's face, and he remained silent for the remainder of the meal. The southern travelers chuckled at what they later described as "Not a Bad Joke."[17]

For others, such images were no laughing matter. An Indiana paper reported that one of its subscribers had recently received several envelopes with an enclosed image of Lincoln. There was no marking, except that the picture had "'nigger' written under it." In western Virginia, the postmaster was apparently the culprit in defacing a mailed image of Lincoln. The *Daily Intelligencer* in Wheeling claimed that Lincoln would have the last laugh on the "spiteful clerk." After the election, "'Honest Old Abe' will hit him a lick a good deal more effectual."[18]

Merchants were not above the use of gimmickry, and they helped to commercialize the election through their headlines. The tone depended upon the market. Local merchants most often opted for a neutral reference to the election, perhaps not wanting to offend potential customers. In New York, a Mr. Knox declared that "Democrats, Republicans, and Americans and National Union Men are united" in declaring the new hat at his store "a thing of beauty." A New England merchant claimed that his fashions included "Douglas Stripes! Lincoln Plaids! Bell and Everett Checks!" In Richmond, a dry goods dealer wrote that "DURING THESE EXCITING TIMES," voters should "use their utmost endeavors to have command over their passions." They also should "visit LEVY'S . . . and purchase some of those Dry Goods." The low prices would put them in a good humor. As important, the good deals would convince them that "it is both agreeable and advantageous to be polite and courteous to their fellow men." George Arnold was one of the few local advertisers to make an openly partisan reference, but even this was tongue in cheek. The Pennsylvania merchant announced "'WIDE AWAKE' MEETINGS" at his clothing store. Republicans might find themselves rubbing elbows only with other night owls, however. The store owner had just returned from a purchasing trip, and the headline meant that he was staying open late each evening.[19]

Because they advertised across much of the country, patent medicine dealers went to even greater lengths to avoid offending potential customers. The maker of "Heimstreet's Hair Restorative" targeted "Politicians of all parties." Many of them had become "prematurely 'old and gray headed'" from the excitement surrounding the election. They would be "glad to know" that a bottle of his medicine "will remove all traces of the battle." J. C. Ayer listed the "Mayors of the Great Cities"—including Selma and Tuscaloosa, Alabama; Detroit; Pittsburgh; and Burlington, Iowa—who vouched for his sarsaparilla as an "antidote" for most any disease. A "Dr. Dod" declared that "THE SOUTH AND THE NORTH" all praised his Imperial Wine Bitters. Anyone who doubted might read the testimonials from a "distinguished lady" in Alabama; doctors in Florida and New York; and a father in New Jersey. Disease respected no political or regional boundaries, and Dod assured readers that his medicine cured anything from sore throats and consumption, to "general bad health."[20]

After the election, local and national advertisers went their separate ways. Hometown merchants catered to their customers' political preferences. "Old Abe is elected—The Country is Safe!" predicted the owner of a boot and shoe store in Wisconsin. A Pennsylvania merchant screamed, "Great Excitement in the South! South Carolina in Arms!" The American nation was "in Danger," and this "Glorious Union Must be Preserved!!" A slave trader in Mississippi bluntly declared, "LINCOLN ELECTED! Civil War Anticipated!" Patent medicine dealers, however, remained unperturbed. Even after the Deep South had seceded by the early spring, the makers of "Professor Wood's Hair Restorative" breezily declared their tonic "The Strongest Bond of Union Yet Discovered between the North and the South." The medicine united all Americans in their desire to hear the question: "What has so improved you in appearance?" W. E. Hegan announced that "NEWSPAPERS INDICATE PUBLIC OPINION." In the troubled political times, there was "great confidence to be placed IN A RELIABLE NEWSPAPER," such as the "New Orleans True Delta . . . Cleveland Plaindealer . . . [and] St. Louis Republican." These papers indicated that the American public believed Hegan's "Magnolia Balm" the "perfect and complete remedy" for pimples, freckles, and other "skin blemishes."[21]

Following the election advertisers also kept Lincoln in the headlines, but for different reasons. Merchants recognized that the president-elect fascinated many people. They used his name to pitch their wares, a nineteenth-century version of the modern-day celebrity. The maker of a "hair stimulant" capitalized on Lincoln's decision to grow a beard, asking:

PRESIDENT LINCOLN
DO YOU SEE HIM?
Do you want whiskers?

If yes, one might write and receive a bottle of hair stimulant. After just a few uses any man might have a "full beard" that rivaled Lincoln's. That same man might follow the new president to have his picture taken, at least according to a New York photographer. "Abraham Lincoln, the People's President, the poor man's friend, the man for the times," the studio owner implausibly announced, "will have his photograph taken (if taken at all on his way to Washington) at Holmes's Gallery." Other marketers used Lincoln to market groceries, cooking stoves, and boots.[22]

The public interest in Lincoln created some backlash in at least two marketing campaigns. W. Alvin Lloyd, the publisher of the *Southern Steamboat and Railroad Guide*, took out a "Personal" advertisement in the *New York Herald*. Lloyd was furious that another paper had accused him of blackmailing southern companies to buy notices in his book or be accused of supporting Lincoln's election. Lloyd attempted to turn the tables, huffing that it was "no unusual thing for the black Republican press of this city to resort to all kinds of misrepresentation against those who may be opposed to them politically." Lloyd admitted that he did not care for the new president. "We are a Southerner by birth, education, and in heart," he offered. Still, he was not a "swindler." Lloyd chose his words more carefully than the editors of the *Southern Banner*. That spring, they offered "Wanted—Abraham Lincoln's scalp—Apply at this office."[23]

The other presidential candidates soon slipped from the headlines after the election—except for Douglas. The former Democratic nominee died during the summer of 1861, and northern advertisers found a new market. Readers might buy a "beautiful photograph" of Douglas, set "in mourning embellishment." Potential customers who wanted a more personal connection might purchase from the Douglas family two of his "fine Carriage Horses." The next year, the "Douglas Memorial Association" advertised for contributions. A person became a life member for one dollar, and an "honorary" member of the Board of Trustees for one hundred dollars. Anyone who contributed received a "Diploma of Membership." The certificate was "beautifully engraved" with a "fine portrait of the departed statesman." Those who sent a larger donation also received a "beautiful imperial size Steel Engraving of Judge Douglas."[24]

THE PRESIDENTIAL ELECTION OF 1864

Four years later, when Lincoln stood for reelection, newspaper editors again touted the political importance of their advertising columns, which for pennies a line reached a large number of readers. The *New-York Tribune* proudly declared its circulation higher than "any other newspaper published in America or (we believe) in the world." The paper supported the Republican Party, but merchants might reach customers of any political background. The daily found its readers among the "large majority of school-houses and the decided minority of grog-shops." The *Philadelphia Ledger* had recently raised its subscription price due to the increased cost of white paper. Store owners should not worry, however. The circulation and advertising of the Democratic paper "are larger now than at any period in the history of the establishment." The *Leavenworth Daily Conservative* abandoned any pretense of political neutrality in the sale notices. "The Republicans of Kansas should all advertise in the leading paper," the editor promised. "It will help your business."[25]

Political headlines less often seemed to catch a reader's eye, however, if based on the few references to the election in the advertisements.[26] Four years earlier, merchants had made frequent use of the presidential race in their sales pitch. Now, in 1864, with the war providing ample material for a lead, the election was only one event among many. "Vote! Vote!" and "Latest from the Election" were prompts used by merchants in Illinois and Maine. A Pennsylvania editor had some fun with a notice for "Mrs. Winslow's Soothing Syrup." In children, the medicine promised to relieve pain and "regulate the stomach and bowels." The editor wondered "if it is good for gentlemen who have been seriously disappointed in the election returns?" If so, "we urgently recommend it to the Republican managers of this county, not a few of whom need some 'soothing' preparation badly." The joke might have been as much on the editor, given the relatively few advertising headlines devoted to the election.[27]

Gimmicks drew less notice, but the wide range of politically themed merchandise suggests that voters were still very much engaged with the presidential campaign. Merchants sold badges and other fashion accessories to wear to political rallies and parades. Supporters of the Democratic Party might buy a "Copperhead, or Badge of Liberty." A play upon the derisive name used for the party by its political opponents, the Copperhead was "made of pure copper, highly polished, and artistic." Voters who supported Lincoln might buy a silver-plated "Union League Badge." The badge also sold as a brooch, for women who wanted to display their political sympathies. Democrats and Republicans alike might wear "Patriotic Medals"—the "only correct medallion likeness" of either of the presidential candidates—or hat cords in red, white, and blue to "Show Your Color!" Church and Clark, two merchants in San Francisco, induced partisans to literally light up the night. Their rockets, candles, and torches were "Sure to Bring Out All the Voters!"[28]

Contemporary observers used the political symbols to draw conclusions about the momentous issues of the presidential campaign. Pandering to racial stereotypes, Democrats ran a story about a "big negro" who seized a McClellan badge from a "lady's bosom" while she walked down the street. Rather than rushing to the woman's defense, Republican onlookers cheered and hooted. In a New Hampshire newspaper, a Union private wrote that he wore a Democratic pin on the morning of the election. His commanding officer told him to remove the trinket, or he would have to perform a "knapsack drill" until he died. The editor argued that only through such voter intimidation had Lincoln won reelection. Republicans countered by equating their badges with patriotism. A Michigan newspaper ran a story on a Union soldier who took leave from a military hospital to vote in Lansing. Wounded in the leg and "obliged to travel on crutches," the man "goes in for 'a vigorous prosecution of the war,' and wears a Lincoln badge." At a Republican rally in New England, a veteran argued that what political badge a soldier wore mattered less than his military uniform. The men in the army favored fighting the war through to Union triumph—a Republican campaign platform.[29]

William Thayer believed the issues of the election were so important that even children should be mobilized by reading *The Pioneer Boy and How He Became President.* Many youngsters had already seen and, in some cases, experienced the war's disruptions and sacrifices. As James Marten shows in his work on the Union home front, the fighting was appearing regularly in children's games and magazines by 1864. Publishers recognized that Thayer's readers were likely too young to vote but claimed the work taught important life lessons. "It shows what the qualities of honesty, industry, patience and perseverance will do for any boy who will try," asserted one notice. Another announcement asked parents to "BUY IT FOR YOUR BOY." Critics savaged the book as too simplistic. One reviewer scoffed that Thayer portrayed young Lincoln learning to write his name in the dirt as one of the great accomplishments in world history. However, Thayer had received an endorsement from Robert Todd Lincoln, the president's son, who claimed to be "very much pleased by the book." Thayer had been "singularly successful in avoiding errors, as I find I have, at some time, heard nearly every thing you narrate from a 'Reliable Gentleman.'" The younger Lincoln's praise boosted sales, and Thayer claimed a whopping nine thousand books ordered within a few months of the publication.[30]

Readers who wanted more information on George McClellan and the Democratic platform had fewer options because the party's convention did not meet until the end of summer. A former Union general, McClellan had authored several military titles that were still readily available. Because of the lateness of the campaign season, his political writings were accessible only in cheaply produced pamphlets. The letters and speeches of Clement Vallandigham, however, were reportedly having a "large sale." A vocal critic of emancipation and a former congressman, Vallandigham helped to shape the

Democratic platform. His *Record on Abolition, the Union, and Civil War* was "handsomely printed on good paper" and included a "very finely executed steel engraving." For those wanting a more intimate portrayal, a "biographical memoir" published by Vallandigham's brother also was for sale. The book was "of unusual value and interest; entirely authentic and reliable." According to the publishing company, Vallandigham was even more in demand than Lincoln. The memoir "is wanted everywhere, immediately by hundreds of thousands."[31]

A campaign chart praised McClellan as the "HERO OF ANTIETAM." Published by Charles Lubrecht, the lithograph included a colored picture of McClellan, a "sketch of his life," and excerpts from his acceptance letter for the presidential nomination. Lubrecht declared that the image "ought to decorate the wall of every Democratic voter." Republicans quickly protested that the Union soldiers were the real heroes of the fighting in western Maryland and turned their scorn upon the former general. A New York correspondent claimed that he had walked around much of Albany in the days before the election. "I can truthfully say," he wrote, "that every drunken or suspicious character, whom I have met, who expressed preferences at all, was in ecstasies over the 'hero of Antietam.'" Another correspondent claimed to have met a friend and longtime Democratic supporter in southern Illinois. The reporter told the man that three or four train cars had recently passed, full of soldiers shouting "unbounded enthusiasms for the hero of Antietam!" The friend replied that he had not heard such good news in some time. As they were preparing to say good-bye, the reporter commented that there was "one thing I had like to have forgotten." The man leaned in, expecting "still stronger evidence of the popularity of his candidate." The cheering men? They were "*all rebel prisoners of war!*"[32]

Northerners seeking a supposedly objective study of the presidential campaign might purchase Edward McPherson's *Political History of the United States during the Great Rebellion*. McPherson was a Republican congressman from Pennsylvania, but the publishers downplayed his politics. They claimed he had included the "most important Documents" in the nation's history, from the Declaration of Independence through the current presidential platforms. The inclusiveness made the title the "most important now before the American people," and one sought after by "very intelligent voters." Reviewers praised the work as thorough and well organized. The selected documents demonstrated the "integrity and capacity of the administration" and the "transcendent importance of the principles involved in our struggle for union, freedom, and law." That directly challenged Democratic claims that Lincoln had become a "tyrant" who had expanded the war effort beyond his constitutional authority. Lincoln was reportedly so pleased by McPherson's work that he agreed to edit one of his 1865 speeches for a later inclusion in the volume.[33]

While merchants hawked their wares, the political parties used the advertising columns to help mobilize voters. As in 1860, Democrats and Republicans attempted to build a sense of community through public ceremonies. Flag raisings had replaced pole raisings, reflecting a more national outlook by the war's fourth summer. In Philadelphia, Republicans invited readers to share the moment when they unfurled the "largest Lincoln and Johnson Banner in the world." Not to be outdone, Republicans in the nation's capital extended a 40-foot flag "bearing the name of Lincoln and Johnson" across Pennsylvania Avenue. The organizers excitedly announced that the "President has been invited and is expected to attend." The proceedings might have become a bit too enthusiastic. Shortly after, the Democratic National Association announced the "new and magnificent flag procured in place of the one destroyed by persons in the Republican and Abolition torch light procession . . . will be thrown to the breeze." Other political activities included parades, barbeques, and concerts.[34]

The parties again used shorthand appeals to explain why a vote mattered, and here differences emerged from 1860. During that year, the parties had portrayed their candidate as the best able to promote the "peace and prosperity" of the country. Events obviously, and quickly, had proven otherwise. Now the parties offered very different visions of the nation's future. By the war's fourth autumn, the Democrats claimed that only they supported "the Union and the Constitution." The Lincoln administration had trampled civil liberties through the enforcement of the military draft and the emancipation of the slaves in Confederate-held territories. "Shall we sink into despotism?," asked another Democratic announcement. The seemingly endless and bloody war continued only because the president and his political allies had gone well beyond the original war aim of preserving the Union. By 1864, the choice was clear. The Democrats offered "UNION! In an honorable, permanent and happy PEACE!" The Republicans offered "DRAFT! Universal anarchy, and ultimate RUIN!"[35]

In an almost unprecedented occurrence, then or now, open disagreement of the Democratic platform received advertisement in New York's *Sun*. Moses Taylor announced that he was chairing the "Convention and Mass Meeting" of Democrats opposed to a negotiated peace with the Confederacy. He invited "all of the Democratic faith" who "retain their respect for the manhood and patriotism which animated the Democratic Party in the days of Jackson." This included anyone who "cannot endure the shame of seeing their country's flag lowered to a tottering foe ever ready to trample it in the dust." The goal was to remove the "degrading concession" announced at the national convention in Chicago that "'THE WAR' so nobly fought by our brave army and navy 'WAS A FAILURE.'" Another Democratic notice in the same paper attempted to patch over any differences by promising "Union, Harmony, and Victory!" Left for the reader to determine was whether this meant victory at the polls, on the battlefield, or both. The infighting made some party members nervous. On the day of the election, Democrats had to remind their comrades to "devote the day to save your country."[36]

Republicans had their disagreements on postwar policies toward the South, but they found ample room for unity in the battlefield successes of the Union army. Recent victories at Atlanta, Mobile, and the Shenandoah Valley in Virginia headlined the notices for many campaign rallies. Other announcements highlighted the army officers invited to speak. Republicans now had the advantage of campaigning as the war turned decidedly in favor of the Union. Not surprisingly, the language of the Republican campaign announcements reflected a renewed military fervor. "Let our enemies see that patriots can and do appreciate Union victories whether they are won by bullets or ballots," thundered one notice. Another advertisement reminded voters that even if not a "soldier with a knapsack," they should be "in the field and . . . enlisted for the Union." As Republican voters went to the polls, they should remember to "Keep Your Eyes on That Flag . . . that to-day is waving over so many victorious fields."[37]

Lincoln won reelection, and advertisements for victory celebrations made clear the significance for the Union war effort. The president struck a conciliatory tone in his second inaugural address in March, famously urging

Americans to move forward together "With malice toward none; with charity for all." Notices for Republican bonfires and parades carried a more ominous message for any northern Democrat (or Confederate) reader hoping that the fighting might end in anything but the destruction of slavery and a complete Union victory. In Burlington, Iowa, an advertisement in the *Daily Hawk-Eye* rejoiced in the "glorious results" of the presidential election and the "crushing of the copper head party." Local Republicans were confident that the "great rebellion will soon go down in blood." Voters in central Pennsylvania purchased advertising space in the *Juniata Sentinel*, a weekly published in Mifflintown, to proclaim: "Victory! Union Forever! Father Abraham and Uncle Andy elected! No Compromise with Rebels!" As far away as Oregon Territory, Republicans hailed the reelection of Lincoln. The triumph of the president was the greatest of the many "Union Victories in 1864!" Now the final work of the Union was to "Push on the Column!"[38]

....

Politics remained in the advertising columns following the assassination of Lincoln that spring, when images of the martyred president flooded the northern market. Merchants emphasized the lifelike nature of the pictures as a way to mark the historical significance of the moment and to commemorate the fallen leader. William Rice advertised the "best likeness" of Lincoln that fit perfectly into a photographic album. He would mail it to "any part of the country" then under federal control. Another photographer of course claimed that he had the "Finest Likeness of the Late President yet presented." Potential customers should not just take his word for it but instead rely on the "judgment of [Lincoln's] widow and several intimate friends." There was about the picture that "indescribable something which assures even those who never saw Mr. Lincoln that it is a correct representation of his strong and good face." Other merchants touted their images of Lincoln as the "best steel engraving," a "splendid steel engraving," and of a "superior finish and most correct of any in circulation."[39]

Although not as numerous, images of John Wilkes Booth received a wide promotion. Card photographs of Booth were not uncommon in the Northeast prior to 1865 because of the actor's stage fame and good looks. They spread rapidly after the assassination, helped, in part, by the federal reward offered for his capture. One editor reminded his readers that a recently published image of the assassin "is said to be correct." Should any citizen recognize him, they should immediately "bring him to light" and claim the bounty. After Booth's death, the likenesses allowed people to see the man who had now become so infamous. A Massachusetts photographer offered a "splendid likeness of Booth, sitting or standing." He was so confident that northerners would want one of the two poses that agents selling the image "can easily make $5 a day." George Russell, a photographer in the Montana Territory, claimed to have a "correct photograph" of the assassin. Individuals who "are anxious to see how the greatest scoundrel in America looked when living" should stop by his store. Other merchants advertised the "best likeness of Booth, the assassin, in existence" and the "most accurate picture of the assassin Booth."[40]

Such images played a key role in the trials of the supposed conspirators. Federal troopers recounted how they displayed photographs of Booth to local residents as they pursued him into the countryside of northern Virginia. That might not have been very much help, one witness claimed, because the image a "very poor one." She believed Booth was a "better looking man." In damaging evidence against Mary Surratt, one of the defendants, a Union captain claimed to have found images of Confederate officials at her boardinghouse. Even more incriminating, he discovered a photograph of Booth "hidden in the back of a little picture." That evidence was so shocking to some onlookers that local officials in Louisville, Kentucky, reportedly made it illegal for merchants to profit by selling any more of assassin's images.[41]

In addition to the photographers, book dealers and other merchants attempted to commercialize the assassination. Publishers moved with remarkable speed. By late May, J. B. Hawley had released *The Assassination of President Lincoln.* The Cincinnati-based publisher declared that he had focused his "whole force and entire attention to bringing out a perfectly reliable record of the whole affair." No one should go without a copy: "Every American citizen—man, woman and child—will read it as an item of interest to-day, and which will pass into the annals of American history and be quoted as one of the greatest events, even to the most distant future." That summer, L. P. Brockett published *The Life and Times of Abraham Lincoln.* The book ran 750 pages, with a "beautifully illuminated cover" and "fine engravings." The title reportedly had sold seventy-five thousand copies in the two months following its publication. Agents who wanted to canvass for the book should move quickly, before more books flooded the market. The publisher crowed: "Much desirable territory remains uncanvassed. There is room for men of backbone." For those who simply wanted to mark time, a merchant in Buffalo appealed for agents to sell the "Lincoln watch." The lightweight timepiece "looks like silver" and sold for thirty-five cents. An ambitious young man might make up to two hundred dollars a day selling the watch at "Cattle Shows and Fairs." That might seem a high figure, but the merchant reminded readers that the Lincoln watch was the "greatest thing ever invented to sell." Other men and women might buy music written upon the death of Lincoln, as well as subscribe to a "monument fund" established in his honor.[42]

The marketing of Lincoln was less conspicuous in the former Confederate States, more because of material shortages than any lingering political hostility. Through the end of 1865, very few advertisements ran for images of Booth or of Jefferson Davis, Robert E. Lee, or any other ex-Confederate official. Still, some notices offered photographs and engravings of the sixteenth president. In Baltimore, a hotbed of Confederate sympathy during the war, a local merchant advertised for agents to sell card photographs of the "Late President." The picture was "taken from a painted portrait and is considered an excellent likeness by every one that has seen it." In Nashville, E. C. Middleton was completing an oil-color portrait of Lincoln. Mrs. Lincoln had reportedly seen the work, and Middleton rather implausibly claimed that the president's widow testified to the "correctness and lifelike character" of the work. A Mr. Geers in Savannah, Georgia, offered an image of Lincoln that seemed to transcend time. In a "beautiful picture" available at his store, the assassinated president "Is not dead but liveth."[43]

By the late spring, many northerners believed they had found evidence of southern complicity in the crime. They pointed to an advertisement that had run in an Alabama newspaper in late 1864, asking for donations to help assassinate Lincoln and other federal officials. With $1 million in funds—payable to a "Box X" in Cahaba—the anonymous assassin promised not only to give the Confederacy "peace" but to "satisfy the world that cruel tyrants can not live in a 'land of liberty.'" Union newspapers soon republished the notice, but with little commentary. One editor later explained that the offer seemed "mere braggadocio" rather than a legitimate threat. In late May, however, federal officials arrested the man who had paid for the notice. A lawyer in Selma, George Washington Gayle claimed that he had placed the advertisement only as a joke. Subsequent hearings cast doubt upon that as a line of defense, with one witness describing Gayle as "distinguished, even in Alabama, for his extreme views on the subject of slavery and the rebellion, and as an ardent supporter of the Confederacy."[44]

Gayle eventually received a presidential pardon, but, in the spring of 1865, Frederick Frelinghuysen used the advertisement as an opening to condemn the Confederacy. Speaking at a public ceremony on April 19, the then attorney general of New Jersey argued that while the notice may have inspired Booth, the real killers of Lincoln were "Human Slavery and Rebellion against Freedom." According to Frelinghuysen, the slave system had cursed the nation since its beginnings. Now, while in "agonies of its dissolution," that system "has dealt a blow upon him, who, as God's instrument, . . . has vanquished it." The "other murder" was the "offspring" of slavery: the pride of slave owners to defy the democratic process. That "foul spirit" had caused them to rebel "without cause, and without the assignment of any cause, against the fairest and best government of the world." Any northerners who "would trace the crime to its proper source" must not point to the newspaper advertisement but "accept the truth that the murderers are the two foul powers" that he had named. The Union had effectively triumphed in the Civil War by the time of Lincoln's assassination, but, as historian Caroline Janney has recently argued, national reconciliation would present its own battles.[45]

Later that same year, a novel by Dion Haco politicized the assassination notice even more extensively. *J. Wilkes Booth, the Assassinator of President Lincoln* recounted the crime from the actor's perspective. In the story, Booth and the fictional Larry McDonald, a member of the Knights of the Golden Circle, pen the newspaper notice (which Haco included word for word). Several months later, on the night of the assassination, two of Booth's conspirators are talking inside Ford's Theatre. When one of them expresses discouragement that no money had yet arrived from Confederate contributors, the other man corrects him. The point was to have the advertisement reprinted in northern newspapers. From that exposure, "sympathizers and friends North of the Potomac" had already contributed tens of thousands of dollars. "Only fancy a 'loyal newspaper' advertising gratuitously for funds to help us in killing off their vagabond leaders," he gloats. "Sharp as they appear to be they are as blind as a three day old kitten." Within one week after the republication of the announcement, "our friends in Wall Street sent us all the profits they had made in their gold operations for a week, and it was no small sum either." Although intended as a plot device to explain where Booth had received his funding, Daco had foreshadowed some of the political battle lines of the postwar era. Republicans charged that the Democrats were a party of disloyalty, and that the Copperheads and Knights of the Golden Circle had posed a serious internal threat to the Union war effort.[46]

Before the public's attention turned to the political battles of the Reconstruction years, Samuel Gardner, a longtime newspaper editor, wondered what politicians might learn from advertisers. A lot, he thought. In an essay on "Style," he argued that the individuals who ran notices had really thought about their words and expressions "because it concerns them in the tenderest point, their pockets." Every line made a point because every line cost money. "When tautology is an expensive sin, it is at once corrected," he asserted, "and repetition then becomes an unheard-of fault." Any reader might appreciate merchants' conciseness by placing their notices alongside "windy editorials" and, even more tedious, reprinted political speeches. He believed that members of Congress would become much more effective communicators if they were charged a small fee for everything from "gross expletives of language" to "outrageous waste of good words, which convey no perceptible freight of ideas." He concluded that American democracy might work best if politicians had to keep the "fear of the reckoning of accounts, and not of critics, before their eyes."[47]

As Gardner acknowledged, the advertising columns had played a significant role in the nation's political life. They had helped the parties to reduce their platforms to easily remembered slogans and to build a sense of political community. Amid the hype, the notices emphasized that individual voters had a simple choice in helping to shape vastly different futures for the United States. Advertisers also recognized that citizens' political engagement extended beyond the act of casting a ballot, as significant as that was. They marketed a range of mementos, including badges, biographies, and lithographs. These wares sometimes drew a strong response from readers, from images of Lincoln to the McClellan campaign chart. As the war drew to a close in the spring of 1865, the notices even commercialized the president's assassination. Additionally, the public reaction to Gayle's announcement requesting funds for the murder helped to shape some of the battles of the postwar era. What guilt did slave owners bear in causing the war? Were Democrats traitors to the nation? Americans would wrestle with these questions, but, between 1861 and 1865, the advertisements had demonstrated that they would fight one another as fiercely in the political arena as on the battlefield.

CHAPTER 4

The Armies

In the spring of 1861, Francis Adams had caught, by his own description, the "soldier fever." After reading a recruiting notice in the *New York Herald*, he enlisted in a cavalry regiment. "There was something attractive about the advertisement," he later remembered, "as there was also about the wild, dashing life of a trooper." That Adams had found the opportunity to fight for his country through the advertising columns was not unusual in itself; Americans had often turned to the newspaper for help in raising their armies. Most recently, during the Mexican War, recruiting officers had run notices for volunteers who were "able and willing" and "well disposed." Yet the scale of these efforts paled by comparison to that of the Civil War. Between 1861 and 1865, the Union and the Confederacy mobilized more than three million men. A higher percentage of the population was under arms than in any of the nation's other conflicts to that time. Newspaper advertisements helped to recruit the Yankee and Rebel armies that went to war following the bombardment of Fort Sumter, and to keep them in the field over the next four years.[1]

THE VOLUNTEERS OF 1861

Raising Union and Confederate volunteers required spreading the word, and military advertisements ran frequently during the spring and summer of 1861. The *New-York Daily Tribune* ran two columns of recruiting notices in early May, more than twice the amount of space devoted to "financial" and "steamboat and railroad" promotions. The *New Orleans Daily Crescent* ran announcements from the Cronan Guards, Pickwick Rifles, Quitman Guards, and other military companies in early June, taking up nearly a full column. That autumn, the *Cincinnati Daily Press* ran military notices across multiple pages and under "New Advertisements," "Special Notices," and "Local Matters." The surge in business allowed some editors to discount their advertising rates. The *Memphis Daily Appeal* charged only ten cents a line for military notices, one-half of the regular rate, while the *Brooklyn Daily Eagle* announced that it would run calls for troops at a "great reduction" from the usual price.[2]

Recognizing the widespread readership of the newspapers, the federal government encouraged military recruiters to place notices. In a memorandum issued that fall, then secretary of war Simon Cameron authorized the monies spent on advertising as "properly chargeable against the fund for collecting, drilling, and organizing volunteers." Only a handful of other expenses were permitted—such as purchasing medicines and renting campgrounds—showing the perceived importance of the advertisements to the Union war effort. Within days, however, Cameron's directive had caused some controversy. Andrew Curtin, the governor of Pennsylvania, grumbled that, without his approval, some men were "publically advertising" for volunteers. These "sundry persons" were drawing away potential recruits from his authorized efforts. He correctly pointed out that the interlopers were abusing the "authority that has been thus given" and should be "stopped without delay."[3]

Curtin's complaint about men recruiting without his permission reflected the local orientation of the mid-nineteenth-century United States. Low-ranking military officers (colonels, captains, and lieutenants) worked with community leaders to help fill the ranks of their companies (one hundred men) and regiments (ten companies). Once mustered, their units received a home-state numerical designation. The 8th Alabama, for example, was raised in west Alabama; the 71st Pennsylvania was recruited in Philadelphia; and the 73rd New York was drawn from New York City. Because men went into the military with their brothers, cousins, and friends, a recruiting notice penned by a neighbor-turned-lieutenant had far more influence over them than would have any national advertising.[4]

Union and Confederate officers who hoped to raise companies and regiments had little precedent to draw upon for their notices. The Mexican-American War, the nation's last major conflict, had ended in 1848, only thirteen years earlier. Yet the number of volunteers raised during the two years of fighting was relatively small—by Civil War standards—at about seventy-five thousand officers and men. The regular army also ran recruitment notices, but only infrequently. With sixteen thousand officers and men in 1860, the army did not need many recruits. Looking for "able bodied, unmarried men," peacetime recruiters emphasized pay, clothing, and medical care. These were not inconsiderable incentives for young men. Soon, however, the Union and the Confederacy had mobilized hundreds of thousands of soldiers. Many of these volunteers expected a short and victorious war, but the human costs mounted. The Battle of Bull Run in late July 1861, the first major fighting of the war, resulted in five thousand soldiers killed, wounded, and missing. To the time, the losses were the highest casualties suffered by American armies.[5]

Looking back at the start of the war, Chauncey Burr, the editor of the *Old Guard*, a monthly journal published in New York, blamed the recruiting notices for helping to create a "popular excitement" that had hoodwinked men into the army. Writing in 1864, he argued that several enthusiasms had swept the American people in recent years, including national tours by Jenny Lind, a well-known Swedish opera singer, and, later, the Prince of Wales. Nothing, however, compared to the war furor of 1861, the "most senseless and reckless of all the delusions which preceded it." Love of country had nothing to do with getting men to volunteer. Instead, he claimed, it "was gotten up by advertisements, play-cards, hand-bills, immense posters, transparencies, bands of music, and all the tricks resorted to in political campaigns." The poor men in the ranks had committed to the war as a "jolly lark." Had they known the bloodshed and hard fighting that awaited them, "not one in five thousands would have gone into it for thirty minutes."[6]

In the recruiting notices, there is some suggestion of war as an adventure. More men seemingly wanted to volunteer following the bombardment of Fort Sumter than either government could process into the military. Recruiting officers implied a prestige gained by joining their military unit. A Missouri sergeant wanted cavalry recruits who "must be of that intelligent and sprightly appearance which should characterize mounted men." A North Carolina captain wanted "good" men who were willing to "be governed by the Regulations and Articles of War." Other recruiting officers wanted "Bold Hearts! Brave Arms!," "strong, athletic men," and "energetic, able-bodied patriots." Some recruiters offered a hard sell and emphasized there was no time to dawdle.

A cavalry company had space for only "a few more men," while an infantry company needed just "5 or 6 more men." A captain advertised in the *Daily Ledger and Texan* that there remained only a "few vacancies" in his company. Because of the limited space, he accepted "good men only." Another recruiter announced that his company was "filling up fast"; any interested men needed to immediately "make application" to him.[7]

More often, advertisements used ideology to explain why men should volunteer. In northern newspapers, notices cast the war as a struggle to protect American republicanism. The nation was not dissolvable whenever a group of people was unhappy with the outcome of an election, or else the Republic would never work. Northerners should rally "for your Country's cause" and "Around the Flag" to demonstrate "Our Union Now and Forever!" "To Arms, To Arms," should fly the "Minute Men of '76" and all "Patriots." Another notice encouraged men to fight for "Our Flag and Our Country" and "The Constitution and The Union." In New England, "Patriotic Men" were asked to strike a "blow for the Old Flag" and to make "The Stars and Stripes Forever." Quoting from "E Pluribus Unum," a poem by George Cutter, an Ohio recruiting officer reminded his readers that a "'nation of Freemen'" would crumble when "its stars shall be trailed on the ground." They might avoid such an inglorious fate by volunteering for "THE WAR FOR THE UNION."[8]

By contrast, Confederate notices portrayed the war as a struggle for the liberties of white southerners against a "sectional tyranny." Captain Perry Guerry argued that true patriots were "Haters of the Usurpers and Lovers of the Sunny South!" A man might perform the "noblest act of his life" by enlisting to "fight for his country." The struggle would not come easily. Advertisements in Tennessee and Virginia cautioned that the "South will have to fight to stay free of northern despotism." But "fight we must and conquer we will." Lieutenant John Tate urged "able-bodied men" to join him "under the Confederate flag during our struggle for independence." Other recruiters encouraged men to "serve their country, in this hour of her need" and to "join us in the Southern cause."[9]

In addition, recruiting notices emphasized duty. Northerners and southerners believed that male citizens had a responsibility to defend the nation, and their appeals to duty were almost interchangeable. "Young men, your country needs your services," ran an advertisement in Macon, Georgia. A recruiting officer in Newark, New Jersey, reminded readers that "Our country expects every man to do his duty." Other recruiters declared, "We want brave men, who are willing to meet the enemy and do their duty"; and "No true son of the South can avoid his duty." Confederate advertisements sometimes varied the theme by emphasizing duty to a state. The tension between national and state power plagued the fledgling nation through the war, but not in the advertising columns. P. H. Nelson, attempting to raise a regiment in Charleston, argued that South Carolina had a duty to help Virginia. With the fighting at Bull Run, "Southern blood has been shed on the soil of a Southern State." Virginians had "proven their devotion to the cause of Southern Independence, and South Carolina is now called on to furnish more troops. . . . Will not the patriotism of our people respond to this call?" They did, and Nelson went to war as the lieutenant colonel of the 7th South Carolina.[10]

Confederate announcements had the advantage of appealing to the very immediate threat of Union invasion. Federal offensives into Rebel territory proved a rallying point for southerners. "Our Soil Is Invaded" and "Repel the Assaults of the Ruthless Invader," headed appeals for troops in Alabama and Georgia. In attempting to raise a cavalry regiment in Columbus, Kentucky, in early 1862, Captain William Lillard appealed to refugees after Union forces had occupied Louisville. "Those who have been bound to leave their homes to escape the prosecution of Lincoln's soldiery," Lillard fumed, "can now have a chance to meet their oppressors with arms in their hands." While recruiting in Upcountry South Carolina, Sergeant Robert Maxwell appealed for men to "come forward in defense of our common country in this her hour of peril." When they did, "the enemy will soon be driven from our beloved Confederate soil."[11]

The Confederacy had no monopoly on worries about invasion of state and home, and Union advertisements played upon similar concerns in the Border States. Recruiting troops in Rolla, Missouri—a state that suffered greatly from guerrilla fighting—C. P. Walker urged his fellow citizens to "Defend your country from the prowling traitors who would drive you and your family from your homes and crimson the soil of Missouri with fraternal blood." Harkening to the Revolutionary generation, Walker thundered: "Shall we submit to have the best government in the world broken up? . . . Rally by the stars and stripes as your fathers rallied and the war will soon be ended and our country saved." Colonel James Wallace urged residents of eastern Maryland to "Rally." The Confederates in northern Virginia might advance at any time into the Eastern Shore: "It is high time that Marylanders are armed and prepared to protect themselves against advancing Rebels." A Union recruiter in northern Kentucky showed that turnaround is fair play. Kentucky had attempted neutrality only to have Confederate soldiers "invade" the state in the autumn of 1861. "Shall we stand by," he asked, "and see our homes, families and friends despoiled by a ruthless band of Tennessee soldiery? Never!" Perhaps with a greater sense of ardor than geography, a lieutenant in northern Ohio urged men to join his cavalry company because the "battle sound is near our doors."[12]

Other factors prompted men to volunteer beyond ideology and duty, including the opportunity to serve in a supposedly well-known regiment. If based on the advertising columns, the Union and Confederacy had several "best" regiments. Two New England regiments claimed the title on the same newspaper page. The 6th Maine touted that its soldiers were the "Best Volunteers in the Service." The 11th Maine, however, in the advertising square just below that of the "best volunteers," described itself as the "best in the service." All of this would have been news to men thinking about volunteering for Major General Benjamin Butler's division in Boston. "YOU ARE RIGHT BOYS!" claimed an advertisement for Butler. "This is the best Division that has been raised during the war." In Columbus, Georgia, a Confederate artillery captain admitted that he accepted only volunteers "from the finest element." He planned to maintain his standards. He cautioned prospective volunteers that "many already have applied." If accepted, a new recruit should feel himself fortunate to serve "in the best company."[13]

Recruiters also appealed to a desire for action. An advertisement for the 20th Indiana pledged that new volunteers would serve in the "Advance of the Grand Army." Stationed with the Union Army of the Potomac outside of Washington, D.C., the Hoosiers would "move with the first rank." A notice signed by "Committee" in Denver, Colorado, hoped to raise a "company of mountain rangers for purpose of marching at once to the seat of the war." That might be a long march, depending on where the reader placed the "seat of the war." Distance aside, the notice exhorted: "Patriots! Turn out, and let Colorado have a finger in 'the Secession Pie.'" The mountain rangers might meet in battle "The Devoted Band" if marching to the east. An unidentified Confederate recruiting officer hoped to raise five thousand to ten thousand cavalry soldiers in southern Georgia and northern Florida. The Devoted Band would immediately ride north and burn New York and Philadelphia. Its commander grimly reasoned that the "shortest path to peace is to bring desolation to the invaders."[14]

Editors often referenced the recruiting notices and added their own reasons why men should fight. They reminded readers to "refer to Capt. Colley's notice"; "see the Orderly Sergeant's notice"; and "see Lieut. Hodgkins' call." There was some bravado, with men encouraged to "test your skill at a 'long shot'" by joining the sharpshooters, and to "aid in making the brazen lips of cannon speak in thunder to the foe" by volunteering for the artillery. More often, they reinforced the ideology already expressed in the announcements. C. W. Willard, the editor of the *Daily Green Mountain Freeman*, informed those men interested in volunteering that they would find the call for troops "in another column." He assured them that the 3rd Vermont was as "good as any" regiment from the state and that they should hurry to help in the "sublime work of saving the country." Another editor declared that the military advertisements "elsewhere in to-day's paper, speak for themselves." By volunteering, men would "show their devotion to the cause so dear to every patriot."[15]

As casualty lists lengthened, editors drew attention to announcements run by military officers who were, in the words of one Louisiana newspaper man, "experienced in war business." In Ohio, that included R. E. Phillips. The lieutenant was, according to the local editor, a "man of sense, and understands himself. He has 'seen service,' and therefore knows how to take care of his men." His notice was in another column, and, for those interested, it read, "Now is the time for you to enlist!" A Georgia editor declared that he took "pleasure in calling attention to Capt. Rudler's advertisement." That officer's military experience was "so well known throughout the South, his numerous friends will be glad to learn that he is about to take the field, where his services are so much needed." Any men interested in going to war "can not do better than to join this company." In New Hampshire, readers should "See [the] advertisement" run by Charles Hapgood. The newly appointed captain possessed "commanding form, stentorian voice, excellent judgment, and [is] thoroughly skilled in military tactics." He had opened a recruiting office, and the company was "fast filling up—It affords a very favorable opportunity for enlistment and service."[16]

The editor of the *Louisville Daily Courier* scoured the advertising columns to boost Confederate morale, in this case by disparaging Union recruiting efforts in Kentucky. Despite supposed plans by Yankee authorities to raise several military units, "it seems that not even the 1st Regiment is yet full, for the Cincinnati papers contain advertisements for recruits to fill up the 1st Regiment." The same papers reported that recruiters hoped to enlist men in northern Ohio and southern Indiana "for the Kentucky regiment." He mocked, "Hadn't they better open a recruiting office in Massachusetts, also?" In early 1862, James Gordon Bennett, the editor of the *New York Herald*, turned the tables. He reprinted the "following rich item" from a Richmond newspaper: "Recruited Wanted—Read all the calls for recruits in our advertising columns, and voluntarily take your place in one of the many companies which need you, before you are forced to bear arms *nolens volens*." He caustically asked if this was the "WAY THE REBELS GET VOLUNTEERS (?)"[17]

It was not, of course, and Union and Confederate recruiters appealed to different visions of the nation's future. Northerners might fight to preserve the benefits of the American Republic for future generations; southerners to protect their freedoms from the perceived tyranny of a sectional majority. Other recruiters cast the war as an opportunity for adventure and action. As battle and disease took its toll, editors added their own caveats. They encouraged readers to volunteer, especially under officers with already demonstrated military experience. Thus, newspapermen and other contemporary observers who portrayed soldiers as hoodwinked into volunteering did their readers no favors. The recruitment notices demonstrated that Yankees and Rebels had a deep understanding of why they fought, and a willingness to risk their lives for the cause. They would not do so recklessly, if judged by appeals to volunteer under an officer already seasoned by some of the war's hardships.

THE VOLUNTEERS OF 1862 AND AFTER

Accounts of Civil War recruitment often focus on the heady days of 1861, when men rushed to the colors and women and children gathered to cheer them to the front. The reality is that hundreds of thousands of Union and Confederate soldiers went into the military during and after the war's second full year. These men made the transition from civilians to soldiers under something of a cloud. The Union and Confederate governments instituted a military draft during 1862 and 1863, the first conscription laws in the nation's history. The federal government and local communities also offered volunteers a large bounty. There still were recruiting rallies and military parades, yet the drafts and bounties combined to give contemporaries a sometimes dim view of these later enlistees. A Kentucky newspaper encouraged wives to shame their husbands into enlisting as "One way to recruit." A Massachusetts newspaper scolded parents for holding onto their sons in the hope that the war would soon end. "We hear some fathers say their sons may enlist 'if necessary,'" fumed the editor. "Is it not necessary now?" The seeming inability of the Union to raise the armies to close out the rebellion rippled into the western territories. Published in Fort Whipple, the *Arizona Miner* worried that no white settlers would move to the West and risk attack from American Indians because the federal government had pulled almost every regular army soldier to fight in the East.[18]

Recruiting advertisements published after early 1862 suggest that many of the men who volunteered were married and had families. This is not to say that captains and lieutenants no longer sought the unencumbered. The 2nd Delaware artillery wanted only "young men" who were "active, sober, and intelligent." The 55th Ohio took only "Brave, able-bodied young men." Yet recruiting officers acknowledged the sometimes competing demands upon men's loyalty, especially when describing the bounty for volunteering. In Roxbury, Massachusetts, a citizens committee provided volunteers with a sliding bounty based on family size. Married soldiers received a one-time payment of eight dollars, while soldiers with a wife and children at home might receive up to eighteen dollars (unmarried soldiers received a payment of four dollars). The "Citizens Volunteer Committee" in Philadelphia also promised help to husbands and fathers. Men might "now enlist under the most advantageous conditions, and while assisting their country in this crisis, can secure ample provisions for the families during their absence." Confederate communities were no less generous. Volunteers who enlisted in the Concordia Sharpshooters in Natchez, Mississippi, received a $120 bounty for their wives, and twenty-five dollars for each child. Men who enlisted in a regiment raised in New Orleans during the spring of 1862 received the assurance that the local community would make sure that their families were "provided for."[19]

Volunteers might serve in any number of military duties, reflecting the increasing totality of the fighting by 1862. At the start of the war, Union and Confederate newspapers overwhelmingly ran notices for infantry and cavalry regiments, and artillery batteries. These three branches still dominated, but the ferocity of the conflict had opened opportunities for other forms of military service. The Union and the Confederacy ran advertisements for marines to serve aboard naval ships and, by 1864, guards for increasingly crowded prisoner-of-war camps. Along the western frontier, men might join a militia cavalry company to pursue "marauding Indians who have been murdering and robbing." The troopers should expect to be in the saddle for up to one month. With much of the war fought in the South, the Confederacy appealed for disabled soldiers to serve in "home guard" companies. The home guard would muster "only in cases of necessity, and for the defense of our homes and families." The Union countered with the Invalid Corps. Soldiers in this "Corps of Honor" would serve primarily as a military garrison in northern cities. In New York, soldiers were grouped by the type of injury they had suffered. Men were organized into separate companies based on whether they had "lost" an arm or a leg. As important as guarding a railroad hub or supply point, the Invalid Corps freed able-bodied soldiers to serve at the front.[20]

Beginning in early 1863, Union recruiting notices appealed for African American soldiers. By the end of the war, about 10 percent of the soldiers and sailors who had served in the Union military were black men. The vast majority of these volunteers were former slaves and recruited in the South. A number of notices ran in northern newspapers, however, the first time that the military had openly recruited black men in the nation's history. The notices generally were straightforward. R. Colson, a recruiter for the United States Colored Troops, told any men interested in volunteering simply to show up outside his office at two o'clock every afternoon. Vincent Colyer attempted to recruit in Albany for the "only regiment of colored men authorized in New York." A white officer in the 23rd United States Colored Troops declared that he although he wanted volunteers, they must have a "fair common school education." An advertisement for a war rally in the *Detroit Free Press* listed a reason why black men should volunteer. The "colored people of Detroit and vicinity" met in the basement of a Methodist church in mid-September. A series of speakers addressed the "war and COLORED VOLUNTEERING." At the close of the meeting, "an opportunity will be given to every patriot to enroll himself among his country's defenders." Should the Michigan soldiers experience combat, the federal government would give "pensions to all wounded, and to the families of all who may fall."[21]

There was considerable public backlash in the Union against the recruitment of black soldiers, and a Massachusetts-born historian and bibliographer used a notice from the Revolutionary era to attempt to diffuse the criticism. In *An Historical Research Respecting the Opinions of the Founders of the Republic on Negroes as Slaves, as Citizens and as Soldiers*, George Livermore acknowledged that many northerners believed the formation of black regiments was not in keeping with the ideals of the Founding Fathers. He, however, reprinted a runaway announcement for a "Molatto Fellow" that had run in the *Boston Gazette* in late 1750. Crispus Attucks was never apprehended, and when he next appeared in a Massachusetts newspaper twenty years later, "it was under very different circumstances. He was no longer a fugitive slave, but a hero and a martyr." The notice was a clear reminder that Attucks was, at one time, held in bondage. And yet, through the shedding of his "precious blood," the former slave had demonstrated that black men were willing to fight and, if need be, die, for their country.[22]

The book helped to swing northern opinion toward the enlistment of black soldiers. An Indiana editor claimed that Livermore's work demonstrated that Americans had mistakenly come to associate slavery with black men and women and "have been blinded to his good traits of character, and have done great injustice to the capacity of the race." Attucks and other black patriots had demonstrated that they would fight if offered the opportunity. That moment had arrived with the Emancipation Proclamation. "Organize them into regiments," he declared of the newly freed slaves. "Let them not only assist in building fortifications, &c., but let them fight." A New York editor claimed that Livermore had clearly documented that, following the death of Attucks, George Washington and other military leaders had permitted black men to serve in the American army. "Let us ponder these lessons from our own history," he encouraged. Livermore was so persuasive in arguing for the enlistment of black soldiers that President Lincoln reportedly gave him the pen he had used to sign the Emancipation Proclamation. Had the runaway notice for Attucks not gone unmet, the flow of the nation's history might have taken a different course by 1863.[23]

Despite the broadening of the war effort, Union recruiting notices emphasized the preservation of the American Republic. As after the bombardment of Fort Sumter, the nation transcended the individual. In late 1862, men in Concord,

New Hampshire, received encouragement "to join the grand forward movement which is soon to scatter the enemies of the Republic, sustain the honor of our Flag, and vindicate the supremacy of the laws." Readers in upstate New York opened the advertising columns to the blare of "Patriotism, Duty, and Interest all require you to enlist. . . . Your country needs you!" In Indiana and Kansas, men read that they had the "chance now of crushing out the rebellion, and once more witnessing the supremacy of the Stars and Stripes," and "It is the duty of every loyal man to come forward." "Rally Once Again" to "Protect Your Country's Flag," ran notices for Ohio infantry regiments in the *Gallipolis Journal.* In Boston, men were reminded that "now is the time" for them to "do *their* share in putting down this rebellion." By contrast, in her deeply researched study on soldiers' motivations, historian Chandra Manning argues that northern officers and enlisted men increasingly recognized the destruction of slavery as necessary to make the Union worthy of salvation. Unlike the recruitment notices, letters and diaries showed a considerable evolution in what was thought to constitute the meaning of American democracy.[24]

By late 1862, Confederate notices warned that the destruction of slavery would fundamentally alter the South's social order. "Will you accept tyranny and slavery?" ran an advertisement in Richmond. "Fight for the right!" Other Confederate notices encouraged men to fight in the "holy cause of Freedom," "For Freedom and Love of Country," and "in defense of country." In their notices, many recruiters pointed to specific Union offensives. They referred to Union armies in the Mississippi River Valley as "vandal enemies" making a "desolating march." A Louisiana newspaper raised the specter of black Union soldiers marching out from the recently occupied Baton Rouge: The "Beautiful valley of the Red River must not be allowed to pass to mercenaries and our wives subject to brutal lust." The *Carolina Watchman* attempted to rally new recruits to help defeat successful Union attacks along the coast. "The struggle now going on is for life or death," warned the paper. "Subjugation is political, social, and moral death."[25]

Also receiving frequent mention in the notices was avoidance of the draft. The overwhelming number of Union and Confederate soldiers gave "willing consent" to their military service, to borrow the phrasing of historian James McPherson, but the advertisements portrayed the other options as limited, at best. A New York artillery battalion urged readers to "be an honorable volunteer rather than a conscript." A Kentucky cavalry regiment warned, "DON'T

BE DRAFTED." Entering the army as a draftee was a "disgrace" that would follow a man into the postwar: "Will it be said that you waited to be drafted before protecting the government that has provided you peace and happiness?" An artillery officer in Vicksburg, Mississippi, offered the "Last Chance to Escape Conscription" by volunteering in his battalion. Given the choice between honor and disgrace, "it behooves every man to volunteer rather than await conscription." Other Union and Confederate recruiting headlines declared, "Come In Out of the Draft," "Last Opportunity," "Avoid the Draft," and "Last Chance."[26]

Should appeals to pride fall on deaf ears, recruiting officers offered practical reasons for avoiding the draft. Volunteers chose their units, unlike draftees, and recruiters extolled the virtues of their regiments and batteries. A Tennessee regiment promised that soldiers "will be armed with the best arms in the Confederacy." The 8th Alabama "will be ranked among the first in the service"; while the Macon Light Artillery was "one of the best companies in the Confederacy." An infantry officer in Georgia promised that his regiment would receive posting to Florida, "the most desirable position in the Confederacy." Northerners read that the Stanton Cavalry in Pennsylvania was a "Select Corps." "The Pleasantest Branch of the Service," headed an advertisement for the United States Navy and the Mississippi River Squadron. Serving aboard a western gunboat offered "no long marches, good quarters on shipboard and good pay and benefits of prizes taken." The land-bound might join the 2nd Colorado forming in Denver. The regiment was "expected to be employed only for the defense of Southern Colorado."[27]

The infantry often came in for a pounding. Captain C. Burks encouraged men to join his artillery battalion forming in Staunton, Virginia. Otherwise, "all conscripts will be put in the Infantry." A Union captain made the same point. His company in the 7th Iowa Cavalry needed "a few more good men." Draftees "will be forced to serve as infantry." The 1st Ohio Heavy Artillery promised "No Marching nor Picket Duty." According to a New York artillery officer, the absence of marching and picket duty was significant because "the most unpleasant and dangerous part of a soldier's duty is avoided." An Illinois cavalry lieutenant added that mounted on horseback was the "most agreeable" way to serve. A Maryland cavalry captain agreed. The cavalry "as regard to health and excitement, is preferable to any other." Still, for those men who enjoyed marching, Lieutenant Rowland appealed for a "few good men . . . wishing to see service." Joining the 91st Indiana was the "Last Chance to Avoid a Draft."[28]

In addition to choosing their unit, volunteers received a bounty. A recruiting officer for the 49th Ohio reminded readers that volunteers received a $302 bounty. Men needed to hurry: "In three days, the time for which bounties are offered will expire." Recruiting for the 2nd Minnesota Cavalry, M. C. Russell declared "Enlist and Avoid the Draft." Volunteers received a $102 bounty. The 1st South Carolina offered volunteers a $50 bounty, while the 3rd Wisconsin light artillery touted the "highest premium offered." A captain in the "1st Washington Territory Infantry" promised a $100 bounty. The amount was not as high as offered by some regiments in the East. The benefit, however, was that the unit was likely to muster. Only authorized volunteers received a federal bounty, and the 1st Washington was the "most thoroughly organized regiment along the West Coast." Colonel William Bartlett in Worcester, Massachusetts, combined the best of all worlds. He explained, "You can avoid the draft and obtain the following bounties and (what is better still) serve your country" by enlisting in the 57th Massachusetts.[29]

DRAFTEES AND SUBSTITUTES

Some men were not swayed by bounties and appeals to volunteer, prompting more direct government involvement. In the spring of 1862, the Confederacy passed a conscription act. With some exceptions, all men between the ages of eighteen and thirty-five (later extended to forty-five) were subject to military service. The following summer, the Union passed the Enrollment Act of 1863. Here too, almost all adult male citizens were subject to possible conscription. Although a vast extension in national power, and one almost unimaginable to Americans only a few years earlier, the draft actually brought only a relatively few men into the ranks. In terms of raising military manpower, however, the draft was a success. Far more men volunteered for the Union and Confederate armies to avoid the perceived shame of conscription than otherwise might have served.[30]

The public ridicule faced by men who opted not to enlist was enormous. In his study on the northern home front, Matthew Gallman argues that newspapers, magazines, and other "published material" filled their pages by "belittling those weak-kneed, cowardly, despicable types who came up with ridiculous schemes to avoid the draft." The message to "ordinary citizens" was clear: those "who run or dissemble or cheat are worthy of the nation's scorn." Yet, the advertising columns offered ample opportunities for men to legitimately avoid military service. The two national governments allowed for exemptions based on occupation, medical disability, family circumstance, and other reasons, and examination boards took frequent newspaper space. Readers of the *Iredell Express* in North Carolina learned that the "State Medical Examining Board" would interview "all persons claiming exemption . . . on account of mental or physical disability" in five different cities and towns over a two-week period in the spring of 1864. The *Boston Post* announced that an examining board was meeting in late July 1863 to determine "exemptions on account of disability, alienage and other causes." If a man eligible for the draft had a note claiming a medical exemption from a doctor not on the examining board, papers needed documentation. Lieutenant R. L. Henderson, the enrolling officer for the draft in Meridian, Mississippi, recommended that any man who had claimed, but not yet received, an exemption needed "to call at this office." James Linn, a lawyer in Lewisburg, Pennsylvania, informed drafted men that he would, for a fee, help to file their paperwork for an exemption.[31]

The Union allowed a draftee to pay a commutation fee if he could not claim an exemption, a policy that sparked its own advertisements. The three-hundred-dollar commutation fee was beyond the reach of most northerners. "Draft Insurance" provided a solution. Groups of men pooled together their money, with the sum used to pay the commutation fee for any unfortunate individual. The amount each man had to pay varied depending on the number of "subscribers." A draft insurance group in Philadelphia advertised a twenty-five-dollar subscription. In New York, another draft insurance group promoted a one-hundred-dollar fee for one year; and a $150 fee for two years. The "Mutual Exemption Fund" in St. Louis saw fewer of its members drafted in 1864 than anticipated. Each subscriber received back one-half of the one-hundred-dollar fee he earlier had paid. The next year, G. A. Colby encouraged men to purchase a policy in the Chicago Draft Insurance Company. He reasoned that the premium was cheaper than having to pay for a substitute after the draft. This was not a decision to put off until the last moment. When the government issued a new troop quota, "MEN AND NOT FIGURES ARE WANTED." Con men preyed upon the many northerners who could not afford draft insurance. An advertisement that listed only a mailing address in

Philadelphia offered a one-dollar pamphlet that explained how to secure a draft exemption. Once the reader had the pamphlet, he would need to spend another ten to fifteen dollars for undisclosed reasons to secure the exemption. Another pamphlet offered by "Lex" in Little Falls, New York, informed "DRAFTED MEN IN THIS OR OTHER STATES" that he had a surefire plan to "release" them from conscription by an "honorable and certain method." The reader had to send one dollar to receive the information.[32]

Other than receiving an exemption or, in the Union, paying a commutation fee, hiring a substitute was the most widely advertised way to avoid the draft. A drafted man could, with government permission, hire another able-bodied man to take his place in the ranks. The practice dated back to the colonial era. Local militias often mobilized only a portion of their manpower, and for a single campaign. Seventeenth- and eighteenth-century Americans saw substitution as a hard-nosed business, where some men did not want to serve, and other men, whether from a desire for extra money, adventure, or both, would fill the vacancy. During the Civil War, substitution created popular outrage. A wealthy man could buy his way out from the war, whereas a poor man had no choice but to fight and bleed. Substitution so hurt morale in the Confederacy that, in 1863, the government outlawed the practice. In the Union, where the well-to-do man also had the option to buy draft insurance, the trade in substitutes continued through the end of the war. By 1865, 116,000 substitutes had served in the Federal army.[33]

Early in the war, substitution occurred as an individual business transaction. A man willing to serve as a substitute placed a notice in the newspaper. The money pocketed by a Confederate substitute skyrocketed quickly. In the early spring of 1862, prospective substitutes advertised their availability for between three hundred and five hundred dollars. That summer, "able-bodied men willing to serve as substitutes" advertised for $1,200. The next year, the price had surged to five thousand dollars. The Confederate economy suffered from inflation throughout the war but not so much as to account for the astronomical rise in price to hire another man's military service. As the war continued, a substitute could almost name his price. Antebellum southerners often smirked at the seeming obsession of northerners with business, but the market hurt Union substitutes. Competing against the commutation fee, men willing to fight simply did not command the same prices. The money stayed generally between two hundred and five hundred dollars. One potential substitute marketed his services by baldly asking, "Who will pay me the most money to go?"[34]

Confederate newspapers provide some insight into the motivations of the men looking to hire a substitute, because the buyers placed their own advertisements. Most men placing the notices simply wanted to avoid the service. They provided a range of incentives beyond money, primarily highlighting the quality of the local military unit. Substitutes would go into a "pleasant Artillery Company" and a "crack company." An advertiser in the *Daily Richmond Examiner* wanted a substitute for a "good Texas regiment." The stay-at-home patriot would furnish his hired soldier with free transportation to Texas when the war was over. Another man would give a substitute to the 3rd Georgia a "good recommendation" once he had honorably completed his military service. In Vicksburg, Mississippi, a man needed a substitute because he was the only financial supporter of his own family and an elderly parent. In Atlanta, another man had received a medical exemption from military service. He still wanted to hire a substitute to have representation in "our struggle for independence." Z. E. Vaughn in Richmond wanted to hire substitutes for two friends already serving in the army. The friends were needed at home to take care of "their property, which is now turning rapidly to ruin in consequence of their absence." Vaughn saw only opportunity for the substitutes, beyond allowing his friends to return home. The men would have the same chance as any other Confederate soldier to win martial glory. He used as an example Franklin Pierce. The former Democratic congressman had volunteered during the Mexican War, and the distinctions won helped to make him "President of the then United States."[35]

Because the practice remained legal, substitution became a booming and widely touted business in the Union. Brokers advertised substitutes for hire, so, unlike their southern counterparts, northern buyers did not place their own notices. The volume of traffic was staggering. William Leyde advertised that he had men to sell for any "township" in Minnesota that might not meet its draft quota (the federal government assigned districts across the Union a certain number of soldiers they needed to mobilize, based on their population). All worried community officials had to do was consult Leyde "in person or by letter." J. L. Bacon, an "Authorized Substitute Broker" in Georgetown, claimed that he had enough substitutes on hand to supply any community falling short of its manpower quota in Delaware and Maryland.

The Washington Recruiting Agency urged northerners wanting a substitute to hurry: The draft was coming. "Citizens desiring to procure Substitutes for three years, and avoid the heavy expense of one when the draft is made," should contact a member of the agency. A broker in Milwaukee worked on commission and declared that he could have substitutes to any town "as fast as needed."[36]

Brokers needed men willing to serve as substitutes, and here immigrants and African Americans received treatment equal to any native-born and white citizen. Men born in Ireland and Germany were available in many northeastern cities, and the notices for their hire as soldiers emphasized customer service. A broker in Boston claimed to have "30 Aliens" willing to replace a drafted man. For $750, a draftee might have his substitute hired and "in the army within the week." B. F. Levy, another substitute broker, headlined his notice in the *Philadelphia Inquirer*, "ALIENS FURNISHED." The men might be hired "at the lowest rates." Even more important, because everyone had a schedule to keep, "Ladies and gentlemen will receive prompt attention, and can have men mustered in without trouble or loss of time." Two drafted men in New York attempted to undercut the market by appealing directly to "aliens." The unwilling soldiers would give $675 to each substitute—"CASH DOWN"—for taking their place in the ranks. The New Yorkers refused to deal with any brokers, who might charge a commission. Instead, "only the substitutes themselves" were to report to a listed street address during the early afternoons.[37]

Because African American men of military age were present in northern cities in relatively small numbers, they received even more preferential treatment from substitute brokers. In the summer of 1864, a Mr. Holly in the District of Columbia attempted to get a jump on any competitors. He offered $100 to any person who brought a black man by his office, as soon as the new recruit mustered into the army. An unidentified entrepreneur offered free transportation to New York for any "colored men" who wanted to enlist. Beyond the price of a ticket, each substitute would receive a $300 payout "cash in hand." Another recruiter promised young black men $325 once they had enlisted, claiming, "This is no humbug." Other brokers offered substitutes a choice of regiment and the possibility of enlisting in the navy. Conscription, at least, was color-blind, and a notice ran for substitutes for "Colored Persons who have been drafted." Cook, Rother, and Company, headquartered in New

York, offered to find replacement soldiers "at the shortest notice and on reasonable terms." In turn, the "Colored substitutes" would be well compensated as soon as they passed a medical inspection and mustered with an African American regiment.[38]

Notices for substitutes helped men to avoid the draft, but they remained a source of controversy in the Union. In Pennsylvania, the editors of the *Union County Star and Lewisburg Chronicle* accused a Democratic "organ at Harrisburg" of advertising for substitutes "without regard to color." The notice was bogus: "The design is to prejudice the people by the supposition that white and colored men are to go together, but it is announced that colored men are in colored regiments only." A Michigan paper reported on a drafted man who was willing to pay $500 for a substitute but wanted the "right man in the right place." The hired man "must bring sufficient proof that he is the blackest abolitionist in the town where he resides." Issues of politics and race highly colored these writings, but the fact that substitution notices ran at all is what really bothered an Illinois lieutenant. During the late summer of 1864, James Connolly wrote that the "columns of the daily papers I see filled with advertisements of Northern cowards. Oh! How such men are despised here!" The soldiers "who are already in the field must do our whole duty now, for it is daily becoming painfully evident those at home do not intend to do theirs." Advertisements for substitutes had helped to bring men into the ranks but at a cost of divisions within the home front and between soldiers and civilians.[39]

Conversely, notices for Union substitutes helped to boost Confederate morale. That the Yankee army was filled with men supposedly forced to fight became a widely held perception among many white southerners. In one example, a Rebel captain penned a song to the "officers and men" of a Louisiana regiment:

> We've sworn to die or conquer, in freedom's holy fight,
> Though Satan league with Lincoln to crush us in his might.
> The Twenty-Eighth is forming, with Thomas in the van,
> And woe to Lincoln's hirelings who dare its shock to stand.

As the war entered its fourth spring, a North Carolina editor opined that the Confederate army was in fine form. The men had "no idea of anything but fighting out the war as long as the Yankees are on the soil and threatened the liberties of the South, and it never enters their heads that they can be whipped by Lincoln's hirelings." After Appomattox, the editor of *De Bow's Review* found comfort in knowing that the Confederacy had succumbed only to overwhelming numbers. He believed that prominently placed in any Union victory celebrations should be "Nine Hundred and Ninety-Nine Thousand Substitutes."[40]

DISCIPLINE AND DEMOBILIZATION

The mobilization of large armies led to discipline problems, with desertion the most frequent issue. Perhaps as many as three hundred thousand Union and Confederate soldiers deserted, a significant leakage of manpower. Newspaper editors sometimes portrayed these fainthearted patriots as all on the other side. The editor of the *Staunton Spectator* in Virginia accused the Union of knocking newly arrived immigrants "into a state of insensibility" and swearing them into the military. He boasted: "Lincoln will be taught that 'drugged,' 'swindled' and 'kidnapped' soldiers cannot be relied upon in battle, even if they can be kept from deserting their colors long enough to fight one." Other contemporary observers depicted deserters as caricatures rather than as men who were tired, hungry, and, often, disillusioned. A Confederate magazine editor told the story of one military fugitive in Richmond. To pass himself off as an amputee, the man attempted to shove his feet into one boot but succeeded only in falling over and breaking his neck. A northern writer described a group of conscripts arriving to their new regiment. Several of them were "fellows who have reenlisted and re-deserted many times—under different names, of course." When an officer called roll, one of the new men removed his cover, looked into it, and "exclaimed, 'Auch! Sure that's me last name I tuk—Hee-ur, Surr!'"[41]

Military officers recognized the reality of desertion, and they turned to the advertising columns to help track down their missing men. The notices began almost as soon as the armies mobilized during the spring of 1861 and continued through the end of the war. In early 1864, a Union provost marshal recorded placing notices as one of the expenses "incurred in the arrest or pursuit of deserters." The next year, Colonel A. C. Haskell of the 7th South Carolina cavalry demanded that the many absent troopers rejoin the unit near Petersburg. Haskell knew that some of the men had left to protect their homes and families from the Yankee invasion of South Carolina earlier that winter. Still, "cowards make the same excuse." That Union cavalry raids had destroyed much of the railroad running south from Petersburg also was no reason to remain at home: "Brave men will make their journey on foot, or on horseback, and rejoin their posts of duty in the army." Every day men dawdled "they weaken our strength and postpone the hour of victory and peace." Few men heeded the call, and Haskell continued to run the advertisement through the fall of Petersburg and Richmond in early April.[42]

Advertisements featured a physical description of the deserter and a reward for his capture. Like with fugitive slave notices (discussed in chapter 5), the level of detail varied. Most often, the colonel, captain, or lieutenant listed the height, complexion, and ethnicity of the missing man. A few officers provided any distinguishing physical characteristics. Thomas McCaffrey, a Union deserter from Kentucky, had a "peculiar expression of the eyes by which he may be known." John Grant, a Confederate conscript and deserter from Alabama, was tall, at 6 feet, but also had a "florid complexion" and an "ulcer on one of his legs." In Colorado, Andrew Babbit deserted an infantry company. He had "blue eyes, with a wild look" and "several small scars on the small of his back." The reward for the return of the men absent without leave was probably the line that caught many readers' attention. The amount offered generally was between ten and thirty dollars (a sum described by a Confederate colonel as the "usual reward"). Occasionally the amount offered reached as high as fifty dollars, although these advertisements listed no explanation for the increased total. Confederate officials sometimes turned creative as inflation hammered the economy and paper money lost some of its purchasing power. In 1864, J. Rainsford, "of the Supporting Corps" in South Carolina, offered twenty bushels of corn for the capture of Alfred Holley. Stationed near Charleston, Holley is "about 25 or 30 years of age, about 5 feet 10 inches high, blue eyes, dark hair, sallow complexion, and thin visage." That same year, the *Galveston Weekly News* advertised that "any citizen (male or female)" apprehending a deserter from a Texas regiment "will be allowed a furlough of twenty days for any soldier he or she may name."[43]

William Furr attracted especial attention when he absented himself from a North Carolina regiment. A "notorious horse rogue," Furr had reportedly stolen the "fine bay mare" of William Smith, his commanding officer. Furr was fair-haired and blue-eyed but "with a sharp keen look, nose somewhat

Roman, sulky osteer look." Smith offered a five-hundred-dollar reward for his return. Jasper Driggers, a Florida private, drew the anger of his company commander. The lieutenant fumed that Driggers remained absent well beyond the end of a leave, granted as an "urgent and meritorious case." Breaking military regulations was one thing, but Driggers's was an extremely selfish act. Until he returned, no other soldier in the company was authorized to receive a furlough. Readers should watch for Driggers, who had "gray eyes, sandy hair, florid complexion."[44]

Less often, Union and Confederate officers who ran notices for the return of deserters turned to public shame and physical threats. Colonel M. G. Harman threatened to publish the names of men absent without permission if they did not return to the 52nd Virginia in five days: "I feel confident all my men will report immediately, and not suffer themselves to be disgraced." Equally patient to a point, Captain D. C. Farmer of the 5th Texas threatened to arrest and court-martial the deserters of his brigade. "You, your relatives and friends must feel a deep sense of infamy which attaches to the name of deserter," Farmer scolded, "and it is enough to remind you that your services are needed by the side of your comrades in Virginia." Soldiers who returned immediately to their units would receive a full pardon. Charles Pennock of the 11th Ohio would not receive a warm welcome back after the Union private deserted during the spring of 1862. Lieutenant Henry Seymour vowed to seek the "extreme penalty of the law, which is death." Seymour fumed that Pennock had told a "deliberate falsehood" and "took advantage of the confidence placed in him, and *disgraced himself by deserting.*"[45]

A few soldiers improperly listed in the newspapers as deserters fought back. In May 1861, five privates in the Charlotte Grays were horrified to see their names in the *North Carolina Whig.* This was "not so." The men wanted the "inquiring public" to know that they had not deserted. Rather, they had taken an "authorized furlough." Privates John Osborne and Herbert Moose of the 25th Ohio might sympathize. The two enlisted men appeared as deserters in the *Spirit of Democracy,* a weekly paper published in Woodsfield, that fall. Osborne and Moose had, indeed, left camp without permission. However, they slipped out "intending at the same time to return." They were in no way "deserving of the censure which ought to be attached to *genuine* deserters." R. F. Manning saw his name listed as a Confederate deserter in a Virginia newspaper in 1862. "This was an error which has done me a great injustice," he insisted, "and caused my friends pain and mortification." Manning offered to show his honorable discharge, signed by a general, to any readers who might harbor doubts.[46]

Historian Mark Weitz argues that Confederate desertion became so widespread that it contributed to the ultimate collapse of the Rebel war effort, but the notices also helped to steel Union resolve because northern editors frequently reprinted them. Under the heading "Southern Items," a New York paper included a notice placed by a Georgia colonel, calling on his soldiers to each arrest seven deserters. If they did, they would receive a "140 days furlough and $210 reward." Another New York paper included a column on "Advertisements in Rebel Newspapers," on the argument that not the "least among the novel, unique and curious reading in the rebel journals is their advertisements." Among the reprinted notices was one for the arrest of Daniel Anthony, a deserter from the 5th Alabama. The Confederate private had slipped away, along with a "considerable sum" of money he had borrowed from some of his fellow soldiers and his lieutenant's gold watch. In Kentucky, the editor of the *Louisville Daily Journal* claimed to "have open before us" a Tennessee paper, with a notice for the Confederate home guard to capture deserters hiding in the state's strongly pro-Union eastern counties. "Would it be any wonder if the Union feeling in that State should be crushed out," he asked, "when men are placed like bloodhounds on the track of their fellow men to hunt down those who do not wish to bear arms against their country?" To his mind, the Union should immediately launch a military offensive to "liberate" the region.[47]

Other discipline issues emerged in the advertising columns, although never as pervasive as desertion. Theft was the most commonly listed crime, and there were apparently more "horse rogues" in the army than Private Furr. H. H. Hanmer, a stable owner in Union-occupied Nashville, reported a horse and buggy stolen by an Ohio private. Hanmer cautioned that the thief will "no doubt attempt to sell" the stolen items to the army. He cared little what happened to the soldier but offered a twenty-five-dollar reward "for any information that will lead to the recovery of the property." Near Knoxville, John Crozier had stolen his "fine gray mare." The Confederate colonel offered ten dollars to anyone who would return the animal to him. Captain John Hanking, an artillery officer stationed outside of Richmond, returned to his tent one evening in 1863 to find his personal possessions rifled through. Missing was a "gold hunting-case English lever watch" and several items of civilian clothing. Hanking wanted his property back but also justice served. He offered a three-hundred-dollar reward for information on either the "discovery of the stolen goods or the person who stole them." The streets of the Confederate capital apparently were no safer. Lieutenant Henry Orr reported that he was "knocked down and robbed" while walking down Main Street on a recent Friday evening. Orr was hit from behind and unable to see if the assailant wore a military uniform. He did know, however, that gone was his gold watch and $180. He offered a one-hundred-dollar reward for the return of his items or the "detection of the thief or thieves."[48]

With Union armies marching deeply across the Confederacy by 1864–65, soldiers stealing from civilians happened with increasing frequency. For all the reports of Yankee vandals, southern advertisements give a different impression. George Heard, a farmer outside of Atlanta, fumed that a squad of Confederate soldiers—"purporting to be impressing officers"—entered his property and confiscated two horses. The same men went to the neighbor's house and "took from the plough a good horse." The soldiers left a "forged receipt" for the animals. Heard offered a one-thousand-dollar reward for the return of the horses or the identification of the thieves. Matthew Allen, a civilian in eastern Alabama, reported two of his horses stolen: "They are supposed to be taken by [Confederate general] Wheeler's cavalry." To make sure, Allen promised a "liberal reward" for any information. Messrs. Wilson and Luster lost several thousands of dollars in Confederate bonds during a Union cavalry raid in northern Virginia during the summer of 1864. The two men had their suspicions about who actually took the certificates. They cautioned merchants in Richmond not to "receive or trade" for the bonds, and listed a reward for their return.[49]

• •

With an end to the war, veterans returned home. The reception varied by whether former soldiers wore blue or gray. Northern newspapers ran editorials encouraging a warm welcome for veterans. "Soldiers begin to drop down among us almost daily," declared a Connecticut newspaper man in July 1865. "Quite a number of our boys have returned home to go to war no more—we hope. Welcome, boys in blue!" Other editors asked for merchants to give "our soldier boys" jobs and discounted prices on "anything they may require" to resume their civilian lives. The mood in the former Confederate States was far more grim. The Union army occupied the region, and the newspapers ran frequent reminders under headings of "Military Orders." In Alabama, Lieutenant Colonel A. L. Gurney reminded Confederate veterans that the pillaging of "Orchards and Gardens" was illegal. All men "who shall so far forget their manhood as to be guilty of theft or trespass" would be arrested. In St. Louis, former Rebel soldiers were not permitted to ride the steamer *Randolph* until they had received a federal parole. At that point, they might board the vessel to "unequaled accommodations."[50]

Beyond the front page, "work wanted" advertisements indicate that some Union and Confederate veterans shared a common worry about an uncertain future. Whether former soldiers faced a difficulty transitioning to civilian work is not entirely clear because help-wanted sections were a staple of many daily newspapers. Against a backdrop of other people looking for work, some veterans placed their notices. S. Miers hoped to resume his prewar occupation. A doctor in Massachusetts, Miers advertised that he had "returned from the war." He was thankful for "past favors, hoping my old friends will patronize me, as well as the new." William Braithwaite—"a Confederate soldier"—pleaded for work in Harrisonburg, Virginia, in May 1865. With a wife and "several small children," Braithwaite hoped for work as a carpenter. He would work on any task and accept as payment "specie or country produce of any description." Braithwaite promised to work hard and to give "entire satisfaction to those who pay for his services." In Buffalo, an unidentified "young man, a veteran soldier, 19 years old," advertised for a "Situation Wanted." He would happily work in a "Wholesale or Retail store," or any other setting that provided a steady pay. Wherever he worked, the "interest of his employer would be his chief study."[51]

Unfortunately, in looking for work, some Union veterans were targets of scams. Get-rich-quick schemes are not a plague of only the modern day, and they made frequent appearances in the newspapers of the 1860s. The *South Carolina Leader* ran a story in late 1865 about a man who answered a notice for "valuable information forwarded" for ten cents. The information? "Knives are dangerous. Always whittle away from you!" Some former blue-clad soldiers were ripe for such schemes while they looked for work following the end of the war. In July, a New York paper advertised for "Returned Soldiers" who might have a "few hours daily to spare." These men might "learn the particulars of a pleasant business at home" if they sent six cents to a listed address.

Following an additional ten dollars in purchases—specified in a circular sent from the same street address—they might turn a "profit of $8 to $10 per day." That September, veterans "who have been honorably discharged from the service" might write to a Cincinnati address. Only, that is, if they were "in want of profitable employment." For a "small" but undisclosed fee, the heroes of the Union would learn a business that would clear them up to three hundred dollars a month. The sum was enormous for privates who had risked their lives during the war for less than one-tenth of the same amount. "This is no exaggeration but simple truth," the notice claimed. Any men who fell for such schemes in the advertising pages were left to their own devices if they hoped to recover their lost money.[52]

Despite scams and worries, Union veterans had the opportunity to at least commemorate their military service. "Diplomas" abounded for former soldiers to purchase, indicating, despite some scholarly claims to the contrary, they were proud of their service. Generic "Camp and Battle Scenes" printed in four colors headed the diplomas. Among the scenes was one depicting Union soldiers "marching in countless numbers into Dixie with drums beating, colors, flying etc." In the center of the document, space existed for a veteran to record his name, regiment, commanding officers, and "battles you have fought." The completed certificate was a family keepsake. One marketer declared that the "Soldiers Diploma" will "become yearly more valued and honored. Every soldier should have one." Mason and Adams, booksellers in Union-occupied Memphis, described the diploma as a "treasure." After providing their information, soldiers might mail the certificate in a "pasteboard tube" to any address "without injury." Their family and friends would appreciate the gesture: "They will get it framed and preserve it as a remembrance." Other booksellers described the diploma as "beautiful" and, echoing the description of Mason and Adams, "easily framed to preserve as a remembrance." Another merchant claimed that he was "sending thousands" of the keepsakes to soldiers and their families, and encouraged those interested to place their order.[53]

Recruitment notices from the Civil War are often overshadowed in the national memory by those from the two world wars, because they were not mass-produced. Yet, between 1861 and 1865, the advertising columns helped to mobilize and maintain the largest armies yet seen in North America. Many of the men who helped determine the outcome of the fighting received a nudge from the recruitment notices that crowded the daily and weekly newspapers. These announcements often emphasized ideology and duty but also acknowledged that not every man wanted to wear a uniform. Calls for substitutes were frequent, as they were for the capture of deserters. In the Union, beginning in 1863, recruiting announcements appealed for African American soldiers. A runaway notice from an earlier American war helped to assure many northern readers that the raising of black military units kept within the limits of the Constitution they were fighting to defend. With local orientation of mid-nineteenth-century recruitment, the otherwise humble advertising column proved one of the most important tools held by the Union and Confederacy to field the mass armies of citizen-soldiers.

CHAPTER 5

Slavery and Race

Writing in the late 1850s, a British journalist noted that whenever he met an American and the conversation turned to slavery, the visitor would almost invariably denounce *Uncle Tom's Cabin*, the best-selling novel by Harriet Beecher Stowe. He would huff that it was most unjust "for an author to string together a series of atrocities and give it as a picture of life in an actual society." The reporter acknowledged that there was something to be said for the argument, especially on a matter where passions ran so deeply. But he encouraged his readers to make up their own minds by perusing the South's dailies and weeklies. "As a general rule," he explained, "there is no better clue to the civilization which prevails from Virginia to Texas than the advertisements in an ordinary southern newspaper, headed 'Negroes! Negroes!!' or 'Cash for Negroes!'" In these notices, the "whole melancholy drama of slave life is displayed before the reader."[1]

Modern-day scholars have heeded these words and have increasingly mined the notices to draw rich conclusions about slavery as an antebellum institution. In their works on the slave trade and the rise of American capitalism, Steven Deyle and Calvin Schermerhorn have argued that merchants in human flesh were especially "ingenious" in their use of new business techniques, including advertisements. The announcements for the buying and selling of large numbers of men and women "grabbed" readers' attention by reducing the process to a financial transaction.[2] It was more than that, of course, and, in their masterful use of runaway slave announcements, John Hope Franklin and Loren Schweninger demonstrate that these individuals were "Rebels on the Plantation." Enslaved men and women struggled to win their freedom "even if they failed."[3] The secession crisis and the four years of fighting that followed continued to shape the slave advertisements, as well as the southern reaction to them. Northern and abolitionist newspapers, in turn, commented on these advertisements as the Union war aims broadened to include the destruction of slavery. Yankee and Rebel readers might learn much about slavery, even before they turned their attention to the news columns and the wartime discussions of emancipation.

BUYING AND SELLING

The continuity of the slave trade through the war is one of its most striking aspects. Some editors worried that the buying and selling of chattel had decreased following the election of Lincoln in 1860, for fear that the South might "submit" to "rule of Abolitionists." That more reflected proslavery propaganda than the reality of the advertising columns. That winter, announcements ran widely for "GOOD NEGROS," with merchants wishing to buy at the "highest price" and sell at a "fair price." Four years later, as the military tide turned decisively against the Confederacy, notices for the sale of slaves still filled the advertising columns. As Union general William Sherman marched his army through Georgia, Solomon Cohen announced that he had a "large stock" of chattel in Augusta. Readers of the *Daily Southern Guardian* might come by and shop for "house servants, and field hands, and also mechanics." By early 1865, with the Union army poised to strike deeper into Alabama, the *Daily Selma Reporter* announced the sale of a black family. The end of the war brought no immediate relief for two enslaved children in Louisiana and Kentucky. One month after the surrender of Confederate general Robert E. Lee's army in early April, a young girl was advertised as for sale in Shreveport. Later that year, in December, a teenage boy was offered for auction outside of Lexington.[4]

The notices were striking for their confident tone. Even as material goods became scarce due to the Union blockade, slave merchants called attention to the sheer range of peoples and talents they had for sale. They had "LIKELY NEGROES," including a "splendid gardener," a "good seamstress," and a "good farm hand." Robert Ransom gushed about the "valuable servant" he had listed for sale. She was a "splendid washer and ironer," and "one of the best negroes in the city." A slave trader in St. Louis, Corbin Thompson emphasized customer service. Any person interested in conducting business should see him before going anywhere else, because "I pledge myself to give satisfaction." In Staunton, Virginia, a slave dealer would send his stock for viewing, should a potential customer not wish to travel. He had a porter in attendance at the "different Trains and Boats," to escort any slaves to nearby towns and villages.[5]

At least some notices used straight talk as a marketing ploy. Itinerant slave traders often stood accused by disgruntled buyers of passing off sick and lame slaves as healthy. Local dealers, however, wanted to protect their reputations. Thus, in 1860, a T. Bergeron offered thirty-five people for sale. Two of the women were "sickly," and a child was "afflicted." A potential buyer should know that one of the men had a crippled hand. The next year, James Leatherwood sold Millford, a "LIKELY NEGRO BOY." The young teenager was "black" and "well made." But Millford had perhaps suffered some physical and mental traumas because Leatherwood declared him to be "mostly sound." In Crystal Springs, Mississippi, M. N. Robertson established a "slave depot." He promised that any black person sold "by us that does not come up to our representation as per bill of sale, will be taken in exchange." All of this would be done "with as little trouble as possible" to the purchaser.[6]

The professional tone in the slave notices contrasted sharply with the demeaning language about blacks found in southern editorials and letters. The use of "darky" and "nigger" gave whites a sense of power over the men and women around them. Even at the start of the war, when many white southerners assumed that slavery was a benevolent institution, the use of pejoratives for blacks was common. One correspondent argued that northerners only talked about slavery as a moral evil because they did not actually know any black people. But they would "howl worse than a whole forest of hyenas" if they actually met a "real, genuine, long-heeled, flat-nosed, thick-lipped, woolly-headed African slave." When the war turned toward the destruction of slavery, the wording became even harsher. In the same week that the Emancipation Proclamation went into effect in early 1863, a North Carolinian compared black people to animals in a poem on the "aspect and figure" of Abraham Lincoln: "For he looks nor like ape, nor like ourang outang, / Nor like baboon, gorilla, or nigger; / But is made up of things not quite human." Now that the Union army was enrolling black men, a letter writer cautioned "What We May Expect." Rape, murder, and pillage were three of the atrocities. The federal government would forgive any offense committed by a former slave, as long as he wore the "blue badge of tyranny and oppression."[7]

Slave advertisements also differed from other southern writings because they reflected none of the debate over the moral justifications of the institution. Scholars have long argued over the extent to which some southerners felt profound misgivings about holding their fellow human beings in bondage. The unease only worsened when the war had clearly turned against the Confederacy by late 1864. Some believed that God may have been punishing the region for its abuses of the peculiar institution. Such doubts never crept into the sale notices, where slaves remained a highly visible commodity. Their very frequency gave the advertisements an energy and creativity independent of the war-themed headlines. The business of slavery appeared to be not only solid but prospering in the advertising columns.[8]

Yet the wartime notices did not reflect the level of paternalism that characterized the antebellum years. In his work on the domestic slave trade, Steven Deyle argues that, by the 1850s, the notices frequently stipulated that the sellers and buyers would not break apart black families. Whether they acted from humanitarian motives or societal expectations is unclear, but, as Deyle writes, the "ideology of paternalism did have an impact on the way that southerners bought and sold their most valuable form of property."[9] Amid the strains brought by the Civil War, such niceties dropped away. Owners announced that they had families to sell and listed descriptions of individual members. In North Carolina, Wilkes Morris announced that he would sell at auction a "family of valuable negroes." The mother and her three children were each described on a separate line so that the buyer might bid on them separately or together. In Texas, members of several families were available for purchase or "exchange for Cotton." Casting doubt on the prewar claim that slaves received care from "cradle to grave," an Atlanta newspaper ran a notice for an elderly woman. Although stooped by the years, she was still "honest and trustworthy." By 1865, the advertising columns had shown that, whatever else slavery had become, it remained above all else a business transaction.[10]

Many antislavery writers read the notices that way and, during the presidential election of 1860, used them to rally partisan support. Amid the political campaigns, John S. C. Abbott, a minister and, later, historian, published his reminiscences of a journey through the southern states. He recalled a conversation with another northerner while the two men traveled down the Ohio River on a steamboat. The fellow passenger remarked that, from what he had seen of slavery in northern Kentucky, black families enjoyed better living conditions than those experienced by white laborers in the free states. The comment so shocked Abbott that he reprinted an auction notice that, in his words, "penetrates the cabin of the negro," by showing the willingness of owners to separate families. "Mechanics of the North, what say you!" he thundered. "Is your condition like this?" Obviously it was not, and he believed that white northerners should never shrug off the evils of the slave system. That same year, in a congressional speech on the "Barbarism of Slavery," Charles Sumner referenced an announcement for the sale of a sixteen-year-old girl because the "owner has no further use for her." "A sated libertine," he sneered, "in a land where vice is legalized, could not expose his victim with apter words." Republican partisans quickly published the speech and circulated the pamphlet as a campaign document.[11]

Arguing that many northerners gained their knowledge of slavery from reading novels, Samuel Smucker published *The Yankee Slave Driver.* In the story, Richard, a plantation owner, meets Snapp, a slave trader. To prove his credentials, Snapp points to a notice that he had run in a Richmond newspaper describing the decent care of the men and women under his control. Just behind him, however, is a chain gang, with its members sprawled upon the ground in exhaustion. Some of these "wretches" showed clear signs of physical abuse, including a pregnant woman whom Snapp had earlier struck for moving too slowly. Either not caring or choosing not to notice, Richard haggles with the slave trader over a price for the dozens of people up for sale. The deal completed, Richard adds his former slaves to the chain gang, breaking apart their families. Smucker asks his readers to imagine what they might feel in a similar spot, "were you torn away by the decree of some throned despot," from their mothers, fathers, and siblings. "Our poor humanity is ever the same," he reminded them, "however high or however low may be its sphere, and whether the color of its outside coating by white or black."[12]

Following the start of the Civil War, antislavery writers continued to turn the announcements run by slave owners against them. In 1863, Alfred Burnett, a nationally known humorist, turned serious when discussing a notice for an escaped slave in his *Incidents of the War.* The owner described his chattel as "light complexion, nearly white." Burnett strongly suspected that the runaway was the master's illegitimate son or grandson. He suggested that "conservative journals" in the North run the announcement and "comment indignantly on the practice of amalgamation." The experience would be a "good one; and we assure them that the instances are as plenty as blackberries in Dixie." Two years later, Albert Richardson recalled his time spent in the Confederacy as a Union spy. The citizens boasted of the "genial and hospitable" aspects of their society, even while thumbing through newspapers "filled with announcements of slave auctions and long descriptions of the negroes to be sold." He attended several of these flesh markets and was horrified by what he saw. A "light quadroon" young woman was surrounded by "coarse-looking men" who made suggestive comments while they touched her "arms, shoulders, and breasts." A planter suggested that the fondling was necessary because "That's the trouble with niggers, . . . you never can tell how old they are, and so you get swindled." Another auctioneer pitched a teenage girl by warning that "No married man had better buy her; she is too handsome." Richardson fumed that a sight such as these "insults Democracy, belies Civilization, and blasphemes Christianity."[13]

An author for the *Southern Literary Messenger* attempted to turn the tables in a short story by using a fictional advertisement to help expose northerners' double standards. Writing under the pen name "Klutz," he told the story of Towhed Blower, a rich Yankee who visited the South. Blower had two ideas, "and only two: he believed himself superior in every respect to everybody else, and that all men are created equal; two very common Yankee notions." After making some injudicious comments in a hotel bar, Blower is confronted that evening by an angry mob. One of the roughs reads aloud a reward notice for the capture of an agent of the Underground Railroad, and the others loudly voice their suspicions of the new arrival. Blower diffuses the situation by buying everyone another round of drinks. Unfortunately, he imbibes too much and, to show he has no hard feelings, purchases a black man. The next morning, hungover and cash-strapped, he demands a refund from the previous owner. That man suggests freeing the slave since northerners so often advised the same to southern owners. Outraged that he would lose his investment, Blower flatly refuses. His point made, the owner hands back the money, and the humbled Yankee quickly leaves town.[14]

More southerners simply found nothing objectionable about the sale notices so saw no need to defend them. Thomas Wentworth Higginson, later an officer in a black regiment, caught that spirit when, during the late 1850s, he visited a slave pen after reading an advertisement in a St. Louis newspaper. He watched as a planter bought the oldest of three sisters, to wait on his wife. "It was an epitome of slavery," he later recalled, "the perfectly matter-of-fact character of the transaction, and the circumstance that those before me did not seem exceptionally cruel men, made the whole thing more terrible." That the trade in human flesh was "not of special outrage, but of every-day business" made it all the worse. The seemingly ordinariness of the notices beguiled some observers well into the postwar years. In 1900, while looking through an old South Carolina newspaper, a writer for the *Atlantic Monthly* paid particular attention to the advertisements. He noted that merchants "were given moderate rates, and made use of them." Announcements for the sale of slaves were as common as those for social engagements, books, and medicines. Sometimes these dealings separated families, but the owners "were in the main kind-hearted men, who made the best of a bad system handed down to them from an epoch callous to human rights and suffering." He concluded that the white southerners who had placed the notices lived in a world that was "pure and simple, whatever we may think of its narrowness."[15]

RENTALS AND RUNAWAYS

Unlike notices for sales and auctions, those for the leasing of slaves more clearly revealed the war's influences. White southerners often had managed their labor force by renting out slaves for various lengths of time prior to 1861. But the practice of what Jonathan Martin, in his book on slave hiring, terms "divided mastery" boomed after the attack on Fort Sumter. Black laborers were in demand, as the production of war materials increased and the military swept white men into the ranks. In Texas, Major J. D. Thomas wanted to rent "1,000 negro women." No minimum age was listed, but the slaves would "spin and weave cloth for the army." At the Tredegar Iron Works in Richmond, J. R. Anderson also hoped to lease one thousand slaves. He would take families, as long as the gender and ages were "not disproportioned." The men would work the blast furnaces, while the women and children would tend the farms "attached to some of the furnaces and collieries." Other notices called for five hundred black men to work on Piedmont Railroad in North Carolina, and up to 225 people to assist a quartermaster in Georgia.[16]

Confederate officials offered wages to the owners but, initially, also appealed to their patriotism. They reminded slaveholders that allowing enslaved men and women to work away from farms and plantations directly aided the war effort. In Galveston, Texas, B. A. Shephard chaired a committee to raise slaves to work on the city's defenses. The owner must provide a pick and shovel, but otherwise he received thirty dollars a month for each laborer. More important than the money, Shephard appealed to a sense of duty. "Let no time be lost," he declared, "and we will have the beautiful Island City in a condition to fight off the hosts of Lincolndom, should they see fit to come against it." In the midst of bitter fighting in northern and central Georgia during 1864, Captain E. Johnson advertised for one thousand black teamsters. The work was dangerous, because the supply wagons often drove near the battle lines. Owners should bear in mind that procuring the black drivers "puts one thousand white men, now filling the position, in the army."[17]

Patriotism was not always enough, and, by 1862, rental notices assured masters that their "property" would be safe. Where owners had worried about the cruelty of some renters before the war, a lack of physical and medical care, and the possibility of capture by the encroaching Union army were now the two main concerns. The hiring officer at the Shelby Iron Works in Mobile, Alabama, promised that leased slaves would receive the "best of housing, clothing and food." Some workers might fall ill, but the on-site medical staff provided the "best treatment." At the Tredegar Works in Richmond, Anderson assured owners that he had made arrangements for provisions and clothing. He "safely" promised that "servants sent to us shall at all times be well fed and clothed." Additionally, the furnaces were "located in healthy sections of the country, remote from the enemy's lines." Should any slaves be "lost in the service," another Confederate officer advertised, the owner would receive "compensation made by the Government." A South Carolina major took a hard line when he advertised for slaves to complete some road work. The bondsmen would bunk in "good cabins" and, when necessary, receive "needed medical attention." If owners did not agree to hire their slaves, the laborers "will be impressed."[18]

Confederate officers sometimes leased slaves. These men ran notices for a "body servant" to perform menial tasks, especially preparing meals. By late 1861, Charles Bradley had reached his fill of army cooking. Stationed outside of Columbus, Mississippi, he wanted a man "who has had experience" to fix his meals. The owner of the veteran cook would, in turn, receive a "liberal pay." Surgeon J. C. Smith advertised for "two good cooks" but stipulated that they must be women. Perhaps aware that women in a military setting might raise some eyebrows, he promised a "very liberal" pay. An officer in northern Virginia recognized that, if he wanted loyalty and a good meal, paying the cook was more important than paying the owner. He did not want to lease a slave who might attempt to slip away but to hire a free black man. He promised that good wages and treatment "may be expected."[19]

The Rebel officer was right to worry about escape attempts, and fugitive slave announcements formed a mainstay in Confederate newspapers. These notices generally followed a similar style. Owners offered a cash reward, as military officers did for deserters. A bounty hunter, however, did much better by returning a fugitive slave, for which, by early 1862, he could earn as much as $250. Two years later, the sum had almost doubled. Because owners reimbursed slave catchers for their expenses, the reward was highest when offered for a person caught far from his "home." In Richmond, a Confederate major offered four hundred dollars for the arrest and return of his "servant boy." If the black man was captured on the outskirts of the Confederate capital, though, the amount fell to $150. The reward also sometimes was contingent upon the return of property supposedly taken by the escaping slave. Peter Smith promised one hundred dollars for the return of a twenty-year-old black man and a mule to his farm in southern Georgia. If only the mule was returned, the reward dropped to twenty-five dollars. William McAlister cared little about what might be returned to him. The South Carolina slave owner offered a two-hundred-dollar reward for the delivery of his "negro boy," whether dead or alive.[20]

These runaway slave notices often included a physical description. At first glance, the details seem remarkably vague to a modern reader. Owners struggled to describe the complexions of the runaways, arriving at such identifiers as "tolerably black," a "tolerable dark color," a "copper color," a "Ginger cake color," and "black." Oliver Perry was at a loss to remember even the name of his missing slave. The twenty-three-year-old went by Ben "or another name which I do not now recollect." More often, the level of detail was remarkably high for a person whom the owner considered an item of property. John, for example, had a "round face, low forehead," and a scar on his nose. William had on "one arm a cross and anchor and on the other a cross of sailor's work." Sloop-shouldered, Martha "talks and appears like a country negro." By contrast, Louisa walked and stood "very straight."[21]

The notices gave ample, and unintended, testament to the hard life and physical toll of slavery, as well as owners' perceptions about the racial inferiority of their servants. In Mississippi, John was distinguishable because he had only two fingers on his left hand, the result of an accident with a cotton gin. In perhaps a similar mishap while young, Lavonia had sprained her left forefinger. Into adulthood the digit remained "turned considerably back and almost useless." Other individuals had scars from whippings and very "bad pox." That enslaved men and women had demonstrated the mental fortitude to withstand such rigors made little impression upon white southerners, who described the slaves' almost childlike behavior as their most distinguishing characteristic. An unidentified "slave boy" from New Orleans became "confused when roughly spoken to." Henry, a twenty-year-old, had a "dull countenance" and was "remarkably slow and hesitating in his speech." John, a fugitive from Decatur, Georgia, was a "very slovenly negro." Other escapees were described as "easily confused when talking," "not very intelligent," and "slow."[22]

In addition to providing a physical description and the amount of the reward offered, fugitive slave announcements speculated about why the individual was attempting to escape. A goodly number of owners seemed genuinely surprised. They wrote that their slaves had left "without the slightest known cause" and "without provocation." Some white families were so steeped in a paternalistic outlook that they acknowledged no initiative on the part of their bondspeople. Instead, an outsider had "stolen" their property. In late 1862, an Alabama plantation owner offered $150 for the return of his "boy" and one thousand dollars for the "thief who stole him." The reward money was high, but with Union-occupied Pensacola, Florida, nearby, such "thefts have become too common." Two years later, another southerner advertised that a recent Federal cavalry raid outside of Richmond had "carried off" four of his slaves. Should any Confederate soldiers intercept the Yankees, he offered a reward for the return of his property.[23]

Many masters blamed their fellow southerners for luring slaves away from the plantation or farm, an announcement that prompted some calls for unity throughout the rest of the newspaper. Throughout the war, Confederate editors and politicians encouraged their fellow citizens to defend slavery and the racial hierarchy. At the same time, in the early war advertisements, owners blamed a generically described "white man" (although, in one case, a "mean white man") for disrupting their work force. The troublemakers had "decoyed off," "lured away," and "enticed away" otherwise unsuspecting slaves. By 1862, many disgruntled slave owners placed the blame squarely on Confederate soldiers. Sometimes these men were stragglers who were no longer subject to military discipline. More often, the culprits were front-line troops who wanted to relieve the drudgeries of camp life. A black man in Richmond was "taken off by soldiers because he is a good cook." Another man was "led off by someone in the army." Officers should keep a lookout for the stolen property, who was wearing a military-style cap. By early 1863, a leased hospital steward had "gone off with some soldiers." In attempting to improve their own immediate circumstances, these Rebels had created cracks within the very institution they were fighting so hard to defend.[24]

The destination point for escaping slaves varied by the individual and the opportunity. For some fugitives, reuniting with their loved ones overrode any other concern, as it also had during the prewar years. As John Hope Franklin and Loren Schweninger remind their readers, if the "breakup of families revealed the callous nature of many slave trades, it also bore silent testimony to the desperate attempts to maintain family unity in the midst of constant assault on its stability."[25] During the Civil War, a husband ran away to see his wife, a daughter to see her mother, a brother to see his sister, and a man to visit his "relatives." Distance and youth proved no deterrent. Lieutenant John Dorman advertised for Bob, who had escaped near Richmond. The "negro boy" was trying to make his way to eastern Alabama, where his wife lived. In New Orleans, Felix had run away. He likely was hiding aboard a train, to speed the passage to his family in Georgia. After the Union fleet had gained control of Mobile Bay, Alabama, William made his escape. He was attempting to meet with his wife outside of the city and "then induce her to go with him to the Yankee fleet." In Savannah, Georgia, Betsy had escaped. She was eight years old and likely fleeing to her mother on a neighboring farm.[26]

For many men and women, however, the Union army—and, after 1862, freedom—was the goal. In western Alabama, the operator of a sawmill declared that one of his slaves was "making his way to the Yankees in Mississippi." A young black man in Tennessee was last seen wearing a blue "soldier's cap and will probably make his way across the river to join the Yankees." Other fugitives recognized the danger of crossing the front lines. They instead hid in plain sight as camp servants for Confederate soldiers. Wearing a "gray military jacket," Jeff had escaped in northern Virginia. The owner believed that his former slave now worked as a cook for a Confederate mess. Jim also had run away toward the Rebel lines and "will try to pass himself off as a servant of an officer." Other men and women were "perhaps about some of the camps," hoping "for employment."[27]

Some fugitives were captured and, in advertisements for their return, reportedly blamed the confusion of war. Their quick thinking offered at least the possibility of avoiding the harsh punishments that normally awaited returning fugitives. By the 1860s, these individuals often reported that they had not meant to leave their white family, but, in the words of one foiled escapee, "by some accident, they became separated." Outside of Shreveport, Louisiana, a black man had become separated from his owner, a Confederate officer. Although the man had seemingly wandered far into the countryside, he claimed to only have been "in search of his master." In late 1862, William McLain advertised that he had "taken up a NEGRO GIRL" in northwestern Mississippi. The unfortunate teenager claimed to have been "kidnapped" by Union soldiers that fall and had recently "made her escape from the Yankees." When McLain found her, she said she was simply was trying to return to her owner. The Yankees did not apparently welcome one fugitive slave captured near Jacksonville, Alabama. The black man had slipped away from the Union army after soldiers had "impressed" him to work as a teamster. When picked up by Confederate troops, the man claimed to be making his way "home" to Georgia.[28]

• •

Such "return" notices were similar to many southern newspaper articles in that they portrayed slaves as loyal to their white owners and the war effort. For all the hysteria stoked in editorials and letters about the threat of racial amalgamation should the Confederacy lose the war, stories about slaves raising money and supplies for the Rebel cause helped to convince many white readers that their way of life was a part of the natural order. Advertisements about slaves attempting to find their "lost" masters contributed to the perception of harmonious race relations. Should the Confederacy lose the war, freed slaves would be thrown on their own resources by fanatical abolitionists and black Republicans, a freedom that most of them supposedly did not seek. Despite slaves intentionally fleeing toward the Yankee lines, some owners believed that their people had gone missing only because a Confederate soldier or another white southerner had tricked them. From their perspective, the threat to slavery as an institution came more from the upheavals created by the war than the approach of the Union army.[29]

Outside observers read the runaway notices very differently. In 1863, William Pittenger published his memoirs about his involvement in the "Great Locomotive Chase." Captured during the Federal raid to damage a Confederate rail line that ran between eastern Tennessee and northern Georgia, the Ohio private was jailed in a cell with other Union prisoners and Aleck, a free black man accused of being a runaway. "I wonder what those tender soldiers," Pittenger wrote, "who consider it derogatory to their dignity to fight in the same army that blacks do, would think if they were confined with them so closely there was no possibility of getting away." Aleck overcame any objections to his presence by being "kind and accommodating" and doing "everything in his power for us." When the jailer beat the black man in an attempt to coerce a confession, the other prisoners "could not help feeling the sincerest sympathy for him." Pittenger observed that the jailer's brutality toward the Aleck was not unusual in the South. When a slave or a free black was found without a pass, he was arrested and flogged: "This usually brings some kind of confession from him, and he is advertised in accordance with that confession." If no white person claimed the runaway, he was whipped again. The cycle between violence and new confessions and advertisements continued for a year. If the black man remained unclaimed at that time, he was sold at auction to pay for the expense of his imprisonment. "When once arrested his doom is sealed," Pittenger bemoaned, "and in this way many free negroes are enslaved."[30]

Charles Tennant used a runaway notice to counter European offers to negotiate a settlement to the war. In *The American Question and How to Settle It,* the English landowner and politician acknowledged that some foreign observers could not fathom that the Union was willing to spend so much blood and treasure to end slavery. They claimed that black Americans lacked the mental prowess to live independently. That was not the case, Tennant argued. "With regard to their intellectual capacities," he wrote, "considering the means taken to prevent their development, all the evidence establishes their equality with whites." A plea for equality extended well beyond the Union's war aims, even after the Emancipation Proclamation. As evidence, however, Tennant reprinted an advertisement for a runaway from New Orleans who "talks French, Italian, Dutch, English, and Spanish." The notice demonstrated that black men and women desired their freedom and, once they gained it, possessed the ability to responsibly exercise it.[31]

Harriet Jacobs, an escaped slave writing under an assumed name, highlighted a runaway notice in her autobiography, published in 1861. In this case, the announcement resulted in the capture of Benjamin, her uncle. He had fled after a physical altercation with his owner and had managed to gain passage aboard a ship. A storm struck while the vessel was sailing to New York, forcing it to dock in an unidentified southern port. "There the [runaway] advertisement met the captain's eye," Jacobs continued. "Benjamin so exactly answered its description, that the captain laid hold on him, and bound him in chains." A sympathetic jailer allowed Benjamin's mother to visit, and she pled with her son to beg forgiveness from the owner. He refused and, in a nifty bit of agility, wiggled loose from his chains and sent them to the master. The defiance resulted in "heavier chains" and plans to sell the uncle. Determined to be free, Benjamin again escaped and ultimately fled to New York. The runaway announcements were not just another business notice but rather the remarkable stories of men and women who were willing to take enormous risks to gain their freedoms. Or, as Jacobs titled the chapter, Benjamin was "The Slave Who Dared to Feel Like a Man."[32]

EMANCIPATION AND RACE

While the sale of black men and women formed a mainstay in southern newspapers, northern publishing companies touted slavery as the root of the sectional troubles. Months before the presidential campaign of 1860 and its threats of disunion had swung into high gear, *The Impending Crisis* received wide notice. Authored by southerner Hinton Rowan Helper in 1857, the book charged that slavery was detrimental to the economic mobility of those who did not own slaves. The book attracted still more attention as the election of 1860 loomed. "This is the work that has created so much excitement IN CONGRESS," screamed one notice. A potential customer might buy an abridged edition, with paper covers. However, for a few pennies more, he or she might buy the full volume of 420 pages. Here the denunciation of slavery was full-throated. "Get the unabridged edition" one merchant encouraged, "and have all the power of HELPER'S SHARP PEN!" Whether buying the short or long version of the book, a reader had plenty of company. Announcements placed the title at 137,000 copies already sold, with another 12,000 to 18,000 copies selling weekly. And, declared another bookseller in early March, the "demand continues unabated."[33]

Northerners who wanted a more fast-paced attack on slavery might purchase *Harrington: A Story of True Love.* Published in 1860, the book told the story of a black man kidnapped and sold into slavery. William O'Conner, the author, claimed that the work was based on real life, a point touted in the advertisements. "Its scenes are drawn from the startling events of our own times, without excess of coloring," one notice ran, "and its personal references will be sure to excite curiosity and extend its sale." Another bookseller declared that the novel was the best antislavery novel "yet published by the American Press. It is worth a dozen of Uncle Tom." That last claim bothered at least one reviewer. He acknowledged that the novel's characters were well developed. Yet its "pictures of plantation cruelties are extravaganzas, calculated to make a Southerner feel as if it were a clever attempt to out-herod Mrs. Stowe." He chalked the book up as a poor attempt to capitalize upon the commercial success of Stowe's work. No one, however, argued with the book's physical presentation or its sales figures. Announcements claimed that the novel made for a proud display on "every well supplied literary table." Printed on "nice paper and elegantly and substantially bound in muslin," it was "having a great demand."[34]

For the more devout, George Cheever offered "proof" that God found slavery a moral wrong. In *The Guilt of Slavery,* he reviewed biblical passages on the "subject of Slavery and Slaveholding as a sin against God and man." The result was the "most thorough demolition of all pro-slavery arguments." The Scottish-born minister argued that God had created all people in His image, and holding some of them as chattel imposed man's law on the divine. The hard-hitting attack made the work, according to one merchant, the "Great Book of the Age." Amid the exhaustive research, the pages seemed to fly. "It is neither dry nor uninteresting," another advertiser declared, "and is to the anti-slavery cause a valuable aid."[35]

Helping to prove that bookseller's claim, Cheever's work struck a nerve among many of slavery's defenders. A writer in *De Bow's Review* scoffed that although the minister might have emigrated to the United States, his views could be traced to the first New England colonists. Like the Puritans, Cheever belonged to an "arrogant, self-righteous, conceited race." These were men who thought and acted "on the belief of his own infallibility, and of other people's fallibility." Another southern writer charged that by hurling accusations, Cheever and other antislavery ministers were not "following any example set by Christ and his apostles that we are aware of." An objective analysis of slavery showed that white southerners were the "true friends of the negro," by setting them on the "upward march of civilization." Louis Stephens, the editor of *Vanity Fair,* echoed the charge that Cheever had exceeded his religious authority by condemning slave owners. In a tongue-in-cheek editorial on "Pugilistic Piety," Stephens wrote that the minister had taught him he was wrong to assume the "Christian religion consisted in obeying the precepts of the Supreme Being, and living at peace with one's neighbors."[36]

James Redpath's biography of John Brown proved as controversial as its subject matter. Outspoken in his antislavery advocacy, Redpath declared Brown a "noble old man" and "one of earth's most gentle souls." Even though the attempt to spark an uprising at Harpers Ferry had failed, he praised the abolitionist fighter for "assailing the Slave Power with the only weapon it fears." By midspring, notices claimed that forty thousand copies had sold. The publisher thanked customers for the book's "astonishing success" and promised readers placed on a waiting list that his steam presses were running "night and day." The large sales numbers sparked threats of violence in Boston. At a meeting to discuss the book later that year, a number of "Union men" flooded the room. According to an onlooker, the uninvited guests passed resolutions "denouncing Brown, justifying his execution and lauding Virginia." The meeting's organizers "vainly endeavored to get a hearing" before the police arrived and sent everyone home.[37]

Northern readers seeking a better understanding of the human experience of slavery had to turn to the abolitionist and black press. Here they found a range of books that recounted the horrors suffered by enslaved men and women. *The Kidnapped and Ransomed* told the story of Peter Still. After escaping from slavery, Still reunited with his mother, whom he had not seen in four decades. The book offered illustrations of that heartwarming scene, as well as a fiery introduction by an antislavery minister. Those wanting a "thrilling work on slavery and the slave trade" might read *The Martyrs and the Fugitive.* The work followed the kidnapping of a black family in Africa, the "horrors of the 'middle passage,'" and subsequent sale in the American South. The more visually inclined might purchase *The Revelations of a Slave Smuggler.* The autobiography included "graphic representations" of the slave markets and slave ships. These were not romanticized images but rather scenes "as they actually occur." Several of the illustrations were full-page, offering more vivid detail. The publisher kept the cover price low, however, to keep book "within the reach of the masses."[38]

Booksellers in the black press highlighted heroes in the fight against slavery. Notices ran for *The Nat Turner Insurrection,* as well as for Redpath's biography on John Brown (or the "Glorious Old Man," as one notice described him). Other readers might prefer a biography of Jermain Loguen, the "great Underground Railroad King." The struggle against human bondage also occurred on the floors of Congress, and the speeches of Gerrit Smith, the former Liberty Party presidential candidate and New York senator, were published. "Slavery has no right but to die!" headlined the promotion for that book. Notably absent were the campaign biographies of Abraham Lincoln so strongly promoted in the white press. Salesmen had yet to determine the antislavery credentials of the new president, among longtime veterans of the movement.[39]

Once the war began, advertisers in the mainstream press continued to find a market for books that attacked slavery. James Gilmore published *Among the Pines* in 1862, a collection of essays on topics such as "Slave Life on the Plantation," "Slave Education," and "Slave Religion." Gilmore supposedly had traveled across the South during the late 1850s, and the book drew upon his experiences. There was some debate on whether he actually had witnessed all the events he described, and some reviewers labeled the book fiction. Merchants claimed that Gilmore pulled no punches. His accounts of attempts to uphold slavery—from "chains and tortures" on the plantation to the "mangling of the Bible" in church—led to the book's suppression in the Confederacy. That Jefferson Davis was nervous about Gilmore's work meant "none is better worth reading" among the many titles now appearing on the "vexed and vexing question of Slavery." A customer might join "thousands of people" across the Union reading about the horrors of the institution. While they did, they might proudly leave the book in the family parlor. It was "handsomely bound in cloth and illustrated" and sold at "fine booksellers."[40]

The following year, Augustin Cochin put American slavery into a transatlantic context. A former district mayor in Paris, Cochin had studied the end of slavery in the French colonies. His translated work was, according to the publisher, "THE STANDARD WORK ON EMANCIPATION." Thousands of copies already had been sold, and the "demand is constantly increasing," attracting customers as far away as Hawaii. The *Pacific Commercial Advertiser* boasted that Cochin's work had recently arrived by boat and was ready for sale. In "circulation everywhere," the book revealed free labor as the "best foundation for industry and order." The United States was not striking out on its own in ending slavery but following the precedent set by much of the rest of the Western world. "The importance of this volume to the people of the United States in the present crisis," another advertiser assured, "can hardly be overestimated."[41]

That was no empty hype, according to contemporary observers. A reviewer for the *Atlantic Monthly* marveled at the impressive range of statistics Cochin had compiled to demonstrate the economic superiority of free labor. He acknowledged that the numbers made for a bit of a slog for the reader. The data, however, was the "genius" of the work. Although many abolitionists were passionately committed to the cause, they "have seldom been exhaustively acquainted with the facts of slavery or those of emancipation." Now they had access to facts and figures demonstrating that "production and commerce have not been annihilated by the abolition of slavery, while the moral condition of both races has been manifestly improved." Another reviewer drew an even deeper lesson from the book. Cochin had clearly demonstrated that a "*moral* wrong can never long tend to *material* advantage, and that the laws of *society* cannot be made ultimately to triumph over the laws of *nature*." But for readers worn down by the war's costs, a larger truth was that there was no way that a wrong might "be righted without some suffering by way of expiation."[42]

In many references to slavery in the white press, advertisers played upon deeply held stereotypes, especially in notices for minstrel shows. Announcements for these popular, and cheap, entertainments parodied black men and women as incapable of living in a free society. Bryant's Minstrels advertised *The Raw Recruits*, about a group of freed slaves on a southern plantation who form their own military company. One of the new soldiers found his sense of direction overcome by his sexual appetite, declaring, "I'se gwine down to Washington to fight for Abraham's daughter." A notice for a minstrel show in Minnesota suggested that slaves were only dimly aware of national affairs. One black man rather proudly declared that he himself was "de Cause ob de war." The news caused the onlookers to break into a "GRAND FLING D'ETHIOPE." In 1865, another notice played up the image of happy slaves. The blackfaced actors "present, in superb manner, the Humor and Oddities of Southern Plantation Life in all its broad, original and mirthful phrases." A show in Sandusky, Ohio, took a similar theme, with the performers drawing their inspiration from "Happy Darky Life" in the South.[43]

A tongue-in-cheek fugitive slave announcement in a Nebraska newspaper also found its humor in stereotypes. Sambo Rhett supposedly had placed the notice. In this instance, however, Rhett advertised for the return of his master, who had fled the approaching Union army. The fugitive cussed often, even though he "calls hisself a 'Suddern genman.'" He had a scar on his shoulder from a fight and a scratch above his eye "made by my Dinah when he tried to whip her." For the return of his master, Rhett advertised a higher reward if he was dead. If not, and he "come back to his kind niggers without much trubble, dis chile will receive him lubbingly." A reader might well enjoy these sharp observations on the so-called southern chivalry. But he or she also would chuckle over the dialect, as well as the idea of a former slave placing an advertisement.[44]

P. T. Barnum was one of the few northern advertisers who dealt with black Americans as individuals, in his promotion for William Tillman at the American Museum in New York. Tillman came to national attention in the fall of 1861, while a cook on the schooner *S. J. Waring.* When Confederate pirates boarded the ship, he killed three of them and helped to fight off the others. Barnum missed no beat and had Tillman at his museum to "receive visitors." The "colored steward" would recount his "experiences with Southern chivalry" and display "THE IDENTICAL HATCHET" he had used to help save the ship. Sensitive to his readers' racial outlook, Barnum was careful to avoid overly lionizing Tillman. He announced that after museum-goers had talked with the former crew member, they might tour the other exhibits that featured bears, snakes, and the "wonderful Albino Sisters." Tillman was an oddity for visitors to gawk at, as much as a hero for them to admire.[45]

Over the course of the war, the advertisements in the mainstream press had sent northern readers a mixed message about emancipation and race. Publishers touted books that blamed slavery, and slave owners, for the start of the war. The works received mixed reviews, and yet they gained a large audience. Claims for "immense" sales are obviously open to interpretation, but, even allowing for exaggeration, Helper, Redpath, and Cochin had gained a wide readership. The rankled reaction drawn from some northerners and southerners also indicates their public visibility. When the notices shifted from the causes to the results of the war, however, racial stereotypes dominated. Advertisers had portrayed black Americans as incapable of living in a free society. The dual message dovetailed with other popular literature. As historian Alice Fahs argues, poems, songs, and other writings practiced a form of "racial containment." Individual soldiers might be honored for their heroism, but deeply held assumptions about race "denied blacks full membership in the nation."[46] In this, the advertisements had played a role.

• •

The very real task of helping black Americans make the transition from slavery to freedom fell to the antislavery press and its advertising columns. At the start of the war, former slaves received encouragement to immigrate to Haiti in the *Pine and Palm*, a weekly newspaper published by James Redpath. Here, the Brown biographer hoped to turn "Hayti" into a "great negro nation." He devoted an entire column in each issue to "advertisements and announcements" from the Haitian Bureau of Emigration, an organization that he had helped to found. Redpath encouraged black men and women to migrate as individuals, families, and communities. Once on the Caribbean island, they would find "a welcome, a home, and a free homestead." The ships and passengers sailing to Haiti received prominent listing so that readers knew they were not the first to make the voyage. The trip itself, an agent for the Bureau of Emigration promised, occurred in "perfect comfort." Those individuals still nervous about making the journey might purchase guides and maps. For frequent users, the publisher helpfully recommended the hardcover edition. The volume included a "fine steel engraving of the President of Hayti, and other illustrations." Once there, emigrants might even have the opportunity to make a social call. Lilly Ann Carter, the wife of a missionary and living in Port au Prince, announced that she "would be glad to hear from any of her friends who may have escaped from slavery."[47]

More of the freedpeople wanted to remain in the United States and almost immediately placed notices to help rebuild families torn asunder by slavery. Listed under "Information Wanted," former slaves sought word of spouses, children, and loved ones. Susan Patterson wanted news about Louisa, her daughter. The mother had last seen her child on a plantation in Louisiana, but that was "several years ago." A Mrs. Burk hoped for a reunion with her three children, born in northern Virginia: "When last heard from they were all living on the plantation of Mr. Charles Steward, Arkansas, near Columbia." In late 1865, the "distressed father and mother" of Charles and Josephus Willis sought word of their two boys who had last been seen with a Confederate captain in Virginia. Mr. and Mrs. Willis currently lived in Charleston, South Carolina, and would receive any information "with thanks." For some children, no reunion was likely. In the spring of 1865, the black community in New Orleans held a fair "For the Benefit of Orphans of Freedmen." Later that same year, another fair was held to solicit Christmas gifts for "orphan children under care of the Freedmen's Bureau."[48]

A few wartime announcements attempted to help the former slaves now living in the free states. The Pennsylvania Abolition Society brought "some of the freed people" to Philadelphia. Members hoped to place the former slaves, many of whom "are women with children," as domestic servants. To prevent disappointment, "we should state that many of these people have little or no acquaintance with housework, and are apt to be slow." They were, however, "of good dispositions and willing to learn." In New York, the "Home for Aged Colored People" was desperately short of funds. Samuel Shipley, the treasurer, hoped that "all who can will aid it promptly." Farmers and others with surplus provisions might also leave them at the home. Anyone was welcome to visit and would find themselves "gratified in mingling with the inmates . . . some of them cases of peculiar hardship."[49]

More notices attempted to help black families living in the former Confederate States. In Louisiana, the Freedmen's Aid Association offered prizes for the most productive farmers. The "Crop Premium" paid $250 to the "Freedmen or gang of Freedmen" who raised the "largest crop per hand." The "Stock Premium" awarded twenty-five dollars to the "Freedmen whose working animals are in the best order." Other awards went to farmers with the "best" cotton, tobacco, and sugar. The point was not simply to distribute money. Rather, the prizes demonstrated "to the world" that the freedmen are "as good tillers of the land, law-abiding citizens, and worthy of the title of American citizens," as they had proven "themselves good soldiers on many hard battlefields." Recognizing that successful farming required record keeping, increasing numbers of notices ran for black schools. A freedperson might attend "Evening Adult School" and "Day School" to learn "Common" and "Higher" English. The distinction between the two types of language lessons might seem rather fine. According to another school notice, however, "Let us secure the freedom we have received by the intelligence that can maintain it."[50]

A smattering of announcements appeared for political meetings. Here was perhaps the greatest difference of opinion between the white and black antislavery presses. White abolitionists urged the freedpeople to concentrate on economic advances above all else. Quipped one editor, a cord of wood and a barrel of corn was worth more to a black family than "all the conventions, loyal leagues, and universal suffrage prayer meetings ever held." That line of thought did not stop the "Friends of Universal Suffrage" from running a notice in the *New Orleans Tribune* that summer, inviting the freedpeople to attend a meeting. The organizers acknowledged that black men had their disagreements, like any other group of people, but not in politics. In addition to supporting the federal government and opposing the "re-establishment of slavery," the "colored voters . . . are all united, as one man, to advocate the practical application of the immortal Declaration of Independence." Later in 1865, in South Carolina, the "colored people" of Charleston were requested to financially support a committee traveling to Washington to "secure our rights." Every man, woman, and child should "put in their mite."[51]

The struggle for equality would be painfully slow, but the advertising pages in the black press provided glimmers of hope, real and otherwise. The makers of patent medicines advertised as frequently in the antislavery press as the mainstream press. These notices made no distinctions based on supposed racial differences between white and black customers. In the *Weekly Anglo-African*, Dr. Clarke promised that his "herb pills" cured colic, fever, pains in the stomach. For good measure, the pills were guaranteed to cure "diseases peculiar to the female sex." In another black-run newspaper, a medicine maker asked if readers were "sick, feeble . . . [and] feeling uncomfortable?" If so, a handful of pills would bring almost immediate relief. To nostrum advertisers chasing a profit, all Americans were equal.[52]

Notices in Union newspapers offered a mixed perspective on slavery and race. Booksellers offered a range of titles attacking slavery as a root cause of the war. Yet they focused on the institution rather than on the men and women held in bondage. Minstrel shows widely promoted in the mainstream press portrayed the slaves as a source of comic relief. For the experiences of actual slaves, potential customers had to turn to the abolitionist and black press. To the freedpeople, the many challenges that came with war's end were no laughing matter. The black press, especially, helped these Americans to rebuild families and communities damaged by the experience of slavery, and to look toward the future.

CHAPTER 6

Battlefield and Home Front

Writing in the late nineteenth century for a national magazine, David Dodge wondered how the Confederate domestic economy had withstood the pressures of the Union blockade. Initially he had hoped that contemporary newspaper stories and editorials might provide the answers. The more he dug, however, the more he realized that editors had too little space to work with and recorded only the "most salient events." Additionally, these men often were tight-lipped about "such matters as might dishearten friends, or encourage foes." The limits of these sources brought him to the advertisements. To his mind, the notices held a "peculiar value" because, amid the sales pitch, they offered a "true, because unconscious, presentation of the condition and attitude of the people." Among the announcements that caught his eye was one for mahogany caskets. The undertaker had just received them through the blockade and promised a discount to any interested readers. Given the heavy fighting throughout the war, Dodge acknowledged that there was "much timeliness" to the offer.[1]

For advertisers, the Civil War blurred distinctions between the battlefield and home front. To soldiers, they sold arms and equipment. Almost anything was available for a price, from artillery pieces and muskets to armored vests and, supposedly, submarines. For families and friends at home, merchants announced war-themed entertainments. Dioramas, lectures, and board games claimed to make sense of the battles and campaigns that dominated the newspaper headlines. As the fighting continued, advertisers emphasized sacrifice. They sold bonds to help fund the soaring war costs, and, for the mounting casualty lists, artificial limbs and embalming services. They also marketed a gendered health that played upon readers' insecurities. Yankees and Rebels perused notices for curing "seminal weakness," a malady that threatened to make them less of a man, while their wives and sisters might purchase pills and potions to supposedly prevent "female hysteria." In the advertisements, the fighting that raged between 1861 and 1865 seemed less a divide between soldiers and civilians, and men and women, than a shared experience among potential customers.[2]

ARMS AND ENTERTAINMENTS

Some of the most heated rhetoric of the secession crisis appeared in the advertising pages, where merchants glimpsed opportunity in a rapidly forming Confederate army. Rebel advertisers appealed to a regional identity, in the hope of undercutting "imported wares" from the free states. In Texas, J. C. Short thanked the "Southern people" for their "liberal patronage" of his gun store. In turn, he continued to sell "those Kentucky rifles, warranted to kill an Abolitionist at 400 yards!" Edwin Want offered a breech-loading rifle that was a "Southern Invention and Southern Manufacture!" The weapon was "one of the safest and surest arms ever offered in the South." Other advertisers announced that they had "breech loading rifles," "MINNIE MUSKETS," and "trimmings for uniforms" so that southern militia might "Prepare for War" and "'Look out for the coming times.'" Undaunted, salesmen from New York and Philadelphia ran notices for uniforms, pistols, and other military equipment. These goods were "ready for delivery" and furnished at "short notice." At least some newspaper editors believed that transplanted wives and sweethearts were helping northerners to carry on the advertising wars. A widely reprinted story recounted that many of the first Confederate militia soldiers not only had "Yankee arms in their hands when they muster in warlike parade, but Yankee arms around their necks in the privacy of their own homes."[3]

Samuel Colt placed little faith in mixed marriages and struck back at his southern competitors. A wealthy New England businessman and the mass-producer of the six-shot pistol that bore his name, Colt advertised widely in the South. In Virginia, he argued that his weapon had "No equal in quality and finish." In Texas, he promised that his pistol was "Your one true friend. Six hearts in its body." Should readers doubt this bit of hyperbole, he invited them to try the sidearm: "Then decide which will afford surest protection to your family, your life and your property." Acknowledging the increasing competition from regional gun manufacturers, he pleaded in Alabama, "Don't Desert an Old Friend for a New Face." To local manufacturers who attempted to copy the design of his pistol, he advised, "CAUTION." The notice threatened legal prosecution "wherever the law can reach." Bringing to trial any "pirates" might not have been easy given the breakdown of federal authority in the South, but Colt need not have tried. By the start of the Civil War, he had reportedly sold two thousand pistols to his now Rebel customers.[4]

Following the bombardment of Fort Sumter, Union and Confederate merchants touted everything from "army" socks and shoes to ammunition. Men hoping to avoid the fighting by heading west might purchase "Mountain Rifles" in St. Louis. These lightweight artillery pieces were perfect for "companies crossing the plains." Those readers who wished to stay and fight might purchase "Steel Rifled Cannon" and other "Munitions of War" in New York and New Orleans. In early 1863, Andrew Morse sold "Sub-Marine Armor." At the same time as the *H. L. Hunley* was under construction in Mobile, Alabama, a New England merchant advertised that his armor was "of the most approved construction" and "warranted for any practical depth of water." No submarine had yet gone into action, and only the *Hunley* eventually did (and sank), so a "practical depth" of water was open to the buyer's interpretation.[5]

In Chicago, William Bead drew upon the endorsement of Union general John Wilder to sell the Spencer repeating rifle. The gun featured a rapid rate of fire and a killing range of, according to Bead, "2000 yards!" For the skeptical reader, he ran a letter from Wilder. The Union officer had led a brigade equipped with the repeating rifles during the fighting at Chickamauga, where they won praise for their steadfastness. Wilder wrote that the "confidence inspired by these arms, added to their terrible destructive capacity, fully quadruples the effectiveness of my command." The men now believed they could "not be whipped." Secretary of War Edwin Stanton agreed with Wilder's claim and, by 1865, had reportedly ordered more of the Spencer rifle than any other comparable weapon.[6]

Other merchants offered a seemingly inexhaustible stock of wares for soldiers' convenience and protection. A "military field pocket glass," an early version of a telescope, was "easily carried" and "allows for sight up to 1.5 miles." A "Soldier's Watch" was just "what the name indicates—Solid, Substantial, and always Reliable." The timepiece was warranted to withstand any amount of "Marching, Riding, or Fighting." A man might check the time while sitting on a stool that "never breaks from packing" or a cot that "never sags." As the days grew shorter, a Boston merchant reminded his readers that he sold "Scarfs for the Soldiers." The Union military was not always prompt in issuing clothing, so men readying for nighttime picket and guard duty would find it "just the thing."[7]

To market his "Portable Soup," a South Carolina merchant invoked Confederate generals Robert E. Lee and P. G. T Beauregard. J. W. Jones recognized that soldiers sometimes were too busy to prepare a hot meal. He sold a "small cake" that easily carried in a pocket or blanket roll. When added to water and boiled, the cake dissolved into an "excellent, delicious and stimulating" meal. If no water was handy or the army was on the march, men might eat the cake as a biscuit. The ration had met with "universal approbation" from Confederate soldiers, with even Lee, Beauregard, and "other eminent officers" warmly commending the soup. Lee's battlefield successes, however, might have undercut some of Jones's marketing efforts. One Confederate veteran remembered that the "tangible" proof of the Army of Northern Virginia's many triumphs was the access to captured Union foodstuffs. Portable soup ranked among the most sought-after of the Yankee delicacies, along with coffee and sugar.[8]

In a competitive market, a number of merchants stretched and omitted the truth. In Minnesota, A. J. Vorhes offered soldiers the opportunity to almost single-handedly win the war if they purchased his repeating rifle. His weapon had the "longest range" and "greatest accuracy" of any currently used in North America. More important, Vorhes claimed the rifle fired thirty shots per minute. For readers who may not have fully grasped the math, he worked the numbers. If a soldier fired one shot every two seconds, he was equal in the rate of fire to a "division every two hours." Even if a man might actually achieve the equivalent firepower to the several thousand soldiers in a division, Vorhes left unstated how he was to carry, or even obtain, that much ammunition. William Reid took an opposite tack and marketed a "bullet-proof vest." Made from steel, the vest was "now very generally worn" by the "sons of Mars." Readers might excuse that as a bit of hyperbole, but Reid ran his notices in mid-1863. Few, if any, soldiers wore the vest through the hard marching and sweltering sun of the war's third summer.[9]

There was no monopoly on outrageous claims, and, in Richmond, a "private citizen" advertised for investors to help fund a warship to smash the Union blockade. The vessel would carry top-secret guns, capable of "destroying in a few minutes iron clad Monitors and any ship of any class that may attack it." Once in open water, the Confederate battle cruiser was fast enough to track down Union merchant ships. After some deductions for the captain and crew, the ensuing prize money would be distributed between the shareholders. The glitter of profits ultimately proved a bogus claim. No such ship sailed by 1865, when investors saw their money, rather than any enemy vessels, disappear from sight.[10]

Union and Confederate merchants recognized that such wild claims drew public rebuke, and they advertised themselves as much as their product. They reminded readers that they were neighbors and friends, not some faraway war profiteer. They sold their goods to "Soldiers or Civilians," "Army Officers and Citizens," and "Soldiers in the Army and Our People at Home." At his clothing store in Massachusetts, Horace Sheldon acknowledged that times were hard for many families. He sold socks at "reduced prices" to soldiers and had "blue mixed yarn" for families that wanted to mend a military blouse rather than buy a new uniform. Because hometown merchants sold individually rather than in bulk, their items also were of a high quality. A Mr. Fosters peddled Union sashes that displayed the "best workmanship." In Georgia, a clothier requested that soldiers have their uniforms trimmed at his store. "Such volunteers . . . are always fit well." All of this was done for "our brave" soldiers, who already had sacrificed so much for their nation.[11]

By contrast, the Union and Confederate governments ignited a harsh public reaction over the issuing of sealed military contracts. The massive national expenditures flowing into the coffers of private suppliers of everything from blankets to rations raised fears of corruption. Contemporary observers increasingly worried that contractors placed making a profit above winning the war. According to historian Michael Smith, civilians worried that this "enemy within" threatened the very nature of American democracy by leading the people into a moral and spiritual decline.[12] In late 1862, one northern editor thundered that the sole goal of some businessmen was to "swindle the soldiers and put money in their pockets." An Indiana newspaperman fumed that the Naumkeag Company, Bates Manufacturing Company, and several other eastern "factories" earned hundreds of thousands of dollars through military contracts. The profits "will give a clue to the pertinacity with which New England favors a continuation of the war." A South Carolinian shared the sense of frustration. Confederate business owners stayed home and counted their money while the national government conscripted their workers into the military. These "vipers" and "land sharks" had no concern "except to keep the war raging that they might make money." The public criticism eventually became so loud that the federal government, at least, mandated the public bidding of contracts, often in the newspaper columns.[13]

• •

Union and Confederate readers might learn about the war and its weapons by attending a polyorama panoptique at a theater or meeting hall. First popular during the 1820s, these optical displays used backlights to illuminate large illustrations and paintings set against a thin paper. By the start of the Civil War, the stage operator might adjust the light to make a glowing effect from a bursting artillery shell or to set day into night over a military encampment. One owner described that his projection of a battle "is lighted up with about forty burners, the same in the afternoon as evening. The room is darkened, and it shows well." The use of shadows and depth created a "startling and faithful representation of actual occurrences." Another owner gushed that his polyorama featured "views of Southern scenery." These included "the rank, luxuriant vegetation, the soft tints of the summer sky, and the life-like freshness of the landscape."[14]

These forerunners of today's motion pictures brought to life events that audiences might otherwise only read about in the newspaper. Two months after the clash between the *Monitor* and the *Virginia* off Fortress Monroe during early 1862—the first battle in world history between ironclad warships—audiences in Richmond might enjoy scenes from the "Great Southern Naval Victory at Hampton Roads." Confederate forces eventually scuttled the *Virginia*, but that was beside the point. Using sketches made by a veteran of the fighting, the "miniature naval battle" depicted "correct models of the vessels engaged." After watching the show, one reviewer was all praise. He had been skeptical that the producer could realistically mimic the waves, but not once the lights dimmed. He enthused that "while watching the course of the Virginia through the billows and seeing her pounce upon her foes with eagle-like velocity," an audience member "imagines himself to be in the presence of a real sea."[15]

The next year, in the nation's capital, viewers at Willard's Hall might watch images from the "new great Mirror of Washington and the War." These included the "Levees, Fortifications, Hospitals, Barracks" and other structures built since 1861. W. J. Kent mixed the illustrations in his *Light Phantasmagoria*, showing in the Idaho Territory. He promised "dissolving views" depicting "battle scenes, army officers, . . . and a variety of other wonderful novelties." A polyorama that ran in Ohio offered a "Grand Matinee," with women and children admitted at a reduced price. The display promised the "great events and striking scenes" of the fighting through late 1863. Few other shows attempted to cover so much of the war, "Hence, its great importance and value, especially to the young." After attending another war-themed show that had toured New York, Boston, and "all the principal cities of the Union," the editor of the Amherst, New Hampshire, newspaper *Farmer's Cabinet* encouraged readers to purchase their tickets. "The many testimonials in the hands of the proprietor from the Mayors of the principal cities, and other reliable and distinguished gentlemen," he declared, "are sufficient assurance of the fidelity and beauty of this series of paintings."[16]

Dioramas proved another popular war-themed entertainment because they combined music, singing, and other gimmicks. The painted canvases showed a variety of wartime scenes and stretched up to several thousand feet. In the *Detroit Advertiser and Tribune* in 1864, the owner of a local meeting hall promoted a "Colossal Picture of the War." The "grand picture" gave "all the vivid illustrations of the BATTLE FIELDS OF THE PRESENT WAR," calling to mind "with STARTLING EARNESTNESS the horrors produced by this UNHOLY REBELLION." The display included scenes from the recently concluded campaigns, "making it the only complete History of this mighty struggle ever painted on canvas." An "accomplished pianist" introduced each scene with a variety of songs. The paintings and music made an "entertainment which stands confessedly without a rival in the world." In Richmond's *Sentinel* Lee Mallory announced "War Illustrations" at the Metropolitan Hall. *Jackson Crossing the Potomac* and *Grand Battle of Manassas* were two of the paintings. These "Splendid Displays of Infantry and Cavalry" were accompanied by "young southern vocalists" and "Smith's Popular Battalion Band." The resulting entertainment was "unparalleled."[17]

Advertisers for other dioramas emphasized their lifelike nature and claimed to make even battle a knowable experience. George Goodwin labeled his painting "vast and comprehensive, officially authentic and minute in all its details." The battle images "are depicted with graphic force, and the audience seem to be transported to the scene itself, to witness the furious onslaught and fiery repulse, and listen to the roar of guns and clash of steel." By comparison, all other dioramas were "miserable imitations." That would surprise Messrs. Croppin and Grien, who promoted a "work of art really worthy of patronage" at a church in Richmond. The paintings were "truthful in historical details," including the 1862 battles around the Confederate capital that "hurled back broken the second Yankee crusade." What really made the images was their lifelike depiction of "sieges, battles, marches, bivouacs, etc." The two men ventured that if packed houses and cheering audiences "convey an evidence of public appreciation and taste, this instructive exhibit is a success beyond peradventure."[18]

Some showmen used figurines and models to depict a range of military scenes. *The Great War Show* in Chicago used ninety thousand "moving and acting" figurines to "vividly reenact the principal battles both by sea and land of the Great Southern Rebellion." In Savannah, *The War* used eight thousand miniatures to re-create particular episodes, ranging from the sinking of a Union monitor to the funeral of Stonewall Jackson. The show closed with the Confederate capture of Fort Pillow in Tennessee, and the "Death of the Federal Commanding Officer, Major Booth." With "life like" toy soldiers and ships that actually seemed to march and sail, the display was the "most thrilling of all modern miracles." After watching a show in Pennsylvania in early 1862, one editor claimed that a Mr. Towns, the producer, "must be a Yankee of great patience to whittle out so large an army of men and horses." The moving figurines gave "very general satisfaction to the large audiences" and were "instructive as well as amusing."[19]

Northerners and southerners curious about the war's progress might instead attend a public lecture. Many of the talks focused on a particular aspect of the fighting. In September 1861, a Mr. Paine was ready to discuss his experiences as a Confederate chaplain at the Battle of Manassas, Virginia, only two months earlier. The Presbyterian minister "had the company of distinguished officers" during the fighting, offering "ample advantages." Readers need not worry that Paine filled his talk with too much military jargon. The notice promised that the reverend "illustrates his descriptions and explanation by the aid of a black board." James Pike, a former Union corporal, lectured on the Battle of Chickamauga. He would use maps to illustrate the maneuvers and fighting over the heavily wooded terrain in northern Georgia: "Let every body attend who wants to hear the correct account of the campaign, and see it demonstrated in all its parts, on the largest topographical maps." Rather than chalkboards and maps, a Union chaplain relied upon his oratorical powers to describe the Battle of Gettysburg. The Reverend Warner was an "attractive speaker of easy and graceful address." His talk would detail with "great force and graphic beauty the grand and sublime, but terrific, scenes of the battle."[20]

Other talks focused more generally on "The War" and attempted to draw ideological conclusions. In Minnesota, a Reverend Mr. Fisk argued that "slavery and slavery alone" was the "sin for which God is judging us in this war." To sustain the institution any longer meant "defying God and vowing that we will not repent." Two years later, in Georgia, Henry Law discussed "Our present revolution and our obligations to its martyrs." The topic "is one of the most attractive themes that could employ a gifted mind." Local readers might show "their good taste and patriotism by filling the seats of the lecture room." Slavery and revolutions were matters too important to leave to earthly interpretations, according to D. L. Coonly. His lecture on "Spiritualism," delivered at a school hall in Indiana, discussed the "Spirit view of the present war." He would channel the afterworld again the next evening but allow a "committee selected by the audience" to choose the war-related topics.[21]

Northern readers, at least, who wanted to spend a quiet night at home might play the Civil War as a board game. The notices often provided only the title of the game, assuming readers' general familiarity with the conflict. In late 1863, the owner of a toy store in Boston declared that he was "daily receiving" new games for children. These included the "instructive and fascinating game of Abe and Jeff—The Game of Red, White, and Blue . . . The Game of Battles North and South," and a "great many more new, interesting and instructive Games." He also had "Commanders of our Forces," a "Game for old and young." He encouraged readers to preserve the list of games "FOR REFERENCE IN MAKING CHRISTMAS PURCHASES." Another merchant announced "The Garrison Game" as one of the "best Games of the Season." The game was suitable for players of any age and "will be found to be the very pleasantest entertainment for the family circle." A different perspective from that of a military garrison was offered in "The Game of Besieging, a War Game." Readers not sure what side to take during a siege operation might instead play "THE WAR FOR THE UNION." Newly issued in 1861 and "beautifully printed," the game was perfect for "enlivening the domestic circle."[22]

All of these entertainments perhaps succeeded too well, and soldiers often grumbled that their families and friends could not possibly "know" the war. The hunger, cold, and loneliness of camp and the sheer terror and carnage of battle were experiences that provided common bonds only between the Yankees and Rebels at the front. The backlash against "arm chair" generals found some support in the newspapers. A northern war correspondent criticized civilians for discussing the maneuvers of armies as if they were moves in a game of chess. These men and women "could hardly distinguish gunpowder from oatmeal." Another reporter added that those individuals at home with the loudest opinions on military strategy generally "know no more of war than they do of astronomy." Battle was a unique experience, one that entertainers could not, of course, replicate, no matter how lifelike their images and backdrops.[23]

THE COSTS OF WAR

The Civil War was the most expensive war in the nation's history to that time, and the Union and Confederacy heavily promoted war bonds. During the War of 1812, Congress had borrowed money to help fight the British. These bonds sold to investors, who often marketed them to state and local governments. Such haphazard methods were hardly adequate for war on a much larger scale. By early 1862, the difficulty in raising the financial resources necessary concerned President Lincoln as much as the seemingly slow progress of the Union armies. "The bottom is out of the tub," he anguished upon learning that the Treasury had almost no money. "What shall I do?"[24]

Lincoln's answer came through Jay Cooke and his advertising campaign. The head of a banking firm in Philadelphia, Cooke was friendly with Salmon Chase, the secretary of the treasury. Cooke received an appointment to market and sell war bonds in 1862, and he looked to the newspapers to advertise the "five-twenties" (a 6 percent bond redeemable in no fewer than five years and no more than twenty years). Two years later, he promoted the "seven-thirties," a three-year note at 7.3 percent. The results were staggering, with Cooke raising over $1 billion for the federal government through the two bond sales. His notices were so visible in the daily and weekly papers that one contemporary declared Cooke "almost as well known as Abraham Lincoln."[25]

In his promotions, Cooke made supporting the war effort accessible to the everyday person. He sold bonds in increments of fifty and one hundred dollars. That was no small amount, when a Union private earned thirteen dollars per month. But the sum was manageable, and the holder gained the interest. "Better to put your money into paper," an advertisement for the "five-twenties" reasoned, "than into the ground." As important, he made the bonds appealing to investors by using clear descriptions. In an age when advertisers often played loose and fast with the truth, especially when selling patent medicines, Cooke offered a very detailed account of the transaction. Three years after purchasing of a "seven-thirty," a bond holder received payment "in lawful money." Or, a customer might convert a matured bond into "gold bearing bonds," also backed by the federal government. There was no mystery to the process. A customer went to a local bank or spoke with an authorized agent, placed his money, and waited for the maturation date.[26]

Interest rates were important, but Cooke also wanted customers to feel they were not only investing in a bond but in the Union war effort.[27] According to one notice, a bond holder's financial commitment provided no "stronger evidence of public confidence in the government." A fifty-dollar war bond was not going to propel the Union army to capture Richmond. A fifty-dollar bond would help the Union win the war, however, when it became a part of "Over Fifty Millions" invested in the national government in just two weeks during the spring of 1864: "This indicates confidence, which every victory will strengthen. To achieve victories, the Government needs money to keep supplied the troops." Another advertisement for war bonds appealed: "Our Country! To Arms!" Investors in the federal government were "patriotic citizens" who had "done their duty." A gray-haired farmer in Wisconsin and a widow in New Hampshire might do as much to win the war as a soldier on the front lines. By offering an opportunity to help preserve the American nation, Cooke had made a "people's war" even more democratic.[28]

Beyond the money raised, the success in marketing the "five-twenties" and "seven-thirties" was their use in other advertising headlines. The owner of a dry goods store declared that citizens should invest in war bonds because the United States "should never fall below credit for courage." He, however, accepted credit, if a shopper was momentarily short on cash. A clothier headlined his notice with "A GOOD INVESTMENT." There was no better security "than the 7-30 Loan, but all families have to make other investments in the way of family articles." He stood ready to help by selling his fashions at reasonable prices.[29]

Like Chase and Cooke, Confederate secretary of the treasury Christopher Memminger emphasized profit and patriotism in selling 8 percent bonds at the start of the war. The bond sold in amounts that ranged between fifty and one thousand dollars, with interest payable every six months at "all of our principal cities." The loan was a solid investment for white southerners because of the guaranteed interest. Still, "it is not to this consideration" that Memminger based his appeal. Instead, purchasing the bond helped a southerner to "sustain the cause of his country." If Confederate citizens valued their "life, liberty, honor," then it "is their duty to aid in this war." For potential investors and patriots who remained undecided, Memminger cautioned that the opportunity to purchase a bond was not open-ended. The Confederacy wanted to borrow $15 million. Should "over-subscription" occur, preference would be given to the investors who placed their money first and in the largest amounts.[30]

Confederate editors eagerly supported the bond drive, but the advertising pages told the grim reality. In 1861, the *American Citizen*, published in Canton, Mississippi, reminded its readers that the "war *must* be prosecuted, and the Government *must* be sustained." Purchase of a bond marked the "time when true patriotism manifest itself." Two years later, the *Chattanooga Daily Rebel* proclaimed: "Twelve months after the close of the war, Confederate bonds will command a premium. Mark the prediction." Yet the Confederate economy experienced horrible inflation, and investors soon ran notices attempting to barter their government loan. An unidentified advertiser hoped to exchange his bond for a house "suitable for a small family" in Richmond. Another unidentified investor was willing to exchange his bond at face value for cash. Merchants responded, and the 8 percent bond became a form of exchange. A land speculator in Arkansas offered tracts of land "at very low price" for the government security. In Atlanta, a store owner accepted the bonds in payment for merchandise and accounts past due. By 1864, notices for the auction of bonds became common as investors attempted to salvage what they might. Investors who waited too long were simply out of luck. In Charleston, South Carolina, a notice cautioned that work on a planned statue of Confederate general Thomas "Stonewall" Jackson was close to abandonment. The committee had placed donations in Confederate bonds that have "been totally lost." Unless new benefactors stepped forward, work on the equestrian statue of the "great Confederate general" would not move forward (and, ultimately, did not).[31]

Alongside notices for war bonds, military claims agents offered to collect soldiers' back pay and bounty. There was some precedent in arguing that the nation had a financial responsibility to its defenders. Most recently, in 1860, claims agents had run notices for lands and monies promised by individual states to veterans of previous wars. The number of notices skyrocketed with the mass armies of the Civil War. Men who had received a medical discharge before receiving their bounty money, or who had mustered out before receiving their last pay, all sought what was due them. Other situations were murkier, with prisoners of war and wounded men sometimes not credited with their monthly pay. In New England, B. H. Mace offered to collect any outstanding pay for men who were suffering from a disease contracted while "engaged in the present War against the Rebellion." He patriotically declared, "Let all see how the government provides for her defenders."[32]

Claims agents quickly attempted to distinguish themselves from their competitors. Many of them advertised that they charged no fee if they were unsuccessful in their filing. T. J. Mitchell offered customer service. Once a claim was approved, he would request that the federal government send the certificate directly to the applicant's home and thereby avoid "all unnecessary delay and uncertainty of the mails." For men still unsure why they should file their claim with Mitchell rather than another agent, he referred them to the "officers and men generally of the 3d Mo. Cavalry," with whom he had served throughout the war. In 1863, J. P. Dickson, a Confederate claims agent, touted his prewar experience in working with the "Government at Washington." He was familiar with the extensive paperwork that accompanied any reimbursement application, "for want of which many are subjected to vexatious delays and heavy expenses."[33]

In Maine, a Mr. Hinds argued that success bred more success in filing claims. Over the past year, he had helped, by his count, four thousand Union soldiers to file for their back pay. That meant a lot of time spent in Washington, but the experience had made him "thoroughly conversant" with the paperwork required by the "different bureaus." In late 1865, J. W. Bennett, a former Union officer, touted his financial success. He had collected twenty-four thousand dollars from federal government since the end of the war. This was not in one or two windfalls, but "in sums of $5 to $700." Henry Atherton believed that experience as a regimental officer made him an ideal claims agent. The military service had readied him for the "'red tape' proceedings required both in the army and the various departments in Washington."[34]

Many claims notices blurred the distinction between soldiers and civilians, with agents offering to represent widows and dependent mothers before the Union and Confederate government. In her study of the northern home front, historian Judith Giesberg argues that the ravages of the Civil War often brought "politics into the spaces of everyday life." Claims notices did so by encouraging women to file to receive their deceased husband's back pay. Agents used much the same wording as they did in appealing to veterans: they would "use every effort to have claims promptly paid," with applications "correctly and promptly made, and as promptly collected." A widow or mother only had to provide "evidence of the relationship." As important as the services offered, the notices for grieving families acknowledged that women had made great sacrifices. They had lost their husbands and sons, and the national governments should honor its commitment to them. By forcing the issue, these widows had, in their own way, politicized the personal.[35]

The war's bloodshed loomed larger than even its financial costs, and life insurance agents naturally directed their attention to soldiers. The premiums ran at about 10 percent of the policy value and offered protection to a buyer's family upon his "being wounded and killed." In a notice that probably gave only cold comfort to readers, the New England Mutual Life Insurance Company touted its promptness in completing claims. By late 1861, the firm had already paid eight hundred thousand dollars to widows and orphans. The next year, the Confederate Insurance Company admitted that it could not understand why some men still did not have a policy. Its announcement baldly stated: "Think of your family if you die." A "Life and Limb" insurance company in New York recognized that losing a leg or an arm in battle was perhaps a worse fate than death. A crippled man might struggle to find any livelihood. An insurance officer pleaded that every soldier "should insure his Limbs, thereby providing for *himself*, in case he should be so unfortunate as to lose a limb." The agent added that his was the "only Insurance Company of the kind in the world."[36]

Adding a sense of urgency, notices for prosthetics were a frequent sight. In Union newspapers, salesmen claimed that the federal government would pay for an artificial limb, leading to a fierce competition for customers. The makers of the "Salem Leg" argued their product was the best "in the world" because they had the patronage of the War Department. The American Leg Company countered that they had the "best artificial leg ever" because it was issued by military doctors. "This is a recommendation to the Limb," they concluded, "as Government gives to the Soldiers none but the best." While waiting for their artificial legs, "invalid" men might purchase "easy walking crutches." With an elastic top, the crutches were the "best" and "healthiest" ever made. Former soldiers might buy them "at cost."[37]

With their national government too hard-pressed financially to offer prosthetics, Confederate advertisers drew upon the testimony of maimed soldiers. Jason Hanger sold an "improved artificial leg" in Staunton, Virginia, and printed a letter of thanks from a veteran. The man had suffered an amputation below the knee and had walked with the help of a cane. He threw that away after receiving the limb from Hanger, which he considered the "lightest, neatest and most durable" on the market. G. W. Wells topped even that success story with his company's artificial leg. The fake limb "fits easily, without chafing or any other unpleasant feeling to the wearer." James Field, a soldier in the 25th Virginia, offered his endorsement. Wounded during the summer of 1862, his right leg was amputated to about five inches above the ankle. He wore the limb supplied by Wells with "great comfort and convenience" and was cleared to return to his regiment in only a few more days. He took "great pleasure in testifying to the happy results of Mr. Wells' ingenuity and mechanical skills."[38]

Death itself had become a booming business. Beginning with the first large battles in 1861, undertakers had plied their trade. Embalming the dead was a relatively new art, but a Dr. Holmes staked his claim. From his office in Washington, he had preserved the corpses of a "large number of officers and private soldiers of our army" to the "entire satisfaction" of their loved ones. Skeptical readers might stop by and see an example of his handiwork in a dog he had embalmed one year earlier. The animal still looked lifelike, even after exposure "to the heat of the past summer." Confederate readers hoping to receive the remains of a loved one would instead have to see John Kerr in northern Virginia. He sold "Metallic Octagon Burial Cases" that were made of the "most imperishable materials and enameled inside and out to prevent rust or corrosion."[39]

By the next year, undertakers advertised from locations close to the front lines. John Good had opened an office in western Maryland, to be near the "late battlefield" at Antietam. The proximity to the blood-soaked grounds allowed him to reduce the "cost of bringing home the bodies of the dead." He would ship the corpses in a burial casket that he had designed, offering the "entire absence of any of the unpleasant circumstances" that happened in more cheaply made cases. He assured readers that his design had "given entire satisfaction" and challenged "any comparison with any Casket now before the public." Good would work with any of the "Friends of Our Patriotic Dead" but allowed that "Orders from a distance" would be "promptly attended to." In Virginia, Dr. W. Maclure had "opened an office upon the late battle field" of Chancellorsville. He would embalm and "disinfect" any of the Confederate dead. The process allowed him to send the bodies any distance, even in the heat of the summer. "Perfect success is guaranteed," he assured. More unnervingly, an Indiana undertaker announced that he was traveling with the Union army "in the West." His proximity to any soon-to-be battlefield allowed him to transport corpses "more cheaply than other companies."[40]

William Wood also touted his ability to inexpensively transport the Union dead. A former Massachusetts officer, Wood was leaving for the Union Department of the Gulf and offered to bring back the remains of those men who were "filling a soldiers' grave" in southern Louisiana. He would charge only enough to cover his time and the transportation costs for returning the body to Boston. "Any person who may charge an afflicted family of a Soldier more," he fumed, "is either an imposter, a copperhead, or a fool." Other undertakers claimed to agree. They offered "reasonable terms" to transport "deceased friends at the seat of the war."[41]

Notices for the transportation of soldiers' corpses were, in a sense, also a political statement because they highlighted the inability of the national governments to provide the same service. Not until later conflicts did the federal government attempt to return the bodies of fallen soldiers to bereaved families. Read another way, however, the advertisements confirmed existing gender roles. Notices for undertakers kept many women from traveling to claim the bodies of the deceased at the front, a very male-dominated space through the mid-nineteenth century. Transporting corpses spared wives, mothers, and their families none of the grief but allowed their mourning to occur at home.[42]

• •

Soldiers' obituaries provided some of the details behind the returned bodies. In her study on death and dying during the Civil War, historian Drew Gilpin Faust argues that soldiers hoped to meet their end, should it come, as faithful and true. The concept of a "Good Death" helped northerners and southerners to transcend the otherwise almost unimaginable suffering and grief that surrounded them.[43] Obituaries sought to instill death with a purpose. Men who fell were "brave and true," "beloved by all who knew him," and a sacrifice on the "altar of his country." In late 1861, Private Emil Long "was vanquished" by disease. His family and friends might draw comfort that "he was a good soldier because he loved its country and its institutions." Another enlisted man died three years later, as a prisoner of war. Although far from home when the end came, "His name will be placed in history as one of those martyrs who has given up his life for our Cause." His last thoughts were of his faith and family: "May we all emulate his example."[44]

In the notices for Frank Heard and Robert Hodge, a "good death" failed to hide the war's grim reality. Heard had suddenly taken ill while serving in northern Virginia. Surrounded by his comrades, he "died the death of a soldier." Still, "no kind mother was there to hear his parting words or to raise her heart in earnest prayer in behalf of her dying child; no affectionate sister was there to bid her dear brother farewell." The war had deprived Heard's family, like many others across the Union and Confederacy, of the comfort of his last earthly moments. During the fighting around Atlanta in the summer of 1864, Hodge was shot through the lower jaw. A surgeon amputated the mangled remains, but Hodge lingered for another several weeks. The obituary writer admitted that words were "inadequate to describe the excruciating tortures which he must have endured."[45]

The sister of Orphens Evans used his obituary to rail against the shoddy record keeping practiced by some Confederate officers. The North Carolina private had fallen in 1862, during the fighting around Richmond. His captain or lieutenant had reported the dead man as Hiram Evans. Later, another officer had amended the name to O. H. Jones. "Both were wrong," the sister icily declared. Her sibling was the deceased soldier, a fate the family found out only weeks after: "The blow is a crushing one to father, mother and sisters—the only son and youngest child of the family." The sister was proud that in his death, Evans had illustrated the "character of a patriot and hero." Still, the "officers who prepare lists of casualties in battle are so careless in writing names" that such errors occurred. She reminded these men that "Proper names should always be written plainly."[46]

War-related deaths afflicted more than soldiers. When the Union army occupied New Bern, North Carolina, in 1862, Ann Byran fled to the interior and her granddaughter's house. Elderly and hobbled by a range of ailments, Byran died soon after. The Yankees deserved the blame. The grandmother had talked almost incessantly about "her loved home" and the shock of the sudden departure being "too severe for her." Three years later, Mary Woodward passed away in Virginia. Physically, she had seemed fine. The loss of her only son at Second Manassas had haunted her, however, and the grief had "likely contributed" to her untimely demise. Woodward, in other words, had died from a broken heart.[47]

At least these families knew the fate of their loved ones, and notices for missing soldiers revealed the anguish of those waiting uncertainly at home. The Union and Confederate governments did not issue identification tags, and soldiers sometimes simply vanished from the military rosters. In the spring of 1863, James Wallace, a discharged Indiana private, was sailing home on a steamship. One month later, "nothing has been heard from him." Any information for the family "will be thankfully received." Later that year, the "aged mother" of Tyre Gillespie, a Confederate private, asked for information on "his whereabouts." He had not written home since suffering a wound during the fighting at Fredericksburg. In 1865, Louis Timson, a Union prisoner, was paroled from Andersonville or another of the "rebel 'pens.'" Taken ill, he was last seen in a military hospital. Any person with information on his fate "will confer a great favor upon his anxious family."[48]

Whether Timson's family ever discovered his whereabouts is uncertain, but the advertisements reflected many of the realities of the war. Recognizing the enormous financial costs, the national governments marketed war bonds. The Union was especially successful and sold the securities as an opportunity to strike a blow against the rebellion. Even though the fighting often occurred on distant battlefields, announcements for embalming services and obituaries reminded readers of the human costs of the fighting. The dead, wounded, and missing listed in the casualty lists were also husbands, fathers, and sons. In an era of often sensationalized newspaper headlines, the advertising columns had conveyed to readers the monies spent and the lives lost to determine the nation's future.

MARRIAGE AND MEDICINES

Loneliness was an emotion that connected soldiers and civilians, and many Yankees and Rebels placed notices for "female correspondents." During the antebellum era, Americans had considered courtship a private activity.[49] Now, with the distance imposed by military service, eligible men publicly announced their availability in the advertising pages. Union private John Shuch hoped to exchange letters with "some young lady," for "fun, love, or matrimony." Writing during winter encampment, three "Gay and Festive young Cavalry-men" hoped to hear from "any number" of young women. "Pitch in Girls," they encouraged, "now is your chance, object; fun, love and matrimony, *the* latter preferred." Perhaps displaying false modesty, a Confederate captain realized that he was "making more money than he cares to spend on himself" and hoped instead to lavish it on his future wife. She might contact him through his commanding officer. In Kentucky, William Caldwell and Bryan Wentwork believed humor was the fastest route to a woman's heart. The two self-described "ugly looking soldiers" were stationed in the "romantic city" of Paducah. They would delight in exchanging letters with almost anyone of the "opposite sex who are better looking than themselves." That requirement ruled out few people, since the "profound homeliness" of the privates entitled "either of them to the possession of the famous jack-knife to be awarded to the ugliest men."[50]

Amid worries that perhaps some of the lonely hearts overestimated their good looks, swapping photographs allowed the new acquaintances to determine how far, if at all, to pursue their relationship. A self-described "young soldier in the Army of the Potomac," Leander Wilber hoped to open a correspondence with "some patriotic young lady." If she included a picture, "one will be sent in return." Also in the East, three "young officers" wanted an equal number of "young Ladies" for "Love, Fun, and whatever may follow." The men added, "photographs desired." A "young naval officer" was more direct. He wanted to exchange letters with "amiable ladies between 20 and 30," with a view toward marriage. Given the seriousness of the undertaking, "no notice will be taken of answers not including the lady's picture."[51]

The personal columns became a flashpoint for controversy in early 1863, when a Union soldier claimed that he and his comrades, frustrated at not receiving enough letters from their families and sweethearts, would turn to the advertisements. In a letter to the *Louisville Daily Journal,* he proposed running:

> Wanted! Wanted!—By a half a dozen or a dozen good-looking intelligent, brave, manly, magnanimous soldiers of the *very highest* respectability, *several* correspondents of the fair sex.
>
> Must be in every way fit for, and worthy of being, the wives of heroes.

He had never written a notice and admitted that he did not "exactly understand the style." However, he knew several men who might "write the sweetest love letters, and, as it would enliven camp-life, why not have a few correspondents?" To the potential pen pals, the "Old Soldier" dangled the possibility of an actual romance. Their new friends faced the dangers inherent to military service, but, he assured them, it's "far better to be a *soldier's widow* than a coward's wife."[52]

That logic drew a response from Edith Garnett, a self-described "Buckeye Girl." She acknowledged that answering the personal advertisements was "quite the rage" among her acquaintances. If the "Old Soldier" and his friends would write to her, care of the editor, she might find a "correspondent for each among the Mollies, Matties, Nellies, or Kates, which flourish so fairly" in Ohio. She challenged "those gents who write those sweetest love letters to try their powers of persuasion and see whether a good letter will not be of as much worth as a handsome face." Although she agreed that women should marry only the "loyal and brave," rather than stay-at-homes and shirkers, she cautioned them to not set their hopes too high. "Of course we can write, as the advertisements usually say, for fun, love, or matrimony," she explained. "I say, let us begin with the first, and if he is *the one,* the 'plot may thicken' as fate dictates." Garnett had used the personal columns to support the Union war effort and to assert that her friends, at least, in matters of the heart, would make their own decisions.[53]

Louis Stephens, the editor of *Vanity Fair,* saw only potential dangers in the personal columns, for allowing "advertising vagabonds" to take advantage of, supposedly, women's' self-conceit. He fumed that "some Female Fool . . . Or a few dozen" would see themselves possessing all the requirements listed in a matrimonial notice, such as "Cheerful," "Religious," and "Of Loving Disposition." Under the charms of a modern-day Lothario, they would suffer abuse of their trust, and worse, reputation. "It's the same old story," fumed this editor. Another writer placed the blame for any romantic misadventures upon newspaper editors for even accepting personal notices. He acknowledged that newspapermen were business owners rather than moral censors. Still, a "man's moral responsibilities are in no way changed" because he was an editor. Otherwise, he had become "something which it is very disagreeable to mention." Besides, the author cautioned, an editor's daughter might respond to a matrimonial notice: "You gain, perhaps, twenty, yes, even thirty dollars for the amusing advertisement, and you lose your daughter."[54]

Even though the personal columns were subject to misuse, they offered more of an opportunity for love and romance than other public settings. As Garnett acknowledged in her response to the "Old Soldier," the advertisements allowed women to receive, rather than initiate, the flirtations. By contrast, as daughters and sisters entered into wartime settings as nurses, munitions workers, and government clerks, their sexual behavior came under public scrutiny. Worry that these women might go astray generated gossip and censure about their appearance and actions. A new cloak or hat, or an unguarded comment to a male bystander, were taken by onlookers as evidence of, according to one Civil War historian, the "unchaperoned wife's depravity." The worry over women's morality brought a greater federal oversight, including a congressional investigation into the supposed misbehavior of women employed at the Treasury Department. In both the advertising columns and the workplace, the increased visibility of women had narrowed the divide between public and private lives.[55]

Soldiers who worried that they perhaps had already wrecked their opportunity for marriage through "self-abuse" offered marketers a golden opportunity. Teachings against masturbation were widespread among medical leaders by the 1860s, who argued that the secretion of sexual fluids also drained spiritual and physical energy. Merchants ran sympathetic notices, by claiming that self-pleasure was an almost inevitable part of youth. They wrote for men who suffered from "Errors and Abuses in early life" and that "dreadful scourge of the young, indulged in when alone." Sometimes, the loss of energy occurred without a youngster even knowing what had happened. A New York physician sold pills for those individuals who, as teenagers, had experienced "seminal loss" from "nightly emissions and sensual dreams." If left untreated, the inevitable results included "Sexual Debility, and Impediments to Marriage" and "Nervousness, Consumption, Epilepsy and Fits; Mental and Physical Incapacity."[56]

The ads naturally went beyond acknowledging a problem to offering a solution. One self-described doctor headlined: "Volunteers Attention! Indiscretions of Youth." He promised that "Sores and Ulcers, Blotches and Swellings, can with certainty be radically cured" with a strong application of his lotion. Other medicines might promise the same results, but they simply shifted the affected areas from one part of the body to another. Only his ointment would "remove the homors [*sic*] from the system and leave the Patient a vigorous and healthy man." The afflicted might also write to James Butler in New York, who offered to send the "Marriage Guide" by return mail. Written in "plain language" and illustrated with "numerous engravings," the book offered advice to "those suffering with Seminal Weakness." Union soldiers who would rather not read about their "own *self-indulgence*, in violation of nature's laws" but yet who "dread marriage" might order a bottle of Cherokee Cure. Sent to any mailing address, even to army camps, the "delicious syrup" will "once more make a man of you." The potion sold at a discount for each additional bottle ordered.[57]

That manhood might be restored through the consumption of a patent medicine offered a different understanding of the idea than found throughout the rest of the Union and Confederate armies. Soldiers might prove, or disprove, their manhood through a variety of actions, including bravery and courage, physical toughness, and honor and duty. According to advertisers, however, Yankees and Rebels who had suffered the "errors of youth," even if unintentionally, needed their help. That might be gained privately, with the medicine men offering to ship their wares in "plain and sealed" envelopes. Once arrived, the pills and potions allowed the unfortunate to "cure himself cheaply, privately, and radically." Reinvigorated soldiers might, eventually, start a family to carry forward not only their own but the nation's legacy. The emphasis upon posterity connected medical advertisers back to a public understanding of manhood and the Civil War. As historian Lorien Foote has recently argued, Americans believed that men needed to possess the right qualities for the republic to survive. The war was as much a test of the nation's masculinity as a struggle between competing visions of the nation's future.[58]

Women might appreciate less their husband's newfound vigor, and notices for birth-control medicines were common. Merchants used remarkably circumspect language, recognizing that any attempt at pregnancy prevention was in the gray area between the human and the divine. Readers might see in the notices what they wanted to see. Thus, a Dr. Cheeseman sold "Female Regulating Pills" that supposedly relieved any of the physical discomforts experienced during a woman's "periodic discharge." However, he warned that a miscarriage would result if an expectant mother took the medicine. "Such is the irresistible tendency of the medicine to restore the sexual functions to a normal condition," he touted, "that even the reproductive power of nature cannot resist it." Each box mailed with "*Explicit Directions.*" Another medicine maker offered pills to cure "all those painful and dangerous diseases to which the female constitution is subject." He urged, however, "CAUTION. *These pills should not be taken by Females during the FIRST THREE MONTHS of Pregnancy, as they are sure to bring on Miscarriage.*"[59]

These notices drew a strong public rebuke for allowing readers access to immoralities that ruined, according to one writer, "its victims for this world and the next." He fumed that a "poor, deluded" wife might destroy her future chances for conception by falling for the "artful sophisms of the abortionist," while a "courtesan" might lose her life by "taking drugs" announced in the advertisements. Editors were focused on securing their "'paying advertisements,' no matter who suffers." A magazine writer echoed the theme. Under the fiction that they were not responsible for the content of the advertisements, newspapermen ran promotions for obscene books, thinly veiled as medical texts, and drugs "for purposes which the words used do not even mask." To his way of thinking, editors were as responsible for the notices they ran as a "publisher for the books he publishes." He asked, "Is it not a matter in which all parents and decent people are interested?" For many of them it was, and the opportunity for women to exercise greater control over their family planning closed rapidly after the war. Led by Anthony Comstock, a Union veteran, the federal government banned the advertising and mailing of "Obscene Literature and Articles," including abortifacients, in the early 1870s.[60]

Other medicine makers cast women as the weaker sex and made money by perpetuating this widely accepted stereotype. The maker of a "Stomach Bitters" in New York warned that the "female organization is often as frail as that of a tender flower." The demands of life, especially the uncertainties over loved ones at the front, sent many women to an "untimely grave." A bottle of the bitters would help women avoid this tragic fate: "It infuses new vitality into the frame, and strengthens the whole system." A young woman in New England claimed that her menstruation cycle had left her "sick for five years." She drank four bottles of a medicine prepared by Linas Belcher and, a few days later, was cured. Alfred Speer claimed that his Sambuci Wine was perfect for "FEMALES, WEAKLY PERSONS AND INVALIDS." Ladies should not worry about drinking too much because the wine had no alcohol. Rather than a spinning head, the drink imparted a "healthy tone to the digestive organs, and a blooming, soft and healthy skin and complexion."[61]

Depictions of women as fragile and delicate contrasted with their portrayal in other forms of wartime literature. In poems and novels, wives, mothers, sisters, and daughters bore risks and sacrifices to help the Union and Confederate causes. They became stronger as individuals, especially in not allowing themselves to become overwhelmed by the war's carnage. The "feminized war" claimed for women an equal stake as soldiers in strength of character and love of country. Fear, however, sold more medicine than fortitude. Even in 1865, as women looked toward the future with a hard-won resilience, nostrum dealers ran the same notices as they had earlier. Appeals "To Females" and "Debilitated Ladies" offered to cure "nervous weaknesses," "hysteria," and other "complaints so peculiar to the sex." In marketing toward women's insecurities, advertisers had granted a dubious gender equality that continued well into the postwar years.[62]

• •

In his study on the experience of battle during the Civil War, Gerald Linderman declares that every "war begins as one war and becomes two, that watched by civilians and that fought by soldiers."[63] Whatever its other merits, the argument is less applicable to the advertising columns. Merchants attempted to sell an almost indistinguishable experience. Soldiers might peruse notices for weapons and military goods, while their families attended war-themed entertainments. As casualty lists lengthened, maimed and injured soldiers might purchase prosthetics, while grieving widows and mothers had their loved one's remains shipped home. Appeals to purchase war bonds offered Union and Confederate readers the opportunity to strike a blow for the cause. They might also combat their own physical insecurities and order pills and potions to restore manhood and limit family size. From the advertisers' perspective, soldiers and civilians, husbands and wives, shared a commonality as potential customers. Amid the tremendous upheaval of the Civil War, merchants attempted to find profit in a unified experience that emphasized common bonds and national loyalty.

Epilogue

Memories

In the late summer of 1865, F. W. Smith, an agent for the *New York Daily News*, headlined a notice in a New Orleans paper, "To the People of the South and West." He reminded readers that with the return of peace, "proper advertising and publishing again must be done." Southerners should consider his publication to run their notices because, during the war, federal authorities had temporarily suspended its operations for supposedly expressing pro-Confederate sympathies. "We propose still to advocate the TRUE INTERESTS of the Southern States," Smith declared, "and we hope to find that support and encouragement from their people as our past course and proposed future will justify them in awarding." With a large readership, the newspaper's "advertising advantages" would run "proportionally great."[1] The Confederacy had collapsed and its armies disbanded, but Smith was appealing to his readers' sense of a Rebel identity. Other advertisers took a similar approach, and commercialization marked much of the nation's memory of its largest conflict.

In the aftermath of the Union triumph at Appomattox, northern advertisers focused on the conflict's military aspects. Readers might peruse notices for the "Photographic History of the War for the Union," with images taken by Mathew Brady. Among the many photographs included were *Dead Soldiers in the Trenches*, *Libby Prison*, and *Sherman's Great "March to the Sea."* The point was not to gawk but to provide the "most interesting and characteristic representations" of the "great national struggle." Those interested in the fighting at Gettysburg might also purchase images showing the "position held by the Union and Rebel forces in that terrible fight." Anyone needing a break from such blood-soaked fields might find a chuckle in F. C. Adams's *History of the Siege of Washington.* Depicting the Union defense of Fort Stevens, the book included "HUMOROUS ILLUSTRATIONS" of several "illustrious generals, as they really appeared during the siege." One reviewer, however, believed the jokes were cheaply made. He huffed that there was nothing funny in "ungenerous ridicule of soldiers who, though they failed of success, did their best to overcome great difficulties." The criticism did not keep the publisher from headlining his notice with "GREATEST MILITARY BOOK."[2]

Two years after the end of the war, Jones Brothers, a Chicago-based publishing company, ran announcements for *The Blue Coats,* an anecdotal history of the common soldier. The work told how these men "LIVED, FOUGHT and DIED FOR THE UNION!" The publisher acknowledged that "a certain portion of the war will never go into the regular histories" because it did not feature the generals. Yet the activities of the enlisted men and low-ranking officers, from their campfire humor to battlefield bravery, "if preserved, convey to succeeding generations a better idea of the spirt of the conflict" than dry official reports. The stories of these men "may be called the gossip, the fun, the pathos of the war." Jones Brothers claimed that the book had become so popular that other publishing companies had issued knockoffs. They cautioned customers to "see that the book they buy contains over 100 fine engravings and 550 pages."[3]

That same year, Linus Brockett acknowledged the contributions of noncombatants to the Union war effort with his *Woman's Work in the Civil War: A Record of Heroism, Patriotism and Patience*. Wives, mothers, sisters, and daughters had served as nurses and volunteers, and their sacrifices had helped to preserve the nation. Their stories were told over 850 pages, with sixteen engravings and, for the cost-conscious, a "low price." Expecting perhaps some resistance among readers who preferred books on generals and privates, one notice reminded them that Brockett's work "commends itself to that somewhat numerous class, who have, or who have had—MOTHERS!" Even women needed some encouragement to read the book. The same notice described Brockett's work as selling fast because men liked to read about the "best half" of the world, and asked, "the best half are they not also curious?"[4]

However readers responded to that question, the otherwise extensive focus on the battlefield allowed merchants to restrict the historical significance of the Emancipation Proclamation to the destruction of slavery (as momentous as that was) rather than the postwar struggle for citizenship. In 1866, Derby and Miller issued a steel engraving titled *First Reading of the Emancipation Proclamation before the Cabinet by President Lincoln,* from a painting by F. B. Carpenter. Agents acknowledged the broadening of the Union war effort as one of the "important events in American history" but focused on everything else. In Chicago, a Mr. Mills described the engraving's lifelike detail. Lincoln and his cabinet, even the furniture in the room, were "represented with the utmost accuracy." The editor of a Vermont paper encouraged readers to consider purchasing the engraving to benefit Sidney Southard, the local agent and a Union veteran. The former captain had suffered a leg wound during the war and now wore a prosthetic. "As agent, of course," reminded the editor, "[Southard] has a commission on all pictures sold, and those who purchase of him will thus be doing a kindness to a deserving Vermont volunteer."[5]

In the black press, notices offered a more expansive interpretation of Lincoln's wartime measure. In New Orleans, the Union League announced that its Fourth of July activities included a reading of the Declaration of Independence and the Emancipation Proclamation. Only with the destruction of slavery did all citizens have the opportunity to pursue their own livelihood. In a subscription notice run prior to the off-year elections in 1866, the editor of the *Loyal Georgian* argued that readers should take his paper as a political act. The "soldiers of Lee, Beauregard, Johnson, and Hood" were attempting to elect former Confederate officials to Congress. "We must," he asserted, "convince the South and the Copperheads that revolutions go not backward—that Emancipation is an unchangeable fact—that the glorious Civil Rights Act can never be repealed." Two years later, in San Francisco, a "Committee of Arrangements" ran an announcement for its upcoming celebration of "President Lincoln's Emancipation Proclamation." An invited speaker would read the document, and audience members would follow by singing the "Star Spangled Banner," "John Brown," and "The Battle Hymn of Freedom."[6]

With the Emancipation Proclamation began the large-scale recruitment of black Union soldiers, and readers interested in their experiences might turn to William Wells Brown's *The Negro in the American Rebellion: His Heroism and His Fidelity.* Published in 1868, the book received announcement as analyzing the "services performed by the negro in the late war." Battlefield bravery knew no distinction beyond a blue uniform, with Union soldiers "of one color in the order and energy of their patriotic life." Every family that "has lost a son, husband, or brother in this great rebellion," should read "this truthful and instructive narrative" of black men "in the struggle for their own freedom, the preservation of our glorious Republic, and for universal suffrage." By carrying the sacrifices of black soldiers into the postwar era, these advertisers expanded the meaning of the war from destroying slavery to achieving political equality.[7]

Ultimately, however, in the mainstream press, advertisers had anticipated the national shift toward reunion during the late nineteenth century. At battlefield meetings during the 1880s and 1890s, Union and Confederate veterans focused almost exclusively upon the war's first three years. As David Blight argues in his work on the Civil War in national memory, the attention to the fighting at Gettysburg and Chickamauga, among other locations, allowed the American public to remember a war fought exclusively by white soldiers. The seeming obsession by former Yankees and Rebels on the maneuvers of their military units also allowed them to avoid the causes of the war. Rather than argue over states' rights and abolition, they found common agreement in the bravery and valor of the American soldier.[8] That was a reunionist message already emphasized in the advertising columns, where merchants attempted to sell battles rather than the causes and results of the fighting.

When northern publishing companies ran announcements for biographies of former Union general Ulysses Grant, the public reaction mixed wartime and postwar politics. In 1868, Adam Badeau published the first volume in his *Military History of Ulysses S. Grant.* Announcements heralded the work as written by "one who has been a member of Grant's official household since his earliest rise into public notice, who has access to all official records and correspondence, and enjoyed the constant and familiar confidence of the General himself." That familiarity drew the wrath of John McClernand, a Union general whom Grant had removed from command. McClernand charged that Badeau had spent the war "hanging around General Grant's headquarters as a questionable appendage." The two men had not seen one another since, but he suspected that since the reporter had failed to gain "distinction as a soldier," he was determined to gain notoriety as a "personal traducer and panegyrist." Amid that rather tortured language, McClernand fumed that Badeau had written the history to help propel Grant into the White House, regardless of any damage done to his fellow officers. If all the wartime facts were known, "Gen. Grant would stand very differently in public estimation than he does at present. That time will yet come when the wrong done me and my command will be corrected." McClernand was not the only person upset, and, in Philadelphia, a newspaperman took issue when Badeau received a federal appointment but still continued to work on his military history. The "overburdened tax-payers" in America would hardly approve that the newly appointed diplomat to England "passes a whole winter at Washington in the pursuit of a private avocation."[9]

Also in 1868, Robert Bonner announced a series of articles on Grant's boyhood to run in the *New York Ledger*. Written by Jesse Grant, Ulysses's father, the series offered a "GENUINE ACCOUNT" of the wartime hero's early life. The elder Grant was a natural storyteller, Bonner assured, and his "style is characterized by great pith and clearness." The resulting biography was as "readable as any work of fiction. Every one will wish to see this genuine account of Grant's early life." The editors of the *Cincinnati Inquirer* had some doubts about how genuine, and they sent their own reporter to talk with the elder Grant. The interview veered into contemporary politics, with the president's father reportedly admitting that he did not "blame people much if they are rebel. I am opposed to having the niggers vote." He also would divide the country into the former free states and slave states, arguing that "It would be better for both." In Memphis, the editor of the *Public Ledger* reminded his readers about "another General, a great and good man" who admitted to cutting down a cherry tree when questioned by his father. "To judge of Grant's boyhood by his manhood," he opinioned, "it is hardly probable his father will have any such pleasing incident to narrate of him."[10]

Other merchants commercialized Grant to market their material wares. In Washington, a Mr. Tharpe declared that there were "all sorts of reformers in this country—some of them assailing even the use of tobacco." A few of these diehards had even "attacked General Grant for his excess in the use of the cigar, but without effect upon the hero of the Wilderness." Thorpe invited these individuals to try some of his tobacco. They might find their nerves calmed, leaving them "less disposed to rail against the world for the enjoyment of a pleasant and harmless luxury." Shortly before Grant died from throat cancer in the summer of 1885, Swift's Specific headlined a notice for its medicine with "CANCER OF THE TONGUE. A Case Resembling that of General Grant." Mrs. Mary Comer wrote that she had suffered from throat cancer that had eaten through her cheek. Unable to talk, she had consumed only liquids. A few bottles of Swift's medicine had cured her cheek and upper lip, and "it seems that nature is supplying a new tongue." She happily reported that she now was talking so that her friends might "readily understand her," as well as eating solid foods. After a few doses, others suffering from throat and mouth cancer might experience similar results.[11]

In the former Confederate States, the war received frequent mention as a marketing pitch. Merchants called attention to their military service, to distinguish themselves from their competitors. J. N. Woodward, the superintendent of the American Hotel in Staunton, Virginia, reminded potential guests that he had been "engaged in the late war, in the field, from the beginning to the ending," and only now had returned to the "peaceful pursuits of life." In Augusta, J. W. Bacon announced his leather business. In addition to being "Georgia born," he and his coworkers were "well tried soldiers of the late war." This meant that the men were "honest, honorable, liberal and enterprising." Writing under the pen name "SOUTH CAROLINA," a resident of Edgefield County ran a card thanking the owner of a stable for his recent "kind disposition and liberality." The man had proved "himself on this occasion, as during the late war, a gallant soldier and patriotic citizen."[12]

Love of country took many forms, and, in 1866, a Mr. J. Ennis ran a testimonial for his iron and hardware store from an "OLD CUSTOMER." This individual claimed that "it is well known" that, during the war, when the "Southern ports were blockaded," Ennis's store had a "fine and well assorted stock of goods needed by our people and the Confederate government." These material wares were commanding a high price, and another man might have made his fortune. Demonstrating a "patriotic spirit that was truly commendable," Ennis had charged his customers only the prewar price. The old customer argued that such selflessness deserved the thanks of the "community and of the entire country." Even though Ennis was not a military veteran, potential customers might rest assured that "men who passed a period that created an inordinate and unlawful desire to acquire wealth, and were not contaminated" would offer a fair deal.[13]

Other merchants urged their readers to support southern-made products, a commercial patriotism that stretched back to the prewar years. They encouraged potential customers to shop for "Southern Made Goods" that supported "our own country." In Alabama, the Piedmont Real Estate Company declared that "Every Southern man should insure" in it because "its funds are retained at home, and tend to our financial prosperity." James Gibbs, the owner of a sewing machine company in Richmond, scolded readers for buying overpriced and cheaply made northern machines. "Instead of patronizing home productions," he fumed, "they suffer themselves to become the easy prey of itinerant carpet-bag peddlers of Yankee notions." He, however, "being a Virginian, propose[d] to do a legitimate business in a fair, Virginia way." Based in Baltimore, the Mackenzie brothers announced their "Carriage Goods and Materials." They encouraged merchants traveling northward to "look for their winter stock of goods," to stop by the store. Baltimore was a populous city, with considerable "commercial importance." Perhaps even more significant, it "has commended itself and people to us by their acts of kindness to our friends who, as prisoners, were in that city during the days of the Confederacy." A traveler might shop for a new saddle and, in the transaction, benefit a city that had, at least in this telling, stood by the Confederacy.[14]

Southern medicine makers also made frequent appeals to a regional pride. Pills and potions were the most advertised products in American newspapers by the early 1870s, and the profits—and competition—were enormous.[15] A Tennessee druggist fumed that his "countrymen" sent too much of their money to the North. "Those who are willing to kill you with the sword," he reminded, "burn everything in the South with the torch, and divide our lands with the compass" should not "prescribe and prepare all your Pills." Better products were made in the South and sold by local druggists. He encouraged his readers to exercise "your own judgment, stand upon your own dignity, and buy from those who are qualified to give satisfaction." He had for sale "the 'Great Southern Preparations'" to cure users of, among other ailments, "sick headache," "painful menstruation," and "nervous trembling." Three years later, in New Orleans, a doctor declared that his bitters were better for those suffering an upset stomach than the "nostrums that are draining our Southern country of millions of dollars annually, and affording no relief or benefit to the afflicted." He was a native southerner and had worked in Louisiana since the 1830s. He used only southern products to make his medicine and promised these would restore customers to "health, strength and vigor."[16]

As Reconstruction faltered and, by the late 1870s, ended, merchants' emphasis on a southern identity was a common marketing ploy. Only weeks after federal troops were withdrawn from Louisiana, a New Orleans grocer headlined his announcement:

LOUISIANA REDEEMED
GREAT REJOICING
GOOD TIMES!

To help usher in the "new era of prosperity dawning upon us," this grocer had coffee and tea on sale. During the Christmas season in 1877, a dry goods dealer headlined his notice with "K.K.K." This did not refer to the Ku Klux Klan but, rather, announced that he had "Kris Kringle's Katalogue." Readers might shop for their families and find "First-Class Goods at Reasonable Rates." By cleverly playing off the initials of an organization dedicated to white supremacy, this merchant was attempting to help his readers have a happy holiday season. The nation had achieved reunion by the late nineteenth century, but in the advertising columns, as in many other public forums, reconciliation remained more elusive.[17]

Modern-day readers might recognize that the Civil War has never strayed too far from the advertising pages, with a major soft drink company announcing itself as a "Southern original," and an Abraham Lincoln reenactor pitching everything from insurance to automobile repairs. Such commercialization had occurred during the 1860s, with merchants attempting to link their wares to the war-themed newspaper headlines. Yet, in their hopes of making a profit, Yankee and Rebel advertisers had broadened participation in the contest. Families might purchase a medicine to support southern rights, or a bond to help fund the Union war effort. Often suffering the horrors of their families sold apart, African American men and women placed notices looking for their children. Highly visible, these and other notices drew a strong public reaction. Contemporary observers used political memorabilia to rally support for their partisan cause, and runaway notices to attack the institution of slavery. Newspaper editors referred to the recruiting notices to encourage men to volunteer or, by reprinting desertion and substitution notices, to disparage the other's war effort. Often overshadowed in the popular memory by the creation of a consumer culture during the late nineteenth century, Union and Confederate advertisers had influenced, and commercialized, the most turbulent domestic crisis in the nation's history.

NOTES

INTRODUCTION

1. Joseph J. Belcher, "Newspaper Advertisements," *Harper's New Monthly Magazine* 33, no. 198 (November 1866): 781; "The Herald's 'Personnals,'" *New York Herald*, October 12, 1861; Robert J. Coen, "200 Years of U.S. Advertising," *Advertising Age*, July 5, 1976, 1; Daniel J. Boorstin, *The Americans: The Democratic Experience* (New York: Random House, 1973), 146. The amount of money spent on advertising in 1860 is debated because no complete business records exist. Coen places the total at $22 million. His figure is reached through the use of census data, and scholars consider it to be the most reliable. Boorstin, however, places the money spent on advertising at $50 million. For a discussion of the difficulties in determining the amount of money spent on advertising prior to the late nineteenth century, see Daniel Pope, *The Making of Modern Advertising* (New York: Basic, 1983), 18–30.

2. Frederic Hudson, *Journalism in the United States from 1690 to 1872* (New York: Harper and Brothers, 1872), 470; Henry Sampson, *A History of Advertising from the Earliest Times* (London: Chatto and Windus, 1874), 556–58; George Wakeman, "Advertising," *Galaxy* 3, no. 2 (January 1867): 202–3.

3. George Augustus Sala, *My Diary in America in the Midst of War* (London: Tinsley Brothers, 1865), 42–51. Samuel Phillips Day, also a British journalist, recorded his experiences in the Confederacy. In 1862, during the Union siege of Yorktown, Virginia, he visited nearby Williamsburg. He browsed old copies of the *Virginia Gazette* and found that the advertisements were "very quaint and amusing, although the grammar is not of the best." He reprinted several of them in his *Down South; Or, An Englishman's Experience at the Seat of the American War*, vol. 2 (London: Hurst and Blackett, 1862), 141–42.

4. Among the best and most recent works on advertising and its influences are Lizabeth Cohen, *A Consumer's Republic: The Politics of Mass Consumption in Postwar America* (New York: Knopf, 2003); Pamela Walker Laird, *Advertising Progress: American Business and the Rise of Consumer Marketing* (Baltimore: Johns Hopkins University Press, 1998); Jackson Lears, *Fables of Abundance: A Cultural History of Advertising in America* (New York: Basic, 1994); and Charles McGovern, *Sold American: Consumption and Citizenship, 1890–1945* (Chapel Hill: University of North Carolina Press, 2006). Older titles on advertising that continue to receive mention in the literature include Stephen Fox, *The Mirror Makers: A History of American Advertising and Its Creators* (New York: William Morrow, 1984); Frank Presbrey, *The History and Development of*

Advertising (Garden City, NY: Doubleday, 1929); E. S. Turner, *The Shocking History of Advertising!* (New York: Dutton, 1953); and James P. Wood, *The Story of Advertising* (New York: Ronald, 1958).

5. William C. Davis, "American Civil War Newspapers," Virginia Center for Civil War Studies, Virginia Polytechnic Institute and State University, Blacksburg, https://dcr.emd.vt.edu/vital/access/manager/Index?site_name=American%20Civil%20War%20Newspaper (2016). Recent titles on the press and the Civil War include Andrew Seth Coopersmith, *Fighting Words: An Illustrated History of Newspaper Accounts of the Civil War* (New York: Norton, 2004); Ford Risley, *Civil War Journalism* (Santa Barbara, CA: Praeger, 2012); Brayton Harris, *Blue and Gray in Black and White: Newspapers in the Civil War* (Washington, DC: Brassey's, 1999); Debra Reddin van Tuyll, *The Confederate Press in the Crucible of the American Civil War* (New York: Peter Lang, 2013); and David B. Sachsman, S. Kittrell Rushing, and Roy Morris Jr., eds., *Words at War: The Civil War and American Journalism* (West Lafayette, IN: Purdue University Press, 2008). Works that remain standards in the field are J. Cutler Andrews, *The North Reports the Civil War* (Pittsburgh: University of Pittsburgh Press, 1955); and *The South Reports the Civil War* (Princeton, NJ: Princeton University Press, 1970); and Louis M. Starr, *Bohemian Brigade: Civil War Newsmen in Action* (New York: Knopf, 1954).

6. The link between commerce and patriotism continues through today (see Dana Heller, ed., *The Selling of 9/11: How a National Tragedy Became a Commodity* [New York: Palgrave Macmillan, 2005]; and Ian Frazier, "All Consuming Patriotism," *Mother Jones*, March/April 2002, www.motherjones.com/politics/2002/03/all-consuming-patriotism).

7. *Yazoo City (MS) Whig and Political Register*, July 7, 1843; *New-York Daily Tribune*, December 30, 1846; *Indiana American* (Brookville) July 27, 1855. On the lack of revenue from the notices, see Gerald J. Baldasty, *The Commercialization of News in the Nineteenth Century* (Madison: University of Wisconsin Press, 1992), 11–35. See also Culver H. Smith, *The Press, Politics and Patronage: The American Government's Use of Newspapers, 1789–1875* (Athens: University of Georgia Press, 1977).

8. Hudson, *Journalism in the United States*, 470; Boorstin, *The Americans*, 143–45.

9. "What Is a Square?," *Advertisers Gazette: A Monthly Journal Devoted to the Interests of Advertisers and Newspaper Publishers* 2, no. 6 (April 1868): 4. A general history of newspaper design that now is dated is Albert A. Sutton, *Design and Makeup of the Newspaper* (New York: Prentice-Hall, 1948). By 1860, an advertising square generally ran between eight and twelve lines.

10. Alfred McClung Lee, *The Daily Newspaper in America: The Evolution of a Social Instrument* (New York: Macmillan, 1937), 748–49; Baldasty, *The Commercialization of News in the Nineteenth Century*, 43–56, 59–60; Wood, *The Story of Advertising*, 101.

11. Harris, *Blue and Gray in Black and White*, 11–15; Pope, *The Making of Modern Advertising*, 139–40; *Evansville (IN) Weekly Gazette*, August 31, 1861.

12. *Navarro Express* (Corsicana, TX), September 28, 1860.

13. *Freeport (IL) Weekly Journal*, May 15, 1861.

14. *New York Times*, June 11, 1863; *Brooklyn (NY) Daily Eagle*, April 29, 1861; *Republican and Gazette* (Sterling, IL), June 29, 1861; *Newport (RI) Daily News*, June 5, 1860; *Pittsburgh Daily Gazette and Advertiser*, September 14, 1860.

15. *Indianapolis (IN) Daily Journal*, July 27, 1864; *North American and United States Gazette*

(Philadelphia), February 19, 1861; *Daily Rocky Mountain News* (Denver), August 15, 1862; *Black Republican* (New Orleans), April 15, 1865.

16. *Cape Girardeau (MO) Weekly Argus*, August 10, 1860; *Boston Post*, September 6, 1863; *Syracuse (NY) Daily Courier and Union*, April 1, 1861; *Mountain Democrat* (Placerville, CA), January 3, 1863.

17. *Louisiana Democrat* (Alexandria), April 4, 1860; *Tri-Weekly Miner's Register* (Central City, CO), November 26, 1862; *South-Jersey Republican* (Hammonton, NJ), October 10, 1863.

18. *Albany (GA) Patriot*, November 18, 1865; *Highland (OH) Weekly News*, March 2, 1865; *Louisville (IL) Republican*, January 22, 1862; *Cedar Falls (IA) Gazette*, October 17, 1862; *Frontier Scout* (Fort Union, ND), June 3, 1864; *Tolland County Herald* (Rockville, CT), April 6, 1865.

19. *Burlington (VT) Free Press*, October 26, 1860; "Newspaper Advertising versus Advertising Schemes," *Advertisers Gazette: A Monthly Journal Devoted to the Interests of Advertisers and Newspaper Publishers* 7, no. 1 (April 1873): 47.

20. The tax on advertisements excluded newspapers with a circulation fewer than two thousand subscribers and, for the remaining newspapers, exempted their first thousand dollars in advertising revenue. The congressional debate over the bill was followed closely in many newspapers, including the *Chicago Daily Tribune*, April 2, 1862; and *New York Herald*, November 12, 1862, and December 9, 1862. The tax revenue collected during the war is taken from John Luther Ringwalt, "Advertisement," in *American Encyclopaedia of Printing* (Philadelphia: Menamin and Ringwalt, 1871), 24. An excellent discussion of the advertising tax is found in Randall P. Bezanson, *Taxes on Knowledge in America: Exactions on the Press from Colonial Times to the Present* (Philadelphia: University of Pennsylvania Press, 1994), 89–97.

21. The American Association of Advertising Agencies, which claims to place more advertising volume than any other agency, was established in 1917. A discussion of the rise of agencies after 1865 is found in Pope, *The Making of Modern Advertising* 112–83.

22. Studies on subconscious advertising include Dylan Love, "The Shocking Drink and Incredible Coke History of Subliminal Advertising," Business Insider, May 26, 2011, www.businessinsider.com/subliminal-ads-2011-5 (2017); and Jim Edwards, "The 10 Best Subliminal Ads Ever Made," CBS Moneywatch, October 20, 2011, www.cbsnews.com/news/the-10-best-subliminal-ads-ever-made/ (2017). On the "art of advertising," see an article from the *Chicago Journal*, reprinted in the *Dayton (OH) Daily Empire*, April 21, 1865. The author writes that in advertising, "The purchaser is passive; the seller must be active. The buyer is indifferent. The seller must put a stop to this indifference. Purchasers are led by the eyes. The advertiser lays hold upon those eyes. The advertisement fails that does not become familiar to the eyes—that is not learned by heart by its reader."

23. C. P. Cranch, "An Old Newspaper," *Galaxy* 6, no. 3 (September 1868): 411–16. In another article, an editor reported that a man in New Jersey had found an "original copy of Dr. Franklin's 'Poor Richard Almanac.'" From all the materials that he might have run from the almanac, the editor reprinted an advertisement for securing buildings from lightning strikes (see "Notes and Queries," *Ladies' Repository* 22, no. 8 [August 1862]: 502).

24. Edward Everett Hale, "The Man without a Country," *Atlantic Monthly* 12, no. 73 (December 1863): 665–80.

25. Louise Chandler Moulton, "Out of Nazareth," *Harper's New Monthly Magazine* 28, no.

164 (January 1864): 202–13; Harriet E. Prescott, "Yet's Christmas Box," *Harper's New Monthly Magazine* 20, no. 119 (April 1860): 644–59. On "sentimental" literature, see Mary Kelley, *Private Women, Public Stage: Literary Domesticity in Nineteenth-Century America* (New York: Oxford University Press, 1984).

26. Joseph Mount, "Recollections of a Deaf and Dumb Teacher," *Ladies' Repository: A Monthly Periodical, Devoted to Literature, Arts, and Religion* 21, no. 8 (August 1861): 457–59.

27. James J. Belcher, "Typographical Errors," *Harper's New Monthly Magazine* 32, no. 188 (January 1866): 230; George Wakeman, "Verbal Anomalies," *Galaxy* 2, no. 1 (September 1866): 29–39. On the use of humor, see Jon Grinspan, "Sorrowfully Amusing: The Popular Comedy of the Civil War," *Journal of the Civil War Era* (September 2011): 313–38.

28. "The Molly O'Malley Papers," *Continental Monthly* 2, no. 2 (August 1862): 202–3. See also John Bell Boulton, *Round the Block: An American Novel* (New York: D. Appleton and Co., 1864), 94–95. Boulton has the heroines place a notice to tutor "Ladies in Good Society Who Desire to Improve Their Education." He continues: "There were many points in this advertisement to which Miss Pillbody's modesty took exception; but Mrs. Crull insisted upon them in a way that permitted no refusal. The little bit of bragging was the principal thing, she said. She had always observed that people are inclined to believe bragging advertisements, though they openly profess that they can't be taken in by them."

29. Alice Fahs, *The Imagined Civil War: Popular Literature of the North and South, 1861–1865* (Chapel Hill: University of North Carolina Press, 2001).

30. J. Matthew Gallman, *Defining Duty in the Civil War: Personal Choice, Popular Culture, and the Union Home Front* (Chapel Hill: University of North Carolina Press, 2015).

31. An overview of whether Americans were emancipated or entrapped by their consumer choices through the mid- and late twentieth century is found in David Steigerwald, "All Hail the Republic of Choice: Consumer History as Contemporary Thought," *Journal of American History* 93, no. 2 (September 2006): 385–403.

32. "Table 37—Newspapers and Periodicals in the United States in 1860," in Joseph C. G. Kennedy, *Preliminary Report on the Eighth Census, 1860* (Washington, DC: Government Printing Office, 1862), 211–13. The census data listed 372 newspapers published daily.

33. "Editor's Table," *Southern Literary Messenger* 31, no. 5 (November 1, 1860): 393; Daniel J. Kenny, *The American Newspaper Directory and Record of the Press: Containing an Accurate List of All the Newspapers, Magazines, Reviews, Periodicals . . .* (New York: Watson and Co., 1861), 116–17.

34. Even the oversized pages of mid-nineteenth-century newspapers, by comparison to today, encouraged "communal reading" practices. A larger sheet made the columns easier for several people to read at the same time, and to alternate reading out loud (see Isabelle Lehuu, *Carnival on the Page: Popular Print Media in Antebellum America* [Chapel Hill: University of North Carolina Press, 2000]). The practice of reading the advertisements to other people drove Julia LeGrand Waitz, a resident of New Orleans, to distraction. In the spring of 1863, she wrote that a well-intentioned housemate worked through the newspaper almost every morning: "Every advertisement, every negro arrest is drawled out and stumbled over. She sits in her room, has the door opened between us and begins before we are dressed in the morning. It is a mania with her and we are dying under it" (see her diary entry for March 1863, in *The Journal of Julia Le-*

Grand, New Orleans 1861–1863, ed. Kate Mason Rowland [Richmond, VA: Everett Waddey, 1911], 195–96). Reading the newspapers aloud, even the advertisements, extended into popular culture references (see Mary A. Howe, *The Rival Volunteers; Or, The Black Plume Rifles* [New York: John Bradburn, 1864], 290).

Chapter 1. THE WAR AS THE LEAD

1. *New-York Daily Tribune*, February 6, 1858; *Indiana State Sentinel* (Indianapolis), May 15, 1851; *Burlington (IA) Daily Hawk Eye*, October 20, 1860; Oliver Wendell Holmes Sr., "Bread and Newspapers," *Atlantic Monthly* 8 (September 1861): 346–48. The *Daily American Telegraph* (Washington, DC) and *Meigs County Telegraph* (Pomeroy, OH) were two newspapers that changed their names to reflect the importance of the new technology. For the influence of the telegraph on American news and newspapers, see Menahem Blondheim, *News over the Wires: The Telegraph and the Flow of Public Information in America, 1844–1897* (Cambridge: Harvard University Press, 1994).

2. *Charleston (SC) Tri-Weekly Courier*, November 15, 1860; *Philadelphia Inquirer*, November 7, 1860; *McKean Democrat* (Smethport, PA), November 29, 1861; *Winchester Virginian*, June 6, 1861. The mixing of news and advertisements in the daily press is detailed in David M. Henkin, *City Reading: Written Words and Public Spaces in Antebellum New York* (New York: Columbia University Press, 1998), 101–35. See also William Huntzicker, *The Popular Press, 1833–1865* (Westport, CT: Greenwood, 1999), 98–100.

3. George Fitzhugh, "The Domain of Fashion," *De Bow's Review* 29, no. 6 (December 1860): 700–702.

4. *Daily Picayune* (New Orleans), March 17, 1861; *Richmond (VA) Whig*, April 3, 1861; *Charleston (SC) Mercury*, December 22, 1860; *Memphis (TN) Morning Enquirer*, February 16, 1861; *Natchez (MS) Daily Courier*, March 13, 1861. The literature on whether a Confederate identity existed and, if so, when it formed, is extensive. Among the standard works not cited immediately below are Paul D. Escott, *After Secession: Jefferson Davis and the Failure of Confederate Nationalism* (Baton Rouge: Louisiana State University Press, 1978); Gary W. Gallagher, *The Confederate War: How Popular Will, Nationalism, and Military Strategy Could Not Stave Off Defeat* (Cambridge: Harvard University Press, 1997); John McCardell, *The Idea of a Southern Nation: Southern Nationalists and Southern Nationalism, 1830–1860* (New York: Norton, 1979); and Emory Thomas, *The Confederate Nation: 1861–1865* (New York: Harper Torchbooks, 1979).

5. *Montgomery (AL) Daily Post*, February 11, 1861; *Constitutional* (Alexandria, LA), April 18, 1861; *Columbus (GA) Enquirer*, February 9, 1861; *Floridian and Journal* (Tallahassee), October 5, 1860; *North Carolina Presbyterian* (Fayetteville), March 9, 1861.

6. *Albany (GA) Patriot*, April 12, 1860; *St. Augustine (FL) Examiner*, November 10, 1860; *Macon (GA) Daily Telegraph*, February 21, 1861; *Houston (TX) Weekly Telegraph*, September 18, 1860. The perception held by many white southerners of northerners as part of a different culture is detailed in George C. Rable, *Damn Yankees! Demonization and Defiance in the Confederate South* (Baton Rouge: Louisiana State University Press, 2015). On a sense of victimhood that helped propel the South toward secession, see Paul Quigley, *Shifting Grounds: Nationalism and the American South, 1848–1865* (New York: Oxford University Press, 2012), 56–63.

7. *Charleston (SC) Mercury,* February 21, 1861; *St. Augustine (FL) Examiner,* November 10, 1860; *Natchez (MS) Free Trader,* February 16, 1861; *Southern Reveille* (Port Gibson, MS), April 5, 1861.

8. *Mobile (AL) Weekly Advertiser and Register,* February 12, 1861; *Florida Home Companion* (Ocala), June 5, 1860; *Daily True Delta* (New Orleans), November 18, 1860; *Dallas (TX) Herald,* March 6, 1861; *Clarksville (TN) Chronicle,* January 11, 1861; *Daily Intelligencer* (Atlanta, GA), November 16, 1860; *Montgomery (AL) Daily Mail,* February 11, 1861; *Federal Union* (Milledgeville, GA), November 11, 1860.

9. *Daily Morning News* (Savannah, GA), February 1, 1860; *Natchez (MS) Daily Free Trader,* March 7, 1861; *Montgomery (AL) Daily Post,* March 12, 1861; *Albany (GA) Patriot,* August 22, 1861; *Belton (TX) Democrat,* March 8, 1861; *Alexandria (VA) Gazette,* November 27, 1860; *Semi-Weekly Standard* (Raleigh, NC), December 1, 1860. On "secession bonnets," see also Catherine Cooper Hopley, *Life in the South: From the Commencement of the War,* vol. 1 (London: Chapman and Hall, 1863), 137. On the secession movement as, literally, a "band of brothers," see Stephanie McCurry, *Confederate Reckoning: Power and Politics in the Civil War South* (Cambridge: Harvard University Press, 2010), 38–84.

10. *Daily Republican* (Lynchburg, VA), December 25, 1860; *Norfolk (VA) Examiner,* March 16, 1861; *Farmville (VA) Journal,* March 21, 1861; *Evening Virginia Sentinel* (Alexandria), March 12, 1861; *Fayetteville (NC) Observer,* December 13, 1860. Worries over sexual violence as a reason to secede are detailed in McCurry, *Confederate Reckoning,* 27–30.

11. *Memphis (TN) Morning Enquirer,* January 26, 1861.

12. On the many ways Confederate citizens helped to build a sense of nationalism, see Anne Sarah Rubin, *A Shattered Nation: The Rise and Fall of the Confederacy, 1861–1868* (Chapel Hill: University of North Carolina Press, 2005), 11–42. Many white southerners counted the Christian church as one of their institutions, but few advertisers made a reference to their faith. Confederate newspapers ran frequent notices from ministers who encouraged readers to pray for their nation and its cause. Merchants, however, made no biblical references to promote their wares, perhaps worried that they risked being profane.

13. "New Southern Enterprises—How to Make Them Succeed," *Charleston (SC) Mercury,* June 25, 1861; William Howard Russell, diary entry for June 1861, in *My Diary North and South* (Boston: T. O. H. P. Burnham, 1863), 320–21.

14. *Sheboygan (WI) Journal,* March 27, 1861; *Holmes County (OH) Republican,* February 28, 1861; *Lynn (MA) Bay State,* March 30, 1861; *La Crosse (WI) Republican,* March 30, 1861; *Red Bluff (CA) Beacon,* November 14, 1861.

15. *Springfield (MA) Daily Republican,* February 18, 1861; *Central Press* (Bellefonte, PA), May 16, 1860; *Fort Wayne (IN) Daily Gazette,* June 27, 1860; *Marshall (MI) Statesman,* October 31, 1860; *Clay County Democrat* (Bowling Green, IN), October 24, 1860; *Cleveland (OH) Morning Leader,* February 11, 1861.

16. *National Anti-Slavery Standard* (New York), June 23, 1860. Advertisers in the antislavery press were otherwise quiet on the growing sectional divide, reflecting the wariness of the movement toward the nation's political atmosphere (see Ford Risley, *Abolition and the Press: The Moral Struggle against Slavery* [Evanston, IL: Northwestern University Press, 2008]).

17. *Glasgow (MO) Weekly Times*, February 28, 1861; *Weekly Border Star* (Westport, MO), February 4, 1860; *Daily Louisville (KY) Democrat*, March 30, 1861, and May 10, 1861.

18. *Boston Herald*, March 13, 1861; *Sheboygan (WI) Journal*, March 27, 1861. The northern reaction to the secession crisis is detailed in Russell McClintock, *Lincoln and the Decision for War: The Northern Response to Secession* (Chapel Hill: University of North Carolina Press, 2008); and Kenneth M. Stampp, *And the War Came: The North and the Secession Crisis, 1860–1861* (Baton Rouge: Louisiana State University Press, 1950).

19. *Florida Peninsular* (Tampa), May 11, 1861; *Rockingham (VA) Register*, May 30, 1862; *Clarksville (TX) Standard*, May 25, 1861; *Macon (MS) Beacon*, September 11, 1861; *Daily Petersburg (VA) Express*, September 17, 1861.

20. *Arkansas State Gazette* (Little Rock), April 26, 1861; *Constitutional* (Alexandria, LA), May 18, 1861; *Federal Weekly Union* (Milledgeville, GA), November 15, 1861; *Daily Ledger and Texan* (San Antonio), June 24, 1861.

21. *Semi-Weekly Mississippian* (Jackson), September 20, 1861; *Rockingham (VA) Register*, May 30, 1862; *Daily News* (Petersburg, VA), June 27, 1862. Unlike Confederate editors and politicians, who sometimes attempted to explain away military defeats, merchants simply ignored them. The fighting at Roanoke Island, Virginia, Forts Henry and Donelson, and Shiloh did not receive any mention in the sales pitches.

22. *Southern Confederacy* (Atlanta, GA), May 10, 1862; *Winchester (VA) Gazette*, May 8, 1861; *Mobile (AL) Daily Advertiser and Register*, February 13, 1862; *True Southron* (Pine Bluff, AR), May 18, 1862. The naval war is detailed in James M. McPherson, *War on the Waters: The Union and Confederate Navies, 1861–1865* (Chapel Hill: University of North Carolina Press, 2012).

23. "An Appeal to Our Friends and the Public," *Southern Field and Fireside*, November 19, 1864; *Charleston (SC) Mercury*, June 25, 1861; *Richmond (VA) Semi-Weekly Enquirer*, September 23, 1862; *Memphis (TN) Daily Appeal*, May 31, 1862. On the desire of southern authors and editors to establish a literary independence from the northern states, see Rubin, *A Shattered Nation*, 25–28.

24. *Vermont Patriot* (Montpelier), October 19, 1860; *Barre (MA) Gazette*, March 21, 1862; *New Hampshire Statesman* (Concord), June 18, 1861; *Ripley (OH) Bee*, November 28, 1861; *Central Press* (Bellefonte, PA) March 28, 1861; *Newark (NJ) Daily Journal*, February 15, 1862; Melinda Lawson, *Patriot Fires: Forging a New American Nationalism in the Civil War North* (Lawrence: University Press of Kansas, 2002), 5. Referring to the past carries some risk to advertisers because they generally are forward-looking in promoting their brand as the "next big thing" (see Pope, *The Making of Modern Advertising*, 11–12).

25. *St. Louis Missouri Democrat*, April 30, 1861; *Western Kansas Express* (Manhattan City), April 20, 1861; *Boston Herald*, August 4, 1862; *Bangor (ME) Daily Whig and Courier*, April 23, 1861. A few merchants ran a block-cut illustration of the American flag (see *Sacramento [CA] Daily Union*, June 22, 1861; and *Willimantic [CT] Journal*, July 28, 1864).

26. *Burlington (VT) Free Press*, July 19, 1861; *Newark (NJ) Daily Journal*, February 15, 1862; *Cleveland (OH) Morning Leader*, June 13, 1862; *Scioto Gazette* (Chillicothe, OH), June 4, 1861; *Daily Advertiser and Farmer* (Bridgeport, CT), May 30, 1861; *Cedar Falls (IA) Gazette*, June 7, 1861; *Whitewater (WI) Register*, September 26, 1862.

27. Articles and editorials in support of sanitary fairs include *American Citizen* (Butler, PA),

May 4, 1864; *Urbana (OH) Union*, December 9, 1863; and *Big Blue Union* (Marysville, KS), May 7, 1864. The sanitary fairs and the creation of a "selfless patriotism" are explored in Lawson, *Patriot Fires*, 14–39. See also Judith Ann Giesberg, *Civil War Sisterhood: The U.S. Sanitary Commission and Women's Politics in Transition* (Boston: Northeastern University Press, 2000).

28. Abby Howland Woolsey to Eliza Newton Woolsey Howland, April 19, 1861, in *Letters of a Family during the War for the Union 1861–1865* (New Haven, CT: Tuttle, Morehouse and Taylor, 1899), 1:39–40; Ruth Hall letter, June 22, 1861, in *St. Cloud (MN) Democrat*, July 4, 1861.

29. *Fitchburg (MA) Sentinel*, April 19, 1861; *Barnstable (MA) Patriot*, April 17, 1861; *Tri-Weekly Cleveland (OH) Herald*, August 23, 1861; *Waterloo (IA) Courier*, May 14, 1862.

30. *Sunbury (PA) American*, October 5, 1861; *New York Herald*, November 23, 1861; *Ashtabula (OH) Weekly Telegraph*, June 21, 1862; *Long-Islander* (Huntington, NY), September 28, 1862; *Rochester (IN) Chronicle*, March 14, 1862; *Vermont Phoenix* (Brattleboro), March 27, 1862; *Dubuque (IA) Daily Times*, July 6, 1862.

31. *Boston Herald*, February 18, 1862. Floyd had a checkered military career. Taking command of Fort Donelson in February 1862, he abandoned the stronghold the night prior to its surrender. He never fled to Canada, via New York, as Jackman suggested, but was relieved of command later that spring. He died the next year (see Charles Pinnegar, *Brand of Infamy: A Biography of John Buchanan Floyd* [Westport, CT: Greenwood, 2002]).

32. Excellent studies of the campaign and battle are James M. McPherson, *Crossroads of Freedom: Antietam* (New York: Oxford University Press, 2002); and Stephen W. Sears, *Landscape Turned Red: The Battle of Antietam* (New Haven, CT: Ticknor and Fields, 1983).

33. *Tioga County Agitator* (Wellsboro, PA), October 22, 1862; *Bangor (ME) Daily Whig and Courier*, November 11, 1862; *Daily Iowa State Register* (Des Moines), December 24, 1862.

34. *Glasgow (MO) Weekly Times*, May 16, 1861; *East Haddam (CT) Journal*, June 19, 1862; *Daily Morning Post* (Pittsburgh), April 8, 1862; *Daily Milwaukee (WI) News*, July 4, 1862; *Daily Louisville (KY) Democrat*, April 30, 1861; *Weekly Mariettian* (Marietta, PA), June 8, 1861. A Confederate merchant was as crude as some of his Yankee counterparts, declaring after some skirmishing in northern Virginia, "Fifteen Thousand Yankees Bite the Dust." Meanwhile, he had "drugs and medicines" for sale (see *Southern Sentinel* [Winnfield, LA], July 10, 1861). The evolution of Union military policy toward southern civilians and property is analyzed in Mark Grimsley, *The Hard Hand of War: Union Military Policy toward Southern Civilians, 1861–1865* (New York: Cambridge University Press, 1995).

35. "Reform Needed," *Vanity Fair* 1 (April 14, 1860): 254; "To Owners of Sharp Sticks," *Vanity Fair* 4 (August 31, 1861): 100; "Proposals for a New Dictionary of the English Language," *Vanity Fair* 5 (May 10, 1862): 229.

36. "Peremptory Sale," *Vanity Fair* 5 (January 18, 1862): 40; "Information Wanted," *Vanity Fair* 5 (May 17, 1862): 243.

37. *Daily Confederate* (Raleigh, NC), April 27, 1864; *Daily Dispatch* (Richmond, VA), August 1, 1864.

38. *Daily Richmond (VA) Enquirer*, September 16, 1861; *Chattanooga (TN) Daily Gazette*, February 6, 1862; *Semi-Weekly Shreveport (LA) News*, February 9, 1864; *Abingdon Virginian*, November 6, 1863; *Rockingham Register* (Harrisonburg, VA), June 20, 1862; *Sentinel* (Richmond, VA), July 10, 1863.

39. *Daily Intelligencer* (Atlanta, GA), March 31, 1864; *Daily Chronicle and Sentinel* (Augusta,

GA), May 24, 1863; *Hillsborough (NC) Recorder*, April 15, 1863; *San Antonio (TX) Daily Herald*, July 10, 1863; *Chattanooga (TN) Daily Rebel*, January 15, 1863.

40. *Fayetteville (NC) Observer*, June 13, 1864, and July 18, 1864; *Mobile (AL) Daily Tribune*, May 26, 1864; *Southern Confederacy* (Atlanta, GA), June 26, 1864; *Semi-Weekly Raleigh (NC) Register*, July 25, 1863; *Montgomery (AL) Sentinel*, October 31, 1863.

41. *Mobile (AL) Advertiser and Register*, January 26, 1863; *Daily Richmond (VA) Examiner*, July 9, 1863; *Petersburg (VA) Express*, January 13, 1863; *Greenville (AL) Weekly Reporter*, April 22, 1865.

42. An exception to the lack of strong words about northerners ran in the *Richmond (VA) Whig*, March 27, 1863. An auction notice for a marble statue claimed that the artist otherwise had no source of income because of the "present destruction of the country" by the Yankee invaders.

43. "Economise," *Augusta (GA) Chronicle*, October 27, 1863; "Confederate Women and the War," *Southern Literary Messenger* 38, no. 2 (February 1864): 127. Excellent discussion on the worries over misplaced priorities and the Confederate home front is found in Drew Gilpin Faust, *The Creation of Confederate Nationalism: Ideology and Identity in the Civil War South* (Baton Rouge: Louisiana State University Press, 1988); and George C. Rable, *Civil Wars: Women and the Crisis of Southern Nationalism* (Urbana: University of Illinois Press, 1989).

44. *Hartford (CT) Weekly Times*, April 10, 1862; *Holmes County Farmer* (Millersburg, OH), June 5, 1862; *Wisconsin State Register* (Portage), October 17, 1863; *Cedar Falls (IA) Gazette*, June 10, 1864. A recent work that argues an antislavery belief was more widely held in the North than is often credited in the scholarly literature is James Oakes, *Freedom National: The Destruction of Slavery in the United States, 1861–1865* (New York: Norton, 2013).

45. *Fremont (OH) Journal*, October 2, 1863; *Detroit Advertiser and Tribune*, April 27, 1864; *Sunbury (PA) American*, January 17, 1863.

46. *Quincy (MA) Patriot*, February 14, 1863; *Vermont Journal* (Windsor), June 20, 1863; *New Hampshire Sentinel* (Keene), August 7, 1862.

47. *Allegany County (NY) Republican*, August 31, 1864. The soldier quotations on the draft riots are taken from Bell I. Wiley, *The Life of Billy Yank: The Common Soldier of the Union* (Indianapolis: Bobbs-Merrill, 1952), 286–87. The best study of the draft riot remains Iver Bernstein, *The New York City Draft Riots: Their Significance for American Society and Politics in the Age of the Civil War* (New York: Oxford University Press, 1990).

48. *Democratic Expounder* (Marshall, MI), August 27, 1863; *Freeport (IL) Weekly Journal*, March 29, 1865; *Salem (IN) Democrat*, November 27, 1862; *Fremont (OH) Weekly Journal*, January 1, 1864; *Highland Weekly News* (Hillsboro, OH), October 9, 1862; *Lexington (KY) Observer and Reporter*, February 25, 1864; *Monroe (WI) Sentinel*, October 29, 1862; *Vermont Journal* (Windsor), August 22, 1863; *Portland (ME) Weekly Advertiser*, May 30, 1865.

49. Stephen Cushman, *Bloody Promenade: Reflections on a Civil War Battle* (Charlottesville: University of Virginia Press, 1999), 88–116. Other examples of inaccurate wartime reporting are detailed in Harris, *Blue and Gray in Black and White*, 129–30.

50. *Evansville (IN) Weekly Gazette*, January 3, 1863. Rather than a full twelve-month cycle, the notice ran from early June 1862 through mid-March 1863.

51. Biographies on Grant are numerous. Among the best and more recent are Brooks D. Simpson, *Let Us Have Peace: Ulysses S. Grant and the Politics of War and Reconstruction, 1861–1868* (Chapel Hill: University of North Carolina Press, 1991); Jean Edward Smith, *Grant* (New York:

Simon and Schuster, 2001); and Joan Waugh, *U.S. Grant: American Hero, American Myth* (Chapel Hill: University of North Carolina Press, 2009).

52. *Daily Intelligencer* (Wheeling, WV), April 17, 1864; *Columbia (PA) Spy*, May 28, 1864.

53. *Knoxville (TN) Tri-Weekly Whig*, July 26, 1864; *Burlington (IA) Daily Hawk-Eye*, August 15, 1864; *Kansas State Journal* (Lawrence), January 19, 1865; *Lancaster (PA) Daily Intelligencer*, December 2, 1864; *Wisconsin State Register* (Portage), October 29, 1864; *Goshen (IN) Democrat*, August 3, 1864.

54. Robert Henry Newell, *The Orpheus C. Kerr Papers* (New York: Carleton, 1863–65), 2:184–85.

55. *Arkansas State Gazette* (Little Rock) May 12, 1865; *North Carolina Daily Times* (New Berne), June 29, 1865; *Staunton (VA) Spectator*, November 21, 1865; *Charleston (SC) Daily News*, November 15, 1865; *Clarksville (TN) Chronicle*, September 8, 1865.

56. *Daily Mississippian* (Jackson), November 3, 1865; *Daily Dispatch* (Richmond), December 22, 1865; *Daily News and Herald* (Savannah, GA), June 24, 1867; *Daily Arkansas Gazette* (Little Rock), November 10, 1867.

57. *Daily News and Herald* (Savannah, GA), June 1, 1868; *Charleston (SC) Tri-Weekly Courier*, November 21, 1868; *American Citizen* (Canton, MS), March 9, 1867; *South-Western* (Shreveport, LA), June 19, 1867.

58. *Columbus (GA) Enquirer*, January 18, 1866. The song lyrics are printed in E. Lawrence Abel, *Confederate Sheet Music* (Jefferson, NC: McFarland, 2004), 235–36.

59. *Daily Richmond (VA) Examiner*, January 9, 1866, and January 26, 1866.

60. *Bedford (IN) Independent*, September 20, 1865; *Tioga County Agitator* (Wellsboro, PA), July 12, 1865; *Decatur (IN) Eagle*, December 1, 1865; *Hillsdale (MI) Standard*, December 5, 1865.

61. *Rocky Mountain Daily News* (Denver), August 14, 1865; *Centralia (IL) Sentinel*, June 29, 1865; *Long-Islander* (Huntington, NY), July 12, 1865.

62. *Buffalo (NY) Morning Express*, October 23, 1865; *Worcester (MA) Palladium*, June 14, 1865.

63. "Two Immense Treats," *Vanity Fair* 4 (November 23, 1861): 237; "Advertising Nuisances," *Round Table* 2, no. 17 (December 30, 1865): 273. On the use of reading notices, see Baldasty, *The Commercialization of News in the Nineteenth Century*, 66–69. The use of reading notices is still popular online (see Dean Rieck, "9 Proven Headline Formulas That Sell Like Crazy," Copyblogger Media, www.copyblogger.com/proven-headline-formulas/ [2006–14]). Rieck writes that advertisers should cast their product as "exciting news." People read "newspapers and magazines because they love news. It's just basic human nature. We're curious. We not only want to know, we need to know. Casting your headline in a way that suggests news, rather than advertising, can have the same powerful appeal of a feature story in the morning paper."

Chapter 2. THE MILLIONS

1. "The Philosophy of Advertising," *Merchants' Magazine and Commercial Review* 23, no. 5 (November 1, 1850): 580–81; *Sun* (New York), April 18, 1861.

2. "Confidence men" supposedly duped many too-trusting Americans, especially, as urban populations increased, newcomers from towns and villages. An excellent study of the topic is Karen Halttunen, *Confidence Men and Painted Women: A Study of Middle-Class Culture in America, 1830–1870* (New Haven: Yale University Press, 1982).

3. *Cincinnati (OH) Daily Press,* May 24, 1861; *Daily National Intelligencer* (Washington, DC), July 4, 1861; *Wisconsin State Journal* (Madison), July 28, 1862; *Detroit Advertiser and Tribune,* February 2, 1863. For book notices in the 1850s, see *Carroll Free Press* (Carrollton, OH), February 28, 1856; and *Yazoo (MS) Democrat,* December 25, 1858. A still standard study of the Civil War in literature is Edmund Wilson, *Patriotic Gore: Studies in the Literature of the American Civil War* (New York: Oxford University Press, 1962). See also Daniel Aaron, *The Unwritten War: American Writers and the Civil War* (Madison: University of Wisconsin Press, 1987).

4. Perhaps lost in the marketing of the book was the fact that some of the early volumes ended with a section on "Incidents, Rumors, Etc."

5. *New-York Daily Tribune,* April 30, 1861; *State Republican* (Eugene City, OR), May 3, 1862; *Hancock Jeffersonian* (Findlay, OH), June 21, 1861; *Daily Dispatch* (Richmond, VA), December 22, 1865. Porter published his memoir shortly before his death in 1910 (see Edward Porter Alexander, *Military Memoirs of a Confederate: A Critical Narrative* [New York: Charles Scribner's Sons, 1907]; see also Edward Porter Alexander, *Fighting for the Confederacy: The Personal Recollections of General Edward Porter Alexander,* ed. Gary W. Gallagher [Chapel Hill: University of North Carolina Press, 1989]). The desire among readers to have supposedly impartial facts on the war is detailed in Fahs, *The Imagined Civil War,* 51–55.

6. *Daily Frankfort (KY) Commonwealth,* May 15, 1864; *Daily Mississippian* (Jackson), June 9, 1862; *Western Citizen* (Paris, KY), December 1, 1865; *Columbia (PA) Spy,* November 11, 1865.

7. *Belmont Chronicle* (St. Clairsville, OH), July 7, 1864; *Delaware State Journal and Statesman* (Wilmington), June 3, 1864; *Cambridge City (IN) Journal,* May 27, 1864; *Centralia (IL) Sentinel,* October 15, 1863; *Chicago Evening Journal,* January 13, 1863; *Vermont Journal* (Windsor), January 10, 1863. That Howe's work stretched to the Union triumph at Vicksburg might have been as much by intent as chronology. The Union 11th Corps, comprised mainly of German American soldiers, fought poorly at Chancellorsville and Gettysburg that spring and summer.

8. *Jeffersonian Democrat* (Chardon, OH), February 26, 1864; *Delaware (OH) Gazette,* September 29, 1865; *Evening Argus* (Rock Island, IL), June 14, 1865; Horace Greeley, *Recollections of a Busy Life: Including Reminiscences of American Politics and Politicians* (New York: J. B. Ford, 1868), 420–21; *The American Conflict: A History of the Great Rebellion in the United States of America, 1860–64,* vol. 1 (Hartford, CT: O. D. Case, 1864), 10. Greely also showed the emphasis on slavery in the full subtitle to his history: *Its Causes, Incidents, and Results: Intended to Exhibit Especially Its Moral and Political Phases, with the Drift and Progress of American Opinion Respecting Human Slavery from 1776 to the Close of the War for the Union.*

9. *Hillsdale (MI) Standard,* May 19, 1863; *Daily Ohio Statesman* (Columbus), April 29, 1863; John S. C. Abbott, *The History of the Civil War in America,* vol. 1 (New York: Henry Bill, 1862), 15.

10. "Our Book Review," *Vanity Fair* 4 (August 10, 1861): 70; *Daily Wabash Express* (Terre Haute, IN), November 19, 1861; *St. Cloud (MN) Democrat,* June 4, 1863. Demand for the work continued into the postwar years. In the mid-1870s, one magazine column described Moore as the editor of the "once highly popular and still useful *Rebellion Record*" (see "Books and Authors," *Appleton's Journal* 15, no. 367 [April 1, 1876]: 442). The trial of William Smith for piracy is detailed in D. F. Murphy, *Full Report of the Trial of William Smith for Piracy, as One of the Crew of the Confederate Privateer, The "Jeff Davis"* (Philadelphia: King and Baird, 1861).

11. "Recent Publications," *Christian Review* 26 (October 1861): 686; "A Page of History," *Pa-*

pers from the Society for the Diffusion of Political Knowledge, vol. 19 (New York: Society for the Diffusion of Political Knowledge, 1863–1864): 221–24.

12. *New York Times*, June 1, 1861; *Delaware (OH) Gazette*, May 20, 1864; *Daily Ohio Statesman* (Columbus), February 14, 1864; *Albany (NY) Journal*, August 8, 1864; *Evansville (IN) Daily Journal*, May 3, 1864; *Quincy (MA) Patriot*, September 2, 1865; *Baltimore Daily Commercial*, December 27, 1865; *Bedford (PA) Gazette*, July 4, 1864.

13. *Daily Richmond (VA) Examiner*, August 5, 1862; *Southern Banner* (Athens, GA), June 24, 1863; *Florida Sentinel* (Tallahassee), July 21, 1863; *Daily Republican* (Lynchburg, VA), August 20, 1863. John Hunt Morgan, a Confederate cavalry officer who gained considerable fame in the South for his battlefield exploits, was the subject of a novel. Published in 1863, *Raids and Romance of Morgan and His Men* offered "all the exciting interest of a first-class standard Romance, and all the Information of a correct history" (see *Charleston [SC] Mercury*, July 21, 1863). The role of heroes in southern wartime culture is analyzed in Paul Christopher Anderson, *Blood Image: Turner Ashby in the Civil War and the Southern Mind* (Baton Rouge: Louisiana State University Press, 2006). Two biographies on Stonewall Jackson were published during the war: Markinfield Addey, *"Stonewall Jackson": The Life and Military Career of Thomas Jonathan Jackson, Lieutenant General in the Confederate Army* (New York: C. T. Evans, 1863), and Catherine Cooper Hopley, *"Stonewall" Jackson, Late General of the Confederate States Army: A Biographical Sketch, and an Outline of His Virginian Campaigns* (London: Chapman and Hall, 1863). However, the notice in the Georgia newspaper reads that a "biographical sketch" by Charles Hallock was "just published."

14. *Worcester (MA) Palladium*, April 12, 1865; *Daily Guardian* (Columbia, SC), December 19, 1862; *St. Paul (MN) Daily Union*, January 21, 1863; *Boston Semi-Weekly Advertiser*, October 8, 1862. Hosmer went on to write widely about the war, with *Outcome of the Civil War, 1863–1865* (New York: Harper, 1907), a volume in The American Nation series, and *The American Civil War* (New York: Harper, 1913). Fontaine published his work under *Marginalia, or, Gleanings from an Army Notebook* (Columbia, SC: Steam power-press of F. G. De Fontaine, 1864).

15. *Chicago Tri-Weekly Journal*, January 26, 1865; *M'arthur Democrat* (McArthur, OH) August 3, 1865; *Bradford Reporter* (Towanda, PA), September 21, 1865; Fahs, *The Imagined Civil War*, 120–49. The idea of "dislodged identities" is taken from Shirley Samuels, *Facing America: Iconography and the Civil War* (New York: Oxford University Press, 2004), see esp. 29–35. The memoir is still in print. See S. Emma E. Edmonds, *Memoirs of a Soldier, Nurse, and Spy: A Woman's Adventures in the Union Army*, introd. Elizabeth D. Leanord (DeKalb: Northern Illinois University Press, 1999).

16. *Daily National Intelligencer* (Washington, DC), February 2, 1847; *Weekly Flag and Advertiser* (Montgomery, AL), July 16, 1847.

17. *Republican Banner* (Nashville, TN), October 27, 1861; *Southern Banner* (Athens, GA), June 24, 1863; *Burlington (VT) Free Press*, March 14, 1862. The poor detail listed on newspaper maps is described in Harris, *Blue and Gray in Black and White*, 12–13. See also David C. Bosse, *Civil War Newspaper Maps: A Historical Atlas* (Baltimore: Johns Hopkins University Press, 1993).

18. *Fitchburg (MA) Sentinel*, June 27, 1862; *Covington (KY) Journal*, June 14, 1862; *Erie (PA) Observer*, February 21, 1863; *Boston Daily Advertiser*, May 5, 1862. The praise from McClellan soon proved problematic. The Union general was sacked from command in November for his excessive caution in attempting to bring the Confederate army to battle. His sales pitch apparently too

closely linked to McClellan to simply drop the endorsement, Hazard withdrew his advertisement from the newspapers.

19. *Smoky Hill and Republican Union* (Junction City, KS), October 11, 1862; *Rocky Mountain Daily News* (Denver), October 23, 1862; *Xenia (OH) Sentinel*, June 21, 1864; *Western Kansas Express* (Manhattan City), November 2, 1861; *Housatonic Republican* (Falls Village, CT), August 16, 1862; *Daily Dispatch* (Richmond, VA), November 3, 1864.

20. *Lamoille Newsdealer* (Hyde Park, VT), May 30, 1862; *Democratic Press* (Eaton, OH), October 23, 1862; *Chicago Times*, March 22, 1864; *North Branch Democrat* (Tunkhannock, PA), December 10, 1862; *Goodhue Volunteer* (Red Wing, MN), March 12, 1862.

21. "Sad Case of Pictorial Paralysis," *Vanity Fair* 5 (May 24, 1862): 250; "Advertisement Extraordinary," *Vanity Fair* 5 (June 28, 1862): 309.

22. James Hosmer, diary entry, March 18, 1863, in *The Color-Guard: Being a Corporal's Notes of Military Service in the Nineteenth Army Corps* (Boston: Walker Wise, 1864), 91; Alonzo Miller to Sarah Miller, May 27, 1864, in *Diaries and Letters, 1864–1865* (Prescott, WI: n.p., 1958), 122; Abby Howland Woolsey to Jane Eliza Newton Woolsey, April 26, 1862, in *Letters of a Family during the War for the Union*, 360; *Augusta (GA) Chronicle*, September 30, 1863; John Beauchamp Jones, diary entry, November 1864, in *A Rebel War Clerk's Diary at the Confederate States Capital*, vol. 2 (Philadelphia: J. B. Lippincott, 1866), 482.

23. *Bedford (IN) Independent*, February 15, 1865; *Burlington (IA) Daily Hawk-Eye*, August 15, 1864; *Columbia Democrat and Bloomsburg (PA) General Advertiser*, June 11, 1864; *New-York Daily Tribune*, June 1, 1861; *Herald and Torch Light* (Hagerstown, MD), May 31, 1865; *Liberty (IN) Herald*, May 27, 1863; *Daily Southern Guardian* (Columbia, SC), December 19, 1862; *Charleston (SC) Mercury*, August 27, 1864; *Cleveland (OH) Morning Leader*, August 23, 1861. Photography studios eagerly sought images of well-known military officers. E. H Anthony, a well-known photographer in New York, asked "friends or relatives of prominent military men" to "confer a favor by sending us their likeness to copy. They will be kept carefully and returned safely" (see *Western Citizen* [Paris, KY], December 11, 1863).

24. *Emporia (KS) News*, February 22, 1862; *Ripley (OH) Bee*, November 14, 1861; *Connersville (IN) Weekly Times*, March 21, 1861; *Boston Daily Advertiser*, May 13, 1862; *Indiana (PA) Messenger*, April 12, 1862.

25. *National Principia* (New York), December 10, 1863; *Weekly Anglo-African* (New York), February 22, 1862; *Liberator* (Boston), July 11, 1862.

26. *Philadelphia Inquirer*, October 15, 1862, and November 3, 1864; *Weekly Perrysburg (OH) Journal*, March 18, 1863; *Daily Union and American* (Nashville, TN), June 18, 1864; *Plymouth (IN) Weekly Democrat*, August 11, 1864; *Marshall County Republican* (Plymouth, IN), July 28, 1864.

27. *Barre (MA) Gazette*, March 28, 1862; Harvey Munsell to "My dear Little Cousins," December 13, 1863, in *Soldiers' Letters from Camp, Battle-field and Prison*, ed. Lydia Minturn Post (New York: Bunce and Huntington, 1865), 472; Wilder Dwight to Family, January 28, 1862, in *Life and Letters of Wilder Dwight: Lieut.-Col. Second Mass. Inf. Vols.*, ed. Elizabeth Amelia Dwight (Boston: Ticknor and Fields, 1868), 349; Hallock Armstrong to Mary Armstrong, July 17, 1865, in *Letters from a Pennsylvania Chaplain at the Siege of Petersburg, 1865*, ed. Mary M. Bronson Armstrong (N.p., 1961), 47.

28. Oliver Wendell Holmes Sr., "Doings of the Sunbeam," *Atlantic Monthly* 12, no. 69 (July 1863): 8; Fahs, *The Imagined Civil War*, 93–119.

29. *South Danvers Wizard* (Peabody, MA), November 2, 1864; *Boston Post*, July 27, 1863; *Highland Weekly News* (Hillsboro, OH), February 28, 1861; *Delaware State Journal and Statesman* (Wilmington), July 22, 1864; *North American and United States Gazette* (Philadelphia), January 1, 1862; *Juniata Sentinel* (Mifflintown, PA), January 11, 1865; *Scioto Gazette* (Chillicothe, OH), December 31, 1861; *Lowell (MA) Daily Citizen and News*, November 19, 1861; *Memphis (TN) Daily Appeal*, June 11, 1861; *Jasper (IN) Weekly Courier*, August 6, 1862; *Daily Chronicle and Sentinel* (Augusta, GA), October 7, 1864.

30. *New York Times*, October 20, 1862; Holmes, "Doings of the Sunbeam," 11–12. Many of the pictures in the 1862 display are reprinted in William A. Frassanito, *Antietam: The Photographic Legacy of America's Bloodiest Day* (New York: Scribner, 1978). Frassanito claims that the images in Brady's studio "horrified" northerners. They undoubtedly did, but only the people who saw them. Few notices for Brady's studio ran in local newspapers during that fall.

31. "The Napoleon of Advertising," in *Cyclopaedia of Commercial and Business Anecdotes*, ed. Richard Miller Devens, vol. 1 (New York: Appleton, 1864), 332; Turner, *The Shocking History of Advertising*, 87–89. Scholarly works on patent medicines are as rare as the trade was prevalent (see James Harvey Young, *The Toadstool Millionaires: A Social History of Patent Medicines in America before Federal Regulation* [Princeton, NJ: Princeton University Press, 1961]; and his *American Self-Dosage Medicines: An Historical Perspective* [Lawrence, KS: Coronado, 1974]).

32. *Republican and Gazette* (Sterling, IL), June 29, 1861; *Anti-Slavery Bugle* (New Lisbon, OH), January 19, 1861; James Gordon Bennett quotation in Lee, *The Daily Newspaper in America*, 317.

33. Medical histories of the war not cited below include Margaret Humphreys, *Marrow of Tragedy: The Health Crisis of the American Civil War* (Baltimore: Johns Hopkins University Press, 2013); Ira M. Rutkow, *Bleeding Blue and Gray: Civil War Surgery and the Evolution of American Medicine* (New York: Random House, 2005); and Frank R. Freemon, *Gangrene and Glory: Medical Care during the American Civil War* (Urbana: University of Illinois Press, 2001).

34. *New York Herald*, July 30, 1861; *New Albany (IN) Daily Ledger*, March 10, 1863; *Louisville (KY) Daily Journal*, November 30, 1861; *Boston Post*, January 15, 1863; *Linn County Patriot* (Marion, IA), June 13, 1863; *Burlington (VT) Free Press*, October 24, 1862.

35. *Ashtabula (OH) Weekly Telegraph*, June 11, 1864; *True Citizen* (New Britain, CT), April 19, 1862; *Franklin Democrat* (Brookville, IN), July 31, 1863; *Aurora (IN) Commercial*, July 31, 1862; *National Eagle* (Claremont, NH), December 12, 1862.

36. *Daily Dispatch* (Richmond, VA), April 24, 1861, and April 1, 1865; *Southerner* (Tarboro, NC), February 28, 1863; *Evansville (IN) Daily Journal*, August 16, 1864; *Baltimore (MD) Clipper*, January 6, 1865; *Xenia (OH) Sentinel*, June 21, 1864; *Decatur (IL) Weekly Gazette*, September 30, 1864; *Moore's Rural New-Yorker* (Rochester), November 1, 1862.

37. *New-York Daily Tribune*, October 14, 1862; *Meriden Recorder* (West Meriden, CT), July 14, 1865. An analysis of veterans' mental health and the transition to civilian life is Eric T. Dean, *Shook over Hell: Post-Traumatic Stress, Vietnam, and the Civil War* (Cambridge: Harvard University Press, 1997).

38. *New York Herald*, November 23, 1861.

39. *Urbana (OH) Union*, October 26, 1864; *Sun* (New York), June 18, 1861; *Bedford (IN) Independent*, February 15, 1865; *Cass County Republican* (Dowagiac, MI), May 14, 1863.

40. *Morning Oregonian* (Portland), January 15, 1864; *New York Herald*, May 25, 1863; *Manchester (NH) Daily Union*, December 27, 1864; *Sacramento (CA) Daily Union*, September 19, 1863; *Leavenworth (KS) Daily Conservative*, July, 27, 1864; *Athens (OH) Messenger*, October 9, 1862.

41. *Vermont Journal* (Windsor), August 26, 1863.

42. *Chicago Tribune*, September 16, 1864; *Christian Repository* (Montpelier, VT). The medicines used in military hospitals are detailed in Michael A. Flannery, *Civil War Pharmacy: A History of Drugs, Drug Supply and Provision, and Therapeutics for the Union and Confederacy* (New York: Pharmaceutical Products Press, 2004).

43. *Virginia Free Press* (Charleston, WV), April 18, 1861; *Daily Louisville (KY) Democrat*, September 16, 1860; *Quincy (IL) Daily Whig and Republican*, June 4, 1862; *Buffalo (NY) Morning Express*, July 1, 1865.

44. *Boston Herald*, February 18, 1862.

45. *Staunton (VA) Spectator*, April 1, 1862, and September 30, 1862; *Daily Richmond (VA) Examiner*, April 18, 1864; *Dallas (TX) Herald*, November 7, 1860; *Daily Chronicle and Sentinel* (Augusta, GA), February 14, 1862; *Camden (SC) Confederate*, December 13, 1861.

46. *Daily South Carolinian* (Columbia), April 11, 1862, and November 12, 1862; *Cincinnati (OH) Daily Press*, November 19, 1862.

47. Report of Surgeon Charles S. Tripler, March 17 to July 3, 1862, in U.S. War Department, *O.R.*, vol. 11, pt. 1, 192. On soldiers and self-care, see Kathryn Shively Meier, *Nature's Civil War: Common Soldiers and the Environment in 1862 Virginia* (Chapel Hill: University of North Carolina Press, 2013). For the advances made, see Shauna Devine, *Learning from the Wounded: The Civil War and the Rise of American Medical Science* (Chapel Hill: University of North Carolina Press, 2014).

48. "Atonement," *Southern Literary Messenger* 38, no. 2 (February 1864): 128; "Letter from a Country Editor," *Vanity Fair* 5 (May 24, 1862): 253; *Humbug: A Look at Some Popular Impositions* (New York: S. F. French, 1859), 26–27.

49. "Revenue of the Commonwealth of Pennsylvania," *Report of the Auditor General, on the Finances of the Commonwealth of Pennsylvania, For the Year Ending November 30, 1862* (Harrisburg: Singerly and Myers, 1863), 5–6; "Patent-Medicine Makers—Morrison, Brandreth, Townsend, etc.," in *Cyclopaedia of Commercial and Business Anecdotes*, ed. Richard Miller Devens, vol. 2 (New York: D. Appleton, 1864), 609; Bouton, *Round the Block*, 94.

50. *Western Sentinel* (Winston, NC), June 20, 1862.

Chapter 3. THE VOTE

1. David W. Mitchell, *Ten Years in the United States: Being an Englishman's View of Men and Things in the North and South* (London: Smith, Elder and Co., 1862), 171–72. The story about the decisive vote to declare war in 1812 was apocryphal. The decision was close, and highly partisan, but not determined by a single vote.

2. Glenn C. Altschuler and Stuart M. Blumin, *Rude Republic: Americans and Their Politics in*

the Nineteenth Century (Princeton, NJ: Princeton University Press, 2000), 79. For a different interpretation, see William E. Gienapp, "'Politics Seem to Enter into Everything': Political Culture in the North, 1840–1860," in *Essays on Antebellum American Politics, 1840–1860*, ed. Stephen E. Maizlish and John J. Kushma (College Station: Texas A&M University Press, 1982), 14–69. On the political culture of the mid-nineteenth century, see Jean H. Baker, *Affairs of Party: The Political Culture of Northern Democrats in the Mid-Nineteenth Century* (Ithaca, NY: Cornell University Press, 1983); Daniel Walker Howe, *The Political Culture of the American Whigs* (Chicago: University of Chicago Press, 1979); and Eric Foner, *Free Soil, Free Labor, Free Men: The Ideology of the Republican Party Before the Civil War* (New York: Oxford University Press, 1970).

3. *New York Herald*, April 5, 1862; Harold Holzer, *Lincoln and the Power of the Press: The War for Public Opinion* (New York: Simon and Schuster, 2014), xvi; Joseph C. G. Kennedy, *Preliminary Report on the Eighth Census, 1860* (Washington, DC: Government Printing Office, 1862), 101–3. According to the census data, 80 percent of the newspapers and periodicals published in the United States in 1860 were "political in their character." The high percentage of partisan papers and magazines among Americans "show how large a portion of their reading is political." An overview of the 1860 presidential campaign is Douglas R. Egerton, *Year of the Meteors: Stephen Douglas, Abraham Lincoln, and the Election That Brought on the Civil War* (New York: Bloomsbury, 2010).

4. *Winona (MN) Daily Republican*, July 19, 1860; *National Republican* (Washington, DC), November 26, 1860; *Oxford (MS) Intelligencer*, July 25, 1860; *Boston Daily Journal*, May 11, 1860; *Jasper (IN) Weekly Courier*, February 27, 1860; *Independent* (Harrisonburg, LA), January 4, 1860.

5. *Arkansas State Gazette* (Little Rock), October 27, 1860; *Southern Banner* (Athens, GA), August 30, 1860; *Altoona (PA) Tribune*, March 27, 1860. The Democratic campaign song also is referenced in Baker, *Affairs of Party*, 284. The lyrics borrowed heavily from "Pibroch of Donald Dhu," a poem by Sir Walter Scott.

6. *Columbia Democrat and Bloomsburg (PA) General Advertiser*, August 28, 1860; *Holmes County Farmer* (Millersburg, OH), October 11, 1860; *Daily Dispatch* (Richmond, VA), November 3, 1860; *Cambridge (MA) Chronicle*, November 12, 1860.

7. "Political Intelligence," *New York Herald*, May 3, 1860; "Senator Seward a Georgia School-Master—The Original Advertisement," *Memphis (TN) Daily Appeal*, September 23, 1860.

8. "Withdrawal of the Southern Trade from New York," *New York Herald*, January 6, 1860; "The Terrors of Submission," *Charleston (SC) Mercury*, October 11, 1860.

9. *Wilmington (NC) Journal*, October 18, 1860; *Dayton (OH) Daily Empire*, August 10, 1860; *Evansville (IN) Daily Journal*, August 7, 1860; *Cincinnati (OH) Daily Press*, September 1, 1860; *Daily Exchange* (Baltimore), September 8, 1860. Shenanigans sometimes also took place at the pole raisings. The *Daily Exchange* reported that a Lincoln pole in Allegany County was "put up by a gentleman of means, a Democrat, who did it as a joke."

10. "The History of the Wide Awakes," *New York Herald*, September 19, 1860; *Freeport (IL) Weekly Journal*, August 8, 1860; *Pittsburgh Daily Gazette and Advertiser*, September 14, 1860; *Essex Banner* (Haverhill, MA), July 20, 1860; *New York Herald*, September 19, 1860, and November 2, 1860; *Whitewater (WI) Register*, September 14, 1860; *Newport (RI) Daily News*, November 1, 1860. See also Jon Grinspan, "'Young Men for War': The Wide Awakes and Lincoln's 1860 Presidential Campaign," *Journal of American History* 96 (September 2009): 357–78.

11. *Daily National Intelligencer* (Washington, DC), September 15, 1860; *Richmond (VA) Whig*, September 18, 1860; *Farmer's Cabinet* (Amherst, NH), October 24, 1860.

12. *New Orleans Daily Crescent*, August 24, 1860; *Daily Dispatch* (Richmond, VA), July 24, 1860; *Cincinnati (OH) Daily Press*, September 14, 1860; *Evansville (IN) Daily Journal*, September 5, 1860; *Cadiz (OH) Democratic Sentinel*, August 15, 1860.

13. "Wooden School Slates," *Scientific American* 1003, no. 19 (November 3, 1860): 298; "True Republicans" to Abraham Lincoln, October 1860, in *The Lincoln Papers*, ed. David C. Mearns, vol. 1 (Garden City, NY: Doubleday, 1948), 291–92; W. S. Hutchinson, "In the Shadow of a Great Tragedy," *Overland Monthly* 13, no. 74 (February 1889): 129–30.

14. *Daily Union and American* (Nashville, TN), August 24, 1860; *Washington Standard* (Olympia), December 15, 1860; *Sunday Transcript* (Philadelphia), August 26, 1860; *Covington (KY) Journal*, September 22, 1860; *Citizen* (Smethport, PA), December 28, 1860; *National Era* (Washington, DC), March 22, 1860.

15. *Cass County Republican* (Dowagiac, MI), June 14, 1860; *White Cloud Kansas Chief*, October 11, 1860; *New-York Daily Tribune*, July 31, 1860; *Burlington (VT) Free Press*, July 13, 1860; *St. Cloud (MN) Democrat*, July 19, 1860; *Macon (MS) Beacon*, July 18, 1860. Some editors poked fun at the sudden public interest in everything Lincoln. Borrowing from a New York paper, the *Macon Beacon* scoffed that a new biography of the presidential candidate listed pressing information such as "His father's name was Mr. Lincoln, his mother's Mrs. Lincoln, and if he had sisters, they were known as the Misses Lincoln." An overview of these publications is Thomas A. Horrocks, *Lincoln's Campaign Biographies* (Carbondale: Southern Illinois University Press, 2014).

16. *New-York Daily Tribune*, September 17, 1860; *Richmond (VA) Enquirer*, August 16, 1860; *New Orleans Daily Crescent*, September 12, 1860; *Connecticut Press* (Hartford), June 16, 1860. An excellent description of political imagery in the 1860 presidential election is Harold Holzer, Gabor S. Boritt, and Mark E. Neely Jr., *The Lincoln Image: Abraham Lincoln and the Popular Print* (Urbana: University of Illinois Press, 1984).

17. *Weekly Standard* (Raleigh, NC), August 1, 1860. Commenting on another commercially produced image of Lincoln, a Mississippi editor scoffed that "it is so ugly" as to give offense to viewers. He admitted that he had examined the picture only from a distance because he had "not the temerity to go too near" (see *Yazoo [MS] Democrat*, August 25, 1860).

18. *Marshall County Republican* (Plymouth, IN), August 9, 1860; *Daily Intelligencer* (Wheeling, WV), August 24, 1860.

19. *New York Herald*, March 21, 1860; *Bangor (ME) Daily Whig and Courier*, October 6, 1860; *Daily Dispatch* (Richmond, VA), November 4, 1860; *Adams Sentinel* (Gettysburg, PA), October 31, 1860; *Western Reserve Chronicle* (Warren, OH), August 8, 1860; *Marion (IA) Herald*, May 31, 1860; *Democratic Expounder* (Marshall, MI), July 26, 1860; *East Floridian* (Fernandina), March 29, 1860.

20. *Daily Louisville (KY) Democrat*, September 16, 1860; *Yorkville (SC) Enquirer*, September 20, 1860; *Daily Hawk-Eye* (Burlington, IA), November 3, 1860; *New York Herald*, November 2, 1860.

21. *Berlin City (WI) Courant*, March 21, 1861; *Daily Intelligencer* (Wheeling, WV), March 25, 1861; *McKean Democrat* (Smethport, PA), November 29, 1860; *Daily Mississippian* (Jackson),

November 27, 1860; *Daily Patriot and Union* (Harrisburg, PA), March 28, 1861; *Natchez (MS) Free Trader,* February 16, 1861; *Ashtabula (OH) Weekly Telegraph,* November 10, 1860.

22. *New York Herald,* February 19, 1861, and February 27, 1861; *Cleveland (OH) Daily Herald,* December 12, 1860; *Athens (TN) Post,* December 7, 1860; *Beaver Dam (WI) Argus,* December 28, 1860; *Daily Mining Journal* (Black Hawk, CO), November 30, 1863. Using Lincoln as a celebrity continued beyond 1860. In the Colorado paper, John Warner, a grocer, declared "Lincoln's Proclamation, No. 2." The proclamation ran, "I, A. Lincoln, President of the United States, Recommend and Advise the good people of the Colorado Territory" to buy their foodstuffs at Warner's store.

23. *New York Herald,* December 10, 1860; *Southern Banner* (Athens, GA), May 8, 1861.

24. *Milwaukee (WI) Daily Sentinel,* June 28, 1861; *Daily National Intelligencer* (Washington, DC), December 8, 1861; *Evansville (IN) Weekly Gazette,* November 1, 1862; *Cape Girardeau (MO) Weekly Argus,* August 20, 1863. In 1863, H. M. Flint published *The Life of Stephen A. Douglas.* The biography offered a "true and faithful exposition" of Douglas's life and "brilliant and instructive career" (see *Chicago Times,* July 7, 1863).

25. *Leavenworth (KS) Daily Conservative,* August 2, 1864; *Santa Fe (NM) Republican,* July 12, 1862. Prospectus of the *New-York Daily Tribune* and *Philadelphia Ledger* in *American Citizen* (Butler, PA), October 12, 1864; and *Ottawa (IL) Free Trader,* December 31, 1864. The *Santa Fe Republican* reminded its readers that it "is the only Union or National paper in New Mexico." Not only that, it "is the only paper published anywhere that circulates to any extent in this Territory." Among the best studies on the presidential campaign of 1864 are John C. Waugh, *Reelecting Lincoln: The Battle for the 1864 Presidency* (New York: Crown, 1997); and David E. Long, *The Jewel of Liberty: Abraham Lincoln's Reelection and the End of Slavery* (Mechanicsburg, PA: Stackpole, 1994).

26. Baker, *Affairs of Party,* 262; Mark E. Neely Jr., *The Boundaries of American Political Culture in the Civil War Era* (Chapel Hill: University of North Carolina Press, 2005), 68–69. There is considerable scholarly debate on whether American voters experienced some political fatigue by 1864. Although high by modern-day standards, voter participation in the election dropped from four years earlier. Baker argues that voters were "not particularly excited" about the presidential race and suggests that the "apathy might be explained by the war." Neely counters that voter turnout is not a "very useful figure" because of the confusion of the war. The argument that Americans were less engaged is "utterly at variance with nearly all the commentators who themselves lived through the Civil War presidential election." The newspaper advertisements certainly suggest that voters were closely engaged with the election and its material culture.

27. *Chicago Tribune,* October 8, 1864; *Bangor (ME) Daily Whig and Courier,* November 9, 1864; *Erie (PA) Observer,* October 20, 1864; *Unconditional Unionist* (Mt. Vernon, IL), February 9, 1864; *Chicago Times,* August 28, 1864.

28. *New York Caucasian,* May 2, 1863; *Long-Islander* (Huntington, NY), April 24, 1864; *Oregon Sentinel* (Jacksonville), November 5, 1864; *Evening Telegraph* (Philadelphia), July 8, 1864; *Quincy (IL) Herald,* October 7, 1864; *Gloucester (MA) Telegraph and News,* October 18, 1864; *Daily Alta California* (San Francisco), October 1, 1864.

29. *North Branch Democrat* (Tunkhannock, PA), November 2, 1864; *Farmer's Cabinet* (Amherst, NH), December 2, 1864; *Lansing (MI) State Republican,* October 5, 1864; *Rutland (VT) Weekly Herald,* November 3, 1864. A discussion of some of the difficulties suffered by Union

soldiers sympathetic to McClellan and the Democratic Party is Jonathan W. White, *Emancipation, the Union Army, and the Reelection of Abraham Lincoln* (Baton Rouge: Louisiana State University Press, 2014).

30. *True Citizen* (New Britain, CT), August 5, 1864; *Chicago Daily Tribune*, September 22, 1863; *New-York Commercial Advertiser*, April 8, 1863; *Daily National Intelligencer* (Washington, DC), June 8, 1863; *Daily Green Mountain Freeman* (Montpelier, VT), June 8, 1863; *Civilian and Telegraph* (Cumberland, MD), June 11, 1863. On children during the Civil War era, see James A. Marten, ed., *Children and Youth during the Civil War Era* (New York: New York University Press, 2012); and his *Children for the Union: The War Spirit on the Northern Home Front* (Chicago: Ivan R. Dee, 2004).

31. *Newark (OH) Advocate*, August 7, 1863; *Dawson's Fort Wayne (IN) Daily Times*, August 8, 1863; *Columbia Democrat and Bloomsburg (PA) General Advertiser*, November 12, 1864; *Dayton (OH) Daily Empire*, October 22, 1864; *Clearfield (PA) Republican*, October 26, 1864; *Chicago Times*, August 24, 1863. Vallandigham also attracted attention in Confederate notices, with two merchants selling his speeches denouncing the Emancipation Proclamation (see *Southern Crisis* [Jackson, MS], February 4, 1863; and *Savannah [GA] Republican*, March 27, 1863).

32. *Daily National Intelligencer* (Washington, DC), September 20, 1864; "Albany Correspondence," in *Western Reserve Chronicle* (Warren, OH), October 5, 1864; "That Cairo Regiment," in *Marshall County Republican* (Plymouth, IN), October 13, 1864.

33. *Jeffersonian Democrat* (Chardon, OH), August 26, 1864; *Daily Ohio Statesman* (Columbus), October 8, 1864; "Critical Notices: Edward McPherson's Political History of the Rebellion," *North American Review* 100, no. 206 (January 1865): 241–42; Noah Brooks, "Lincoln," *Scribner's Monthly* 15, no. 6 (April 1878): 886.

34. *Philadelphia Inquirer*, October 28, 1864; *Daily National Republican* (Washington, DC), September 12, 1864; *Daily National Intelligencer* (Washington, DC), October 27, 1864; *Weekly Perrysburg (OH) Journal*, September 28, 1864; *Sun* (New York), September 8, 1864; *Boston Evening Transcript*, November 4, 1864.

35. *Daily Ohio Statesman* (Columbus), October 29, 1864; *Erie (PA) Observer*, October 27, 1864; *McKean Democrat* (Smethport, PA), January 9, 1864; *Cambridge (MA) Chronicle*, November 5, 1864.

36. *Sun* (New York), November 1, 1864; *Elk Advocate* (Ridgway, PA), November 5, 1864.

37. *Delaware State Journal and Statesman* (Wilmington), October 25, 1864; *Philadelphia Inquirer*, November 3, 1864; *Pittsburgh Daily Gazette and Advertiser*, October 25, 1864; *Eau Claire (WI) Daily Free Press*, November 3, 1864; *South Danvers Wizard* (Peabody, MA), November 2, 1864.

38. *Burlington (IA) Daily Hawk-Eye*, January 5, 1865; *Juniata Sentinel* (Mifflintown, PA), November 9, 1864; *Oregon Sentinel* (Jacksonville), November 12, 1864.

39. *Springfield (MA) Daily Republican*, May 2, 1865, and May 15, 1865; *Boston Evening Transcript*, September 9, 1865; *Portland (ME) Daily Advertiser*, May 30, 1865; *Illinois State Chronicle* (Decatur), June 24, 1865; *Christian Repository* (Montpelier, VT), May 27, 1865. A survey of the emotional reaction to the assassination is Martha Elizabeth Hodes, *Mourning Lincoln* (New Haven: Yale University Press, 2015).

40. *Manitowoc (WI) Pilot*, April 28, 1865; *Norfolk County Journal* (Roxbury, MA), May 14, 1865; *Montana Post* (Virginia City), June 3, 1865; *Woonsocket Patriot and Rhode-Island State Register*, May 19, 1865; *Goshen (IN) Democrat*, May 10, 1865; *Bedford (PA) Gazette*, August 4, 1865.

41. *New York Herald*, May 17, 1865; *Evening Star* (Washington, DC), May 15, 1865; *Ashtabula (OH) Weekly Telegraph*, June 10, 1865.

42. *Daily Union and American* (Nashville, TN), May 30, 1865; *Marshall (MI) Statesman*, May 31, 1865; *Indianapolis (IN) Daily Journal*, August 18, 1865; *Meriden Recorder* (West Meriden, CT), July 14, 1865; *Buffalo (NY) Morning Express*, July 27, 1865; *Brooklyn (NY) Daily Eagle*, July 17, 1865.

43. *Baltimore Clipper*, May 8, 1865; *Nashville (TN) Union and American*, June 14, 1865; *Daily News and Herald* (Savannah, GA), May 30, 1865; *Herald and Torch Light* (Hagerstown, MD), May 31, 1865; *Lexington (KY) Observer and Reporter*, June 14, 1865.

44. *Chicago Tribune*, January 26, 1865; *White Cloud Kansas Chief*, April 27, 1865; "Million Dollars for Assassination," in *The Assassination of President Lincoln and the Trial of the Conspirators*, ed. Benn Pitman (Cincinnati, OH: Moore, Wilstach and Baldwin, 1865), 51.

45. Frederick T. Frelinghuysen, *Obsequies of Abraham Lincoln, in Newark, N.J., April 19, 1865* (Newark, NJ: Daily Advertiser, 1865), 10–13. On northern claims that the slave system was responsible for the assassination of Lincoln, see Caroline E. Janney, *Remembering the Civil War: Reunion and the Limits of Reconciliation* (Chapel Hill: University of North Carolina Press, 2013), 55–62.

46. Dion Haco, *J. Wilkes Booth, The Assassinator of President Lincoln* (New York: T. R. Dawley, 1865), 43–45, 52–53.

47. Samuel Jackson Gardner, "Style," in *Autumn Leaves* (New York: Hurd and Houghton, 1865), 108–11.

Chapter 4. THE ARMIES

1. *Daily Union* (Washington, DC), May 21, 1846; *New York Herald*, June 2, 1846; *Liberty (MS) Advocate*, May 23, 1846; Francis Colburn Adams, *The Story of a Trooper: With Much of Interest Concerning the Campaign on the Peninsula, Not before Written* (New York: Dick and Fitzgerald, 1865), 5–6. Examples of recruiting notices prior to the mid-nineteenth century are found in Wood, *The Story of Advertising*, 54, 58–60; and Turner, *The Shocking History of Advertising*, 61. A general overview of American military mobilization is found in Marvin A. Kreidberg and Merton G. Henry, *History of Military Mobilization in the United States Army, 1775–1945* (rpt., Westport, CT: Greenwood, 1975).

2. *New-York Daily Tribune*, May 2, 1861; *New Orleans Daily Crescent*, June 8, 1861; *Cincinnati (OH) Daily Press*, September 4, 1861; *Daily Ohio Statesman* (Columbus), September 13, 1861; *Memphis (TN) Daily Appeal*, April 24, 1861; *Brooklyn (NY) Daily Eagle*, April 29, 1861.

3. "General Orders, No. 70," War Department, September 3, 1861, in U.S. War Department, *O.R.*, ser. 3, vol. 1, 478; "Appendix," *O.R.*, ser. 3, vol. 2, 932; Andrew Curtin to Simon Cameron, September 18, 1861, *O.R.*, ser. 3, vol. 1, 526. In early 1862, Union general Benjamin Butler complained about competing advertisements in his efforts to raise troops. He was autho-

rized to raise another regiment but found that two units were "endeavoring to recruit by flaring advertisements in opposition to one another." He judged it "not best to mix in the quarrel" (see Benjamin Butler to Daniel Richardson, February 3, 1862, in *Private and Official Correspondence of Gen. Benjamin F. Bulter, during the Period of the Civil War*, vol. 1 [Norwood, MA: Plimpton, 1917], 342).

4. James I. Robertson Jr., *Soldiers Blue and Gray* (Columbia: University of South Carolina Press, 1998), 11–14.

5. *Detroit Advertiser and Tribune*, January 1, 1861; *Chicago Tribune*, February 27, 1860; *Milwaukee (WI) Daily Sentinel*, December 13, 1860; *Memphis (TN) Morning Enquirer*, February 14, 1861. The recruitment of volunteers during the Mexican War is described in Richard B. Winders, *Mr. Polk's Army: The American Military Experience in the Mexican War* (College Station: Texas A&M University Press, 1997); and James M. McCaffrey, *Army of Manifest Destiny: The American Soldier in the Mexican War, 1846–1848* (New York: New York University Press, 1992).

6. "The War—How It Began and What Keeps It Up," *Old Guard* 2, no. 1 (January 1864): 3. The modern-day literature on why soldiers fought is extensive. Influential early works by Bell I. Wiley are *The Life of Johnny Reb: The Common Soldier of the Confederacy* (Indianapolis: Bobbs-Merrill, 1943), and *The Life of Billy Yank: The Common Soldier of the Union* (Indianapolis: Bobbs-Merrill, 1952). Wiley argues that soldiers had little idea why they were fighting, except for their comrades. Two books by nationally recognized scholars that argue soldiers held deep ideological commitments to their cause are James M. McPherson, *For Cause and Comrades: Why Men Fought in the Civil War* (New York: Oxford University Press, 1997); and Reid Mitchell, *Civil War Soldiers: Their Expectations and Their Experiences* (New York: Viking, 1988).

7. *Daily Missouri Republican* (St. Louis), September 5, 1861; *Fayetteville (NC) Observer*, November 21, 1861; *Daily Delta* (New Orleans), January 1, 1862; *Indianapolis (IN) State Sentinel*, July 31, 1861; *Dubuque (IA) Democratic Herald*, July 12, 1861; *Daily Ledger and Texan* (San Antonio), July 3, 1861; *Daily Richmond (VA) Enquirer*, May 10, 1861; *Vermont Phoenix* (Brattleboro), November 21, 1861.

8. *Louisville (KY) Daily Journal*, September 25, 1861; *Pennsylvania Daily Telegraph* (Harrisburg), August 4, 1861; *Alton (IL) Telegraph*, November 22, 1861; *Cleveland (OH) Daily Herald*, November 7, 1861, and December 4, 1861; *Charlestown Advertiser* (Boston), September 4, 1861; *Bangor (ME) Daily Whig and Courier*, November 25, 1861; *Spirit of Democracy* (Woodsfield, OH), October 9, 1861.

9. *Columbus (GA) Enquirer*, August 1, 1861, and August 30, 1861; *Memphis (TN) Daily Appeal*, December 25, 1861; *Daily Richmond (VA) Examiner*, February 24, 1862; *North Carolina Whig* (Charlotte), February 26, 1862; *Daily True Delta* (New Orleans), June 4, 1861.

10. *Macon (GA) Weekly Telegraph*, March 7, 1862; *Newark (NJ) Daily Advertiser*, November 8, 1861; *Independent Republican* (Montrose, PA), March 13, 1862; *Winchester (VA) Republican*, March 7, 1862; *Charleston (SC) Tri-Weekly Courier*, August 13, 1861; *Southern Watchman* (Athens, GA), August 28, 1861.

11. *Mobile (AL) Advertiser and Register*, February 13, 1862; *Albany (GA) Patriot*, September 12, 1861; *Daily Confederate News* (Columbus, KY), January 15, 1862; *Keowee Courier* (Pickens Court House, SC), March 15, 1862.

12. *Rolla (MO) Express*, July 22, 1861; *Easton (MD) Gazette*, November 9, 1861; *Louisville (KY) Daily Courier*, September 25, 1861; *Cleveland (OH) Morning Leader*, October 4, 1861.

13. *Bangor (ME) Daily Whig and Courier*, March 6, 1862; *Boston Daily Advertiser*, January 17, 1862; *Mankato (MN) Weekly Independent*, December 13, 1861; *Columbus (GA) Enquirer*, March 13, 1862.

14. *Indianapolis (IN) State Sentinel*, September 13, 1861; *Daily Rocky Mountain News* (Denver), June 10, 1861; *Opelousas (LA) Patriot*, August 17, 1861.

15. *New Orleans Daily Crescent*, June 4, 1861; *Potter Journal* (Coudersport, PA), June 13, 1861; *Daily Green Mountain Freeman* (Montpelier, VT), August 30, 1861, and November 18, 1861; "Col. Carrington's Rifle Regiment," *Columbus (OH) Gazette*, August 23, 1861; "Volunteering for the War," *Charleston (SC) Mercury*, December 3, 1861.

16. *Shreveport (LA) Daily News*, October 3, 1861; *M'Arthur Democrat* (McArthur, OH), October 31, 1861; "Baker Volunteers," *Augusta (GA) Chronicle*, August 17, 1861; *Farmer's Cabinet* (Amherst, NH), September 20, 1861.

17. *Louisville Daily Courier* article, reprinted in *Fayetteville (TN) Observer*, June 27, 1861; *New York Herald*, February 26, 1862.

18. *Daily Commonwealth* (Frankfort, KY), September 1, 1862; *Charlestown Advertiser* (Boston), July 26, 1862; *Arizona Miner* (Fort Whipple), April 20, 1864. An excellent analysis of Confederate soldiers who volunteered during 1862 and after is Kenneth W. Noe, *Reluctant Rebels: The Confederates Who Joined the Army after 1861* (Chapel Hill: University of North Carolina Press, 2010).

19. *Delaware State Journal and Statesman* (Wilmington), July 28, 1863; *Norwalk (OH) Reflector*, September 30, 1862; *Norfolk County Journal* (Roxbury, MA), August 23, 1862; *Peninsular News and Advertiser* (Milford, DE), July 21, 1864; *Natchez (MS) Daily Courier*, April 29, 1862; *Daily True Delta* (New Orleans), March 20, 1862.

20. *Evening Telegraph* (Philadelphia), July 8, 1864; *Mobile (AL) Evening News*, April 16, 1864; *Carolina Watchman* (Salisbury, NC), June 16, 1862; *Daily Confederate* (Raleigh, NC), March 9, 1864; *Montana Post* (Virginia City), November 26, 1864; *Daily Register* (Petersburg, VA), July 31, 1863; *Huntingdon (PA) Globe*, July 29, 1863; *New York Times*, June 11, 1863.

21. *Philadelphia Inquirer*, July 17, 1863, and March 29, 1864; *Albany (NY) Journal*, January 4, 1864; *Detroit Free Press*, September 15, 1863. The African American military experience during the Civil War is detailed in Joseph T. Glatthaar, *Forged in Battle: The Civil War Alliance of Black Soldiers and White Officers* (New York: Free Press, 1990); Ira Berlin, Joseph P. Reidy, and Leslie S. Rowland, eds., *Freedom's Soldiers: The Black Military Experience in the Civil War* (New York: Cambridge University Press, 1998); and Dudley Taylor Cornish, *The Sable Arm: Black Troops in the Union Army, 1861–1865* (repr., Lawrence: University Press of Kansas, 1987).

22. George Livermore, *An Historical Research Respecting the Opinions of the Founders of the Republic on Negroes as Slaves, as Citizens and as Soldiers* (Boston: J. Wilson, 1862), 114–18.

23. "Negroes as Soldiers," *Madison (IN) Courier*, reprinted in *Daily Evansville (IN) Journal*, February 5, 1863; "Black Soldiers," *New York World*; reprinted in *Chicago Daily Tribune*, December 22, 1862; *Cleveland (OH) Tri-Weekly Leader*, January 13, 1863.

24. *National Eagle* (Claremont, NH), December 11, 1862; *Syracuse (NY) Daily Courier and Union*, December 2, 1862; *Indianapolis (IN) Daily Journal*, June 18, 1862; *Big Blue Union* (Marys-

ville, KS), August 30, 1862; *Gallipolis (OH) Journal*, August 18, 1864; *Weekly Louisville (KY) Democrat*, December 10, 1863; *Boston Semi-Weekly Advertiser*, August 16, 1862. On the argument that Union soldiers served as a vital middle ground between northern civilians and politicians in helping to push the destruction of slavery as a war aim, see Chandra Manning, *What This Cruel War Was Over: Soldiers, Slavery, and the Civil War* (New York: Knopf, 2007). For preserving the Union as a primary motivation for northern soldiers, see Gary Gallagher, *The Union War* (Cambridge: Harvard University Press, 2011).

25. *Daily Dispatch* (Richmond, VA), May 29, 1862; *Dallas (TX) Herald*, October 4, 1862; *Cotton States* (Gainesville, FL), April 26, 1864; *Daily Chronicle and Sentinel* (Augusta, GA), April 1, 1862; *Daily Mississippian* (Jackson), June 9, 1862; *Hinds County Gazette* (Raymond, MS), July 9, 1862; *Semi-Weekly Shreveport (LA) News*, October 28, 1862; *Carolina Watchman* (Salisbury, NC), June 16, 1862.

26. *New York Herald*, July 12, 1863; *Louisville (KY) Daily Courier*, August 12, 1862; *Daily Vicksburg (MS) Whig*, April 9, 1862; *South Danvers Wizard* (Peabody, MA), January 6, 1864; *Philadelphia Inquirer*, February 17, 1865; *Highland Weekly News* (Hillsboro, OH), September 15, 1864; *Daily Ohio State Journal* (Columbus), June 6, 1862; McPherson, *For Cause and Comrades*, 14–29.

27. *Knoxville (TN) Register*, July 6, 1862; *Mobile (AL) Daily Advertiser and Register*, April 5, 1862; *Daily News and Herald* (Savannah, GA), May 26, 1862; *Daily Intelligencer* (Atlanta, GA), August 28, 1863; *Pittsburgh Daily Gazette and Advertiser*, September 30, 1862; *Pioneer and Democrat* (St. Paul, MN), November 12, 1863; *Daily Commonwealth* (Denver, CO), May 15, 1864.

28. *Staunton (VA) Spectator*, September 30, 1862; *Burlington (IA) Daily Hawk-Eye*, April 15, 1863; *Athens (OH) Messenger*, July 9, 1863; *Syracuse (NY) Daily Courier and Union*, April 1, 1863; *Centralia (IL) Sentinel*, February 25, 1864; *Daily Dispatch* (Richmond, VA), May 29, 1862; *Evansville (IN) Daily Journal*, April 1, 1864.

29. *Fremont (OH) Journal*, January 1, 1864; *St. Paul (MN) Daily Union*, December 10, 1863; *Daily South Carolinian* (Columbia), April 11, 1862; *Milwaukee (WI) Daily Sentinel*, January 25, 1865; *Morning Oregonian* (Portland), June 22, 1862; *Worcester (MA) Palladium*, January 6, 1864.

30. Weigley, *A Great Civil War*, 118–19, 234–36; McPherson, *Battle Cry of Freedom*, 428–37, 600–611. On the draft in the Union, see also Eugene C. Murdock, *Patriotism Limited, 1862–1865: The Civil War Draft and the Bounty System* (Kent, OH: Kent State University Press, 1971); and his *One Million Men: The Civil War Draft in the North* (Madison: State Historical Society of Wisconsin, 1971).

31. *Iredell Express* (Statesville, NC), April 15, 1864; *Daily Conservative* (Raleigh, NC), April 7, 1864; *Boston Post*, July 20, 1863; *Daily Clarion* (Jackson, MS), July 19, 1864; *Union County Star and Lewisburg (PA) Chronicle*, April 28, 1864. The public contempt for those men attempting to escape the draft is detailed in Gallman, *Defining Duty*, 125–57. On resistance to the draft, see Albert Burton Moore, *Conscription and Conflict in the Confederacy* (repr., Columbia: University of South Carolina Press, 1996).

32. *Philadelphia Inquirer*, February 17, 1865; *New-York Daily Tribune*, July 25, 1864; *Daily Missouri Republican* (St. Louis), March 4, 1864; *Alleghenian* (Ebensburg, PA), March 8, 1865; *Chicago Tribune*, January 15, 1865; *Chicago Times*, August 4, 1863; *Press* (Philadelphia), June 15, 1863; *New York Herald*, August 8, 1863.

33. Weigley, *A Great Civil War*, 235–36; Robertson, *Soldiers Blue and Gray*, 37–39.

34. *Montgomery County Sentinel* (Rockville, MD), December 19, 1862; *Raleigh (NC) Register*, July 2, 1862; *Daily Dispatch* (Richmond, VA), May 29, 1862, and October 23, 1862; *Southern Confederacy* (Atlanta) April 9, 1863; *Southern Recorder* (Milledgeville, GA), May 19, 1864; *Hartford (CT) Daily Post*, January 18, 1865; *Daily National Intelligencer* (Washington, DC), January 18, 1865.

35. *Daily Southern Guardian* (Columbia, SC), May 9, 1863; *Sentinel* (Richmond, VA), January 1, 1863; *Daily Richmond (VA) Examiner*, August 5, 1862; *Countryman* (Turnwold, GA), September 29, 1862; *Vicksburg (MS) Daily Whig*, June 6, 1862; *Daily Dispatch* (Richmond, VA), January 1, 1863.

36. *Pioneer and Democrat* (St. Paul, MN), March 15, 1864; *Georgetown (DE) Union*, April 7, 1865; *National Intelligencer* (Washington, DC), January 18, 1865; *Milwaukee (WI) Daily Sentinel*, January 25, 1865; *Quincy (MA) Patriot*, December 26, 1863; *Elm Leaf* (East Hartford, CT), November 2, 1864.

37. *Boston Evening Transcript*, July 19, 1864; *Philadelphia Inquirer*, August 23, 1864; *Sun* (New York), August 1, 1864.

38. *Daily National Republican* (Washington, DC), August 9, 1864; *New York Times*, August 5, 1864; *Albany (NY) Journal*, January 1, 1864; *Evening Star* (Washington, DC), July 23, 1864; *New-York Daily Tribune*, September 30, 1863.

39. *Union County Star and Lewisburg (PA) Chronicle*, July 21, 1863; *Grand Haven (MI) News*, October 14, 1863; James Connolly to Mary Connolly, August 16, 1864, in *Three Years in the Army of the Cumberland: The Letters and Diary of Major James A. Connolly*, ed. Paul Angle (Bloomington: Indiana University Press, 1996), 255–56.

40. "Song," *Opelousas (LA) Courier*, January 23, 1864; "The Virginia Army," *Western Sentinel* (Winston-Salem, NC), January 28, 1864; "Journal of the War," *De Bow's Review* 2, no. 5 (November 1866): 541.

41. *Staunton (VA) Spectator*, May 3, 1864; *Western Democrat* (Charlotte, NC), March 14, 1865; *Ann Arbor (MI) Journal*, November 8, 1864; "A Well-Digested Plan for the Relief of Richmond," *Southern Literary Messenger* 37, no. 12 (December 1863): 726–27; "Editor's Drawer," *Harper's New Monthly Magazine* 28, no. 165 (February 1864): 428. The standard work on desertion remains Ella Lonn, *Desertion during the Civil War* (repr., Lincoln: University of Nebraska Press, 1998). See also Mark A. Weitz, *More Damning Than Slaughter: Desertion in the Confederate Army* (Lincoln: University of Nebraska Press, 2005).

42. Report of the Disbursing Branch of the Provost Marshal General's Bureau, January 1, 1866, in U.S. War Department, *O.R.*, series III, vol. 5, 781; *Tri-Weekly (Newberry, SC) Herald*, April 8, 1865.

43. *Daily Commonwealth* (Frankfort, KY), November 20, 1861; *Mobile (AL) Evening Telegraph*, July 14, 1863; *Athens (TN) Post*, April 24, 1863; *Daily Colorado Republican and Rocky Mountain Herald* (Denver), October 23, 1861; *Nebraska Advertiser* (Brownville), January 7, 1864; *Daily Republican* (Lynchburg, VA), March 13, 1863; *Sentinel* (Richmond, VA), November 2, 1862; *Oxford (MS) Intelligencer*, November 7, 1862; *Edgefield (SC) Advertiser*, October 19, 1864; *Galveston (TX) Weekly News*, May 30, 1864.

44. *Daily Bulletin* (Charlotte, NC) December 2, 1863; *Cotton States* (Gainesville, FL), April 16, 1864.

45. *Rockingham Register* (Harrisonburg, VA), July 4, 1862; *Houston (TX) Telegraph*, November 2, 1864; *Weekly Perrysburg (OH) Journal*, May 14, 1862.

46. *North Carolina Whig* (Charlotte), May 7, 1861; *Spirit of Democracy* (Woodsfield, OH), July 3, 1861; *Rockingham Register* (Harrisonburg, VA), December 26, 1862.

47. "Southern Items," reprinted from the "New York Journals," *Daily Picayune* (New Orleans), August 12, 1864; "News From the South," *New York Herald*, January 22, 1862; *Louisville (KY) Daily Journal*, March 14, 1863.

48. *Daily Union and American* (Nashville, TN), April 22, 1862, and June 17, 1862; *Knoxville (TN) Daily Register*, January 19, 1862; *Daily Dispatch* (Richmond, VA), September 8, 1863; *Daily Richmond (VA) Examiner*, June 1, 1863.

49. *Southern Confederacy* (Atlanta) April 6, 1864; *Jacksonville (AL) Republican*, November 17, 1864; *Daily Dispatch* (Richmond, VA), June 29, 1864; *Knoxville (TN) Tri-Weekly Whig*, July 26, 1864.

50. *Meriden Recorder* (West Meriden, CT), July 4, 1865; *Vermont Transcript* (St. Albans), June 16, 1865; *Monticello (IA) Express*, July 10, 1865; *Jacksonville (AL) Republican*, August 12, 1865; *Daily (Little Rock) Arkansas Gazette*, May 30, 1865.

51. *Springfield (MA) Daily Republican*, February 4, 1865; *Rockingham Register* (Harrisonburg, VA), May 12, 1865; *Buffalo (NY)* Morning *Express*, July 7, 1865. For a recent work on the transition of former Union soldiers to peacetime society, see Brian M. Jordan, *Marching Home: Union Veterans and Their Unending Civil War* (New York: Liveright, 2014).

52. *South Carolina Leader* (Charleston), December 23, 1865; *Buffalo Morning Express*, July 18, 1865; *Chicago Tribune*, July 18, 1865; *Detroit Free Press*, September 15, 1865.

53. *Daily Union and American* (Nashville, TN), May 26, 1864, and June 30, 1864; *Corinth (MS) Chanticleer*, September 18, 1863; *Elk Advocate* (Ridgway, PA), March 30, 1865.

Chapter 5. SLAVERY AND RACE

1. *London Times* article, reprinted in Horace Greeley, *Aunt Sally, Come Up! Or, the Nigger Sale* (London: Ward and Lock, 1859), 78–79.

2. Calvin Schermerhorn, *The Business of Slavery and the Rise of American Capitalism, 1815–1860* (New Haven: Yale University Press, 2015); Steven Deyle, *Carry Me Back: The Domestic Slave Trade in American Life* (New York: Oxford University Press, 2005). Also drawing conclusions from the slave notices are Robert H. Gudmestad, *A Troublesome Commerce: The Transformation of the Interstate Slave Trade* (Baton Rouge: Louisiana State University Press, 2003); and Michael Tadman, *Speculators and Slaves: Masters, Traders, and Slaves in the Old South* (Madison: University of Wisconsin Press, 1989).

3. John Hope Franklin and Loren Schweninger, *Runaway Slaves: Rebels on the Plantation* (New York: Oxford University Press, 1999). For announcements from an earlier century, see Lathan A. Windley, *Runaway Slave Advertisements: A Documentary History from the 1730s to 1790*, 4 vols. (Westport, CT: Greenwood, 1983). A number of historical societies and universities also have developed excellent databases on runaway slaves, drawn from the notices.

4. *Dallas (TX) Herald*, November 7, 1860; *Alexandria (VA) Gazette*, December 27, 1860; *Home Journal* (Winchester, TN), November 8, 1860; *Memphis (TN) Morning Enquirer*, January 16, 1861;

Family Friend (Monticello, FL), December 15, 1860; *Daily Southern Guardian* (Columbia, SC), November 3, 1864; *Daily Selma (AL) Reporter,* January 27, 1865; *Shreveport (LA) Semi-Weekly News,* May 6, 1865; *Western Citizen* (Paris, KY), December 1, 1865; *Southern Watchman* (Athens, GA), April 12, 1865.

5. *Yorkville (SC) Enquirer,* December 20, 1860; *St. Mary's Beacon* (Leonard Town, MD), January 12, 1860; *Yazoo (MS) Democrat,* August 11, 1861; *Fayetteville (NC) Observer,* August 22, 1864; *Mobile (AL) Evening Telegraph,* July 14, 1863, and November 19, 1864; *Glasgow (MO) Weekly Times,* May 2, 1861; *Montgomery (AL) Daily Post,* February 18, 1861; *Staunton (VA) Spectator,* November 3, 1863. On slave merchants and the market revolution, see Schermerhorn, *The Business of Slavery,* 33–68.

6. *Sugar Planter* (West Baton Rouge, LA), January 7, 1860; *Wilmington (NC) Journal,* July 12, 1861; *Fayetteville (TN) Observer,* April 18, 1861; *Hinds County (MS) Gazette,* September 26, 1860.

7. *Daily Morning News* (Savannah, GA), March 26, 1861; *Weekly Raleigh (NC) Register,* January 7, 1863; *Fayetteville (NC) Observer,* January 25, 1864; *Charleston (SC) Daily Courier,* May 31, 1862, and January 10, 1863; *Daily Richmond (VA) Examiner,* September 15, 1864; *Natchez (MS) Daily Courier,* November 12, 1862.

8. A recent overview of white southern guilt over slavery is found in William L. Barney, "Rush to Disaster: Secession and the Slaves' Revenge," in Robert J. Cook, Barney, and Elizabeth R. Varon, *Secession Winter: When the Union Fell Apart* (Baltimore: Johns Hopkins University Press, 2013).

9. Deyle, *Carry Me Back,* 223.

10. *Wilmington (NC) Daily Journal,* December 12, 1863; *Galveston (TX) News,* May 30, 1864; *Journal and Confederate* (Camden, SC), July 24, 1863; *Daily Intelligencer* (Atlanta) August 28, 1863.

11. John S. C. Abbott, *South and North, Or, Impressions Received during a Trip to Cuba and the South* (New York: Abbey and Abbot, 1860), 78–80; Charles Sumner, *"The Barbarism of Slavery": Speech of Hon. Charles Sumner on the Bill for the Admission of Kansas as a Free State* (Washington, DC: Buell and Blanchard, 1860), 14.

12. Samuel Mosheim Smucker, *The Yankee Slave Driver, or, the Black and White Rivals* (New York: H. Dayton, 1860), 150–56. Smucker's work was originally published in 1855 but under a different title.

13. Alfred Burnett, *Incidents of the War: Humorous, Pathetic, and Descriptive* (Cincinnati, OH: Ricky and Carroll, 1863), 119; Albert Richardson, *The Secret Service, the Field, the Dungeon, and the Escape* (Hartford, CT: American Publishing Co., 1865), 65–70.

14. "Klutz" [pseud.], "Hannibal, a Nigger, Parts I–IV," *Southern Literary Messenger* 30, no. 6 (June 1860): 410–20.

15. Thomas Wentworth Higginson, "Cheerful Yesterdays," *Atlantic Monthly* 79, no. 476 (June 1897): 780; W. P. Trent, "Gleanings from an Old Southern Newspaper," *Atlantic Monthly* 86, no. 515 (September 1900): 356–64.

16. *Shreveport (LA) News,* July 5, 1864; *Daily Richmond (VA) Examiner,* November 21, 1863; *Southern Confederacy* (Atlanta), July 23, 186; *Cotton States* (Gainesville, FL), March 19, 1864. See also Charles B. Dew, *Ironmaker to the Confederacy: Joseph R. Anderson and the Tredegar Iron Works* (New Haven: Yale University Press, 1966).

17. *Houston (TX) Weekly Telegraph,* January 14, 1863; *Daily Selma (AL) Reporter,* January 19,

1865; *Richmond (VA) Daily Dispatch,* January 16, 1865; *Gate-City Guardian* (Atlanta), July 5, 1864; *Daily Picayune* (New Orleans), August 3, 1861.

18. *Daily Richmond (VA) Examiner,* November 21, 1863; *Mobile (AL) Evening Telegraph,* November 3, 1864; *Daily Selma (AL) Reporter,* January 27, 1865; *Daily News and Herald* (Savannah, GA), February 25, 1862; *Journal and Confederate* (Camden, SC), April 7, 1865. Confederate officers often carried through on the threat to impress slaves (see Jaime Amanda Martinez, *Confederate Slave Impressment in the Upper South* [Chapel Hill: University of North Carolina Press, 2013]).

19. *Memphis (TN) Daily Appeal,* December 25, 1861; *Daily Mississippian* (Jackson), August 7, 1862; *Vicksburg (MS) Daily Whig,* June 8, 1862; *Camden (SC) Confederate,* February 21, 1862.

20. *Richmond (VA) Sentinel,* October 23, 1863; *Lexington (KY) Observer and Reporter,* April 2, 1862; *Albany (GA) Patriot,* May 26, 1864; *Daily Gazette and Comet* (Baton Rouge, LA), November 16, 1864; *Columbia (SC) Phoenix,* March 30, 1865. If a black man stood accused of raping a white woman, the reward for his capture skyrocketed. Two men imprisoned for rape escaped a local jail, and the return brought one thousand dollars for each of them (see *Weekly Conservative* [Raleigh, NC], April 12, 1865).

21. *Western Democrat* (Charlotte, NC), July 14, 1863; *Rockingham Register* (Harrisonburg, VA), December 26, 1862; *Weekly Register* (Point Pleasant, WV), August 21, 1862; *Daily Sun* (Columbus, GA), March 15, 1864; *Edgefield (SC) Advertiser,* June 10, 1863; *Daily Southern Guardian* (Columbia, SC), April 6, 1864; *Southern Intelligencer* (Austin, TX), January 1, 1861; *Camden (SC) Confederate,* April 17, 1863.

22. *Vicksburg (MS) Daily Whig,* January 29, 1862; *Hinds County Gazette* (Raymond, MS), February 8, 1860, and January 22, 1862; *Daily Southern Crisis* (Jackson, MS), February 13, 1863; *Charleston (SC) Mercury,* March 4, 1863; *Richmond (VA) Sentinel,* August 21, 1863, and October 23, 1863; *Covington (KY) Journal,* October 21, 1861; *Daily Picayune* (New Orleans), March 16, 1862; *Fayetteville (NC) Observer,* April 17, 1862.

23. *Daily Conservative* (Raleigh, NC), April 7, 1863; *Daily Clarion* (Jackson, MS), July 19, 1864; *Arkansas State Gazette* (Little Rock), January 24, 1863; *Daily Republican* (Lynchburg, VA), March 13, 1863; *Mobile (AL) Evening Telegraph,* December 17, 1862; *Daily Express* (Petersburg, VA), August 3, 1864.

24. *Daily Picayune* (New Orleans), March 16, 1862; *Southern Confederacy* (Atlanta), July 9, 1864; *Daily Ledger and Texan* (San Antonio), December 1, 1860; *Daily Express* (Petersburg, VA), April 21, 1864; *Confederate Union* (Milledgeville, GA), November 8, 1864; *Richmond (VA) Whig,* March 27, 1863.

25. Franklin and Schweninger, *Runaway Slaves,* 49–74.

26. *Daily Intelligencer* (Atlanta), September 10, 1860; *Chattanooga (TN) Daily Gazette,* December 18, 1862; *Daily Missouri Republican* (St. Louis), March 19, 1861; *Sentinel* (Richmond, VA), November 7, 1863; *Daily Delta* (New Orleans), February 16, 1861; *Knoxville (TN) Register,* September 19, 1860; *Mobile (AL) Evening Telegraph,* November 19, 1864; *Savannah (GA) Republican,* March 15, 1864.

27. *Daily Dispatch* (Richmond, VA), April 18, 1864; *Daily Clarion* (Jackson, MS), July 19, 1864; *Chattanooga (TN) Daily Rebel,* September 10, 1862; *Winchester (VA) Republican,* May 30, 1862; *Farmville (VA) Journal,* April 8, 1862.

28. *Navarro Express* (Corsicana, TX), June 16, 1864; *Memphis (TN) Daily Appeal*, November 10, 1862; *Jacksonville (AL) Republican*, March 16, 1865; *Weekly Standard* (Raleigh, NC), October 15, 1862; *Daily Mississippian* (Jackson), January 14, 1863; *Henderson (TX) Times*, November 21, 1863; *Confederate Union* (Milledgeville, GA), February 9, 1864.

29. Cards of thanks and other notices that indicated black men and women aiding their masters and the Confederate war effort are found in *Daily Southern Crisis* (Jackson, MS), February 6, 1863; and *Camden (SC) Weekly Journal*, August 14, 1862. A plantation owner in Mississippi came at the topic indirectly. He placed a reward for arsonists who had set fire to his house. With the aid of his "servants," he had extinguished the blaze (see *Vicksburg [MS] Whig*, April 9, 1862).

30. William Pittenger, *Daring and Suffering: A History of the Great Railroad Adventure* (Philadelphia: J. W. Daughaday, 1863), 131–33.

31. Charles Tennant, *The American Question and How to Settle It* (London: S. Low, Son, and Co., 1863), 207–9.

32. Harriet A. Jacobs, *Incidents in the Life of a Slave Girl* (Boston: Published for the author, 1861), 33–43.

33. *Alleghenian* (Ebensburg, PA), March 1, 1860; *Daily Evening Bulletin* (San Francisco), January 13, 1860; *Milwaukee (WI) Daily Sentinel*, January 21, 1860.

34. *Racine (WI) Daily Journal*, January 29, 1861; *Anti-Slavery Bugle* (New Lisbon, OH), December 29, 1860; *White River Gazette* (Worthington, IN), February 6, 1861; *Chicago Daily Tribune*, November 24, 1860; "Critical Notices," *Dial: A Monthly Magazine for Literature, Philosophy and Religion* 1, no. 12 (December 1860): 777.

35. *Liberator* (Boston), March 23, 1860; *New York Herald*, May 8, 1860; *Dubuque (IA) Daily Times*, July 15, 1864.

36. "Bonaparte, Cromwell, and Washington," *De Bow's Review* 28, no. 2 (August 1860): 142; W. W. Wright, "Relations of the Negro Race to Civilization," *De Bow's Review* 28, no. 6 (December 1860): 638; "Pugilistic Piety," *Vanity Fair* 2 (October 18, 1860): 191.

37. James Redpath, *The Public Life of Capt. John Brown* (Boston: Thayer and Eldridge, 1860), 7–8; *New-York Daily Tribune*, January 25, 1860, and April 17, 1860; *Western Reserve Chronicle* (Warren, OH), April 11, 1860; *Penny Press* (Cincinnati, OH), February 3, 1860; *Spirit of Democracy* (Woodsfield, OH), December 12, 1860.

38. *Weekly Anglo-African* (New York), January 25, 1862.

39. *National Anti-Slavery Standard* (New York), March 9, 1861; *National Era* (Washington, DC), March 22, 1860.

40. *Albany (NY) Journal*, November 12, 1864; *Newark (NJ) Daily Advertiser*, August 1, 1862; *Burlington (IA) Daily Hawk Eye*, October 20, 1862. The critical reaction to Gilmore's work is detailed in Fahs, *The Imagined Civil War*, 159–62.

41. *New York Herald*, January 3, 1863; *Pacific Commercial Advertiser* (Honolulu), July 2, 1863; *Boston Semi-Weekly Advertiser*, December 23, 1862; *New-York Daily Tribune*, July 25, 1864.

42. "Reviews and Literary Notices: Cochin's Results of Emancipation," *Atlantic Monthly* 11, no. 65 (March 1863): 395–97; "Literary Notices: Popular Edition. Results of Emancipation. By Augustin Cochin," *Continental Monthly* 6, no. 2 (August 1864): 232–33.

43. *New York Herald*, November 23, 1861; *St. Paul (MN) Daily Union*, January 23, 1864; *Fre-*

mont (OH) Journal, February 3, 1864; *Detroit Free Press*, November 10, 1863; *Daily Louisville (KY) Democrat*, November 29, 1860. An excellent, if increasingly dated, analysis of minstrel shows is Robert C. Toll, *Blacking Up: The Minstrel Show in Nineteenth-Century America* (New York: Oxford University Press, 1974).

44. *Nebraska City Herald*, December 26, 1861.

45. *New York Herald*, July 26, 1861.

46. Fahs, *The Imagined Civil War*, 150–81.

47. *Pine and Palm* (Boston), May 25, 1861, and November 16, 1861; *National Anti-Slavery Standard* (New York), January 30, 1865. Redpath's involvement with attempts to emigrate black Americans to Haiti is detailed in John R. McKivigan, *Forgotten Firebrand: James Redpath and the Making of Nineteenth-Century America* (Ithaca, NY: Cornell University Press, 2008).

48. *Black Republican* (New Orleans), May 20, 1865; *New Orleans Tribune*, April 3, 1865; *Christian Recorder* (Philadelphia), February 4, 1865; *South Carolina Leader* (Charleston), December 23, 1865.

49. *National Anti-Slavery Standard* (New York), July 30, 1864, April 8, 1865, and October 7, 1865.

50. *New Orleans Tribune*, December 13, 1865; *Christian Recorder* (Philadelphia), October 29, 1864; *Black Republican* (New Orleans), April 16, 1865.

51. *Columbia (SC) Phoenix*, October 6, 1865; *New Orleans Tribune*, June 23, 1865; *South Carolina Leader* (Charleston), December 16, 1865.

52. *Weekly Anglo-African* (New York), August 10, 1861; *National Anti-Slavery Standard* (New York), October 11, 1862.

Chapter 6. BATTLEFIELD AND HOME FRONT

1. David Dodge, "Domestic Economy in the Confederacy," *Atlantic Monthly* 58, no. 346 (August 1886): 229–43.

2. For different perceptions of the war between soldiers and civilians, see Steven J. Ramold, *Across the Divide: Union Soldiers View the Northern Homefront* (New York: New York University Press, 2013); and Linderman, *Embattled Courage*. Whether the Civil War broke down distinctions between soldiers and civilians also is analyzed in Mark E. Neely Jr., "Was the Civil War a Total War?," *Civil War History* 50, no. 4 (December 2004): 434–58.

3. *Augusta (GA) Chronicle*, February 3, 1861, and March 3, 1861; *Daily South Carolinian* (Columbia), December 13, 1860; *Dallas (TX) Herald*, March 6, 1861; *Staunton (VA) Vindicator*, December 4, 1860; *Raleigh (NC) Register*, February 20, 1861; *Gate-City Guardian* (Atlanta), February 13, 1861; *Weekly Columbus (GA) Enquirer*, February 9, 1861; *Mississippian* (Jackson), December 28, 1860; *Montgomery (AL) Sentinel*, February 15, 1861; *Daily Picayune* (New Orleans), December 30, 1860; *Daily Rough Notes* (Goldsboro, NC), February 25, 1861; *Farmville (VA) Journal*, March 21, 1861; *Anderson (SC) Intelligencer*, December 20, 1860; *Cecil Whig* (Elkton, MD), February 16, 1861.

4. *Daily Intelligencer* (Wheeling, WV), March 20, 1861; *State Gazette* (Austin, TX), August 4, 1860; *Jacksonville (AL) Republican*, August 23, 1860. At least one northern editor suggested that announcements for Colt's pistols ran in Confederate newspapers (see "Important from Virginia,"

Boston Herald, May 20, 1861). The number of sales recorded by Colt is taken from Matthew Warshauer, *Connecticut in the American Civil War: Slavery, Sacrifice, and Survival* (Middletown, CT: Wesleyan University Press, 2012), 49. See also Herbert G. Houze, Carolyn C. Cooper, and Elizabeth M. Kornhauser, *Samuel Colt: Arms, Art, and Invention* (New Haven: Yale University Press, 2006).

5. *Daily Missouri Republican* (St. Louis), March 4, 1864; *Union and Dakotian* (Yankton), November 19, 1864; *Louisville (KY) Daily Journal*, November 30, 1861; *Daily Picayune* (New Orleans), December 16, 1862; *New-York Daily Tribune*, August 12, 1861; *Daily Evening Bulletin* (San Francisco), November 7, 1861; *Boston Post*, January 2, 1863.

6. *Chicago Tribune*, May 25, 1864; "The First Century of the Republic," *Harper's New Monthly Magazine* 50, no. 297 (February 1875): 377. The article reports that the federal government ordered 94,156 Spencer rifles by the end of the war. The battlefield exploits of Wilder's brigade are detailed in Peter Cozzens, *This Terrible Sound: The Battle of Chickamauga* (Urbana: University of Illinois Press, 1992), 393–96.

7. *Daily National Intelligencer* (Washington, DC), June 10, 1861; *Indianapolis (IN) State Sentinel*, October 31, 1861; *Quincy (MA) Herald*, July 31, 1865; *McKean Democrat* (Smethport, PA), January 9, 1864; *Elk Advocate* (Ridgway, PA), February 6, 1864; *Confederate Union* (Milledgeville, GA), January 6, 1863, *Ashtabula (OH) Weekly Telegraph*, June 11, 1864; *Daily Richmond (VA) Examiner*, September 16, 1861; *Essex Banner* (Haverhill, MA), August 15, 1862.

8. *Southern Recorder* (Milledgeville, GA), January 6, 1863; Allen C. Redwood, "A Boy in Gray," *Scribner's Monthly* 22, no. 5 (September 1881): 644.

9. *St. Paul (MN) Daily Union*, February 5, 1863; *Newbern (NC) Progress*, March 29, 1862; *Boston Semi-Weekly Advertiser*, November 26, 1862; *National Eagle* (Claremont, NH), May 21, 1863.

10. *Daily Richmond (VA) Examiner*, April 2, 1863. Confederate readers also had the opportunity to purchase shares in a privateer (see *Daily Picayune* [New Orleans], May 21, 1861; *Charleston [SC] Mercury*, August 21, 1861).

11. *McKean Democrat* (Smethport, PA), January 9, 1864; *Southern Recorder* (Milledgeville, GA), November 21, 1860; *New York Times*, June 1, 1861; *Worcester (MA) Palladium*, February 10, 1864; *Daily Columbus (GA) Enquirer*, December 20, 1862; *Philadelphia Inquirer*, January 2, 1863; *Petersburg (VA) Express*, September 17, 1861; *North Carolina Daily Times* (New Berne), June 11, 1864.

12. See Michael Thomas Smith, *The Enemy Within: Fears of Corruption in the Civil War North* (Charlottesville: University of Virginia Press, 2011), 15–36; and Gallman, *Defining Duty in the Civil War*, 91–122.

13. *Cadiz (OH) Democratic Sentinel*, February 17, 1864; *New York Herald*, August 15, 1861; *Jasper (IN) Weekly Courier*, January 31, 1863; *Natchitoches (LA) Union*, November 27, 1862; *Yorkville (SC) Enquirer*, November 5, 1862.

14. *Fremont (OH) Journal*, December 19, 1862; *Indianapolis (IN) Daily Journal*, January 16, 1861; *Urbana (OH) Union*, January 28, 1863.

15. *Daily Dispatch* (Richmond, VA), May 13, 1862; *Richmond (VA) Whig*, May 16, 1862.

16. *Daily National Republican* (Washington, DC), May 15, 1863; *Boise News* (Bannock City, ID), October 22, 1864; *Burlington (IA) Daily Hawk-Eye*, November 3, 1861; *Daily Ohio Statesman* (Columbus), November 13, 1863; *New York Herald*, July 30, 1861; *Worcester (MA) Palladium*, May 25, 1864; *Farmer's Cabinet* (Amherst, NH), January 13, 1865.

17. *Detroit Advertiser and Tribune*, January 18, 1864; *Daily Union and American* (Nashville, TN), December 8, 1863; *Sentinel* (Richmond, VA), April 13, 1863.

18. *Daily Intelligencer* (Wheeling, WV), October 29, 1863; *Indianapolis (IN) State Sentinel*, March 19, 1863; *Daily Richmond (VA) Examiner*, April 2, 1863.

19. *Chicago Tribune*, April 4, 1865; *Savanah (GA) Republican*, June 14, 1864; *Bradford Reporter* (Towanda, PA), April 24, 1862.

20. *Memphis (TN) Daily Appeal*, September 20, 1861; *Highland Weekly News* (Hillsboro, OH), December 28, 1865; *Evening Star* (Washington, DC), May 15, 1864.

21. *St. Cloud (MN) Democrat*, January 23, 1862; *Chattanooga (TN) Daily Rebel*, July 1, 1864; *Daily Wabash Express* (Terre Haute, IN), December 31, 1861; *Dallas (TX) Herald*, February 12, 1864; *Dayton (OH) Daily Empire*, May 10, 1864.

22. *Boston Daily Advertiser*, December 25, 1861, and December 11, 1863; *South Danvers Wizard* (Peabody, MA), December 21, 1864; *Detroit Free Press*, November 14, 1863; *North American and United States Gazette* (Philadelphia), December 21, 1861.

23. *Lansing (MI) State Republican*, June 25, 1862; *Bedford (PA) Gazette*, May 29, 1863; *Manchester (VT) Journal*, July 22, 1862.

24. Finances during the war are detailed in McPherson, *Battle Cry of Freedom*, 437–50; and Weigley, *A Great Civil War*, 69–70, 204–10.

25. Ellis P. Oberholtzer, *Jay Cooke: Financier of the Civil War*, vol. 1 (Philadelphia: G. W. Jacobs, 1907), 631.

26. *New Hampshire Statesman* (Concord), November 16, 1864; *Lewistown (PA) Gazette*, August 10, 1864; *Fort Wayne (IN) Daily Gazette*, November 7, 1864; *New York Times*, August 28, 1864; *Philadelphia Inquirer*, March 29, 1864; *Linn County Patriot* (Marion, IA), October 27, 1864.

27. For a discussion on Union war bonds and nationalism, see Lawson, *Patriot Fires*, 40–64. Lawson argues that a "self-interested patriotism" motivated many buyers. They gained the interest of the bond and, more indirectly, aided the Union war effort.

28. *Vermont Watchman and State Journal* (Montpelier), May 27, 1864; *New York Herald*, August 8, 1863; *Fremont (OH) Journal*, April 7, 1865; *Cleveland (OH) Morning Leader*, July 27, 1864; *Union County Star and Lewisburg (PA) Chronicle*, July 28, 1863; *Newark (NJ) Daily Advertiser*, November 8, 1862; *Highland Weekly News* (Hillsboro, OH), March 2, 1865.

29. *Vermont Transcript* (St. Albans), June 16, 1865; *Tioga County Agitator* (Wellsboro, PA), July 12, 1865; *Detroit Free Press*, November 21, 1863; *Worcester (MA) Palladium*, April 12, 1865.

30. *Galveston (TX) Weekly News*, April 2, 1861; *Fayetteville (NC) Observer*, September 12, 1861; *Staunton (VA) Spectator*, November 4, 1862; *Raleigh (NC) Register*, October 9, 1861.

31. *American Citizen* (Canton, MS), August 3, 1861; *Chattanooga (TN) Daily Rebel*, January 31, 1863; *Charleston (SC) Tri-Weekly Courier*, August 13, 1861; *Daily Intelligencer* (Atlanta), March 31, 1864; *Wilmington (NC) Daily Journal*, November 30, 1864; *Shreveport (LA) Semi-Weekly News*, October 10, 1862; *Charleston (SC) Daily News*, November 15, 1865. For the role of public finances and the southern war effort, see Douglas B. Ball, *Financial Failure and Confederate Defeat* (Urbana: University of Illinois Press, 1991).

32. *Sun* (New York), January 3, 1861, and March 28, 1861, *Mountaineer* (Salt Lake City, UT), April 21, 1860; *Daily Missouri Republican* (St. Louis), March 18, 1861; *Hartford (CT) Weekly Times*,

August 23, 1862; *Springfield (MA) Daily Republican,* February 25, 1865; *Bangor (ME) Daily Whig and Courier,* October 29, 1861.

33. *Weekly Perrysburg (OH) Journal,* September 28, 1864; *Haverhill Banner* (Essex, MA), November 25, 1864; *Daily Nebraskan* (Omaha), March 10, 1864; *Norwalk (OH) Reflector,* December 22, 1863; *Daily Arkansas Gazette* (Little Rock), July 14, 1865; *Daily Conservative* (Raleigh, NC), April 7, 1865; *Staunton (VA) Spectator,* July 7, 1863.

34. *Aroostook Pioneer* (Presque Isle, ME), June 6, 1865; *Vermont Semi-Weekly Record* (Brattleboro), September 1, 1865; *New Hampshire Weekly Telegraph* (Nashua), June 25, 1864.

35. *Ellsworth (ME) American,* May 12, 1865; *Daily Conservative* (Raleigh, NC), April 7, 1865. On the blurring between the home front and the battlefield, particularly for northern women, see Judith Ann Giesberg, *Army at Home: Women and the Civil War on the Northern Home Front* (Chapel Hill: University of North Carolina Press, 2009).

36. *Daily National Republican* (Washington, DC), August 13, 1864; *Freeport (IL) Weekly Journal,* May 15, 1861; *Indianapolis (IN) Daily Journal,* October 10, 1861; *Southern Confederacy* (Atlanta), September 28, 1862; *New York Herald,* October 25, 1863.

37. *Baltimore Clipper,* January 6, 1865; *Cleveland (OH) Morning Leader,* April 20, 1865; *Daily National Republican* (Washington, DC), August 9, 1864; *New York Herald,* July 12, 1865.

38. *Richmond (VA) Whig,* September 22, 1863; *Daily Richmond (VA) Examiner,* September 30, 1863. Confederate amputees had a much more difficult time transitioning to daily life than the notices suggested (see Brian Crain Miller, *Empty Sleeves: Amputation in the Civil War South* [Athens: University of Georgia Press, 2015]).

39. *Evening Star* (Washington, DC), May 15, 1862; *Daily National Intelligencer* (Washington, DC), April 30, 1862; *National Republican* (Washington, DC), January 1, 1863; *Allegany County Republican* (Angelica Court House, NY), August 31, 1864; *Winchester (VA) Republican,* March 7, 1862; *Southern Confederacy* (Atlanta), August 4, 1861.

40. *Philadelphia Inquirer,* October 23, 1862; *Daily Richmond (VA) Examiner,* June 1, 1863; *Indianapolis (IN) Daily Journal,* March 17, 1863; *Daily Nashville (TN) Patriot,* October 8, 1863.

41. *Cambridge (MA) Chronicle,* November 15, 1864; *South Danvers Wizard* (Peabody, MA), August 24, 1864; *Daily Missouri Republican* (St. Louis), October 15, 1863.

42. Giesberg, *Army at Home,* 143–60.

43. Drew Gilpin Faust, *This Republic of Suffering: Death and the American Civil War* (New York: Knopf, 2008). See also Mark S. Schantz, *Awaiting the Heavenly Country: The Civil War and America's Culture of Death* (Ithaca, NY: Cornell University Press, 2008).

44. *Sunday Transcript* (Philadelphia), October 12, 1862; *Cotton States* (Gainesville, FL), November 26, 1864; *Arkansas State Gazette* (Little Rock), December 20, 1862; *Daily Clarion* (Jackson, MS), July 19, 1864; *Daily Intelligencer* (Atlanta, GA), March 31, 1864; *San Antonio (TX) Herald,* November 9, 1861; *Daily Richmond (VA) Examiner,* May 7, 1864.

45. *Daily Sun* (Columbus, GA), April 8, 1864; *Confederate News* (Jefferson, TX), December 2, 1864.

46. *Spirit of the Age* (Raleigh, NC), August 13, 1862.

47. *Weekly (Raleigh, NC) Standard,* October 15, 1862; *Rockingham Register* (Harrisonburg, VA), March 21, 1865.

48. *Evansville (IN) Daily Journal,* May 11, 1863; *Spirit of the Age* (Raleigh, NC), July 20, 1863; *Semiweekly Standard* (Raleigh, NC), April 10, 1863; *St. Cloud (MN) Democrat,* May 25, 1865.

49. On courtship, see Karen Lystra, *Searching the Heart: Women, Men, and Romantic Love in Nineteenth-Century America* (New York: Oxford University Press, 1989); and Ellen K. Rothman, *Hands and Hearts: A History of Courtship in America* (New York: Basic, 1984). In his study of elite southern planters, Stephen Berry argues that men needed romantic love as a private affirmation of their public ambition, perhaps another motivation for running a personal notice (see his *All That Makes a Man: Love and Ambition in the Civil War South* [New York: Oxford University Press, 2003]).

50. *Gallipolis (OH) Journal,* May 21, 1863; *M'arthur Democrat* (McArthur, OH), November 19, 1863; *Richmond (VA) Examiner,* November 2, 1863, and March 18, 1862; *Chicago Tribune,* August 12, 1864. No John Shuch is listed on the roster of Ohio regiments, so perhaps he advertised under an assumed name. The war, however, found its way into the wedding announcement for Jason Garrison. The Confederate captain for "three long years has . . . been fighting the enemies of liberty and against the Union." During that time, he had "never wavered nor shrunk at the approach of the foe." Now, finally, he has "at last been conquered and absolutely gone into 'the Union.'" His comrades would forgive him, however, when they learned that the "'Union' he has formed, is sanctioned by, at least, one of the fair daughters" of the South. The newly married husband and wife might always have "a Union of Hearts, a Union of Hands" (see *Henderson [TX] Times,* November 5, 1864).

51. *Detroit Free Press,* November 10, 1863; *Fitchburg (MA) Sentinel,* June 5, 1863; *Boston Post,* May 7, 1863; *New York Herald,* August 25, 1863; *Corrector* (Sag-Harbor, NY), February 13, 1864. For the discrepancy sometimes between the described and actual physical characteristics of those individuals placing the notices, see "Matrimonial Advertising," *Vanity Fair* 4, no. 100 (November 16, 1861): 228.

52. "Old Soldier" letter, in *Louisville (KY) Daily Journal,* March 20, 1863.

53. "A Buckeye Girl to 'Old Soldier,'" in *Louisville (KY) Daily Journal,* April 1, 1863.

54. "Matrimonial," *Vanity Fair* 2 (November 24, 1860): 257; "Editor's Easy Chair," *Harper's Magazine* 27, no. 159 (August 1863): 422–23. E. W. Ayers and W. H. Wade, the editors of the *Southern Illustrated News,* refused to accept matrimonial notices on the argument that they were a "Yankee trick." Such announcements allowed unscrupulous newspapermen to earn advertising revenue and unprincipled readers to experience a voyeuristic thrill. They hoped that the "people of the South" would never stoop to such lows and, when pressed, stood by their word. In 1863, they refused to accept the money sent by a Confederate soldier, lecturing, "We accept no such advertisements" (see "Notices to Correspondents," *Southern Illustrated News,* May 30, 1863; and "To Correspondents," *Southern Illustrated News,* June 13, 1863).

55. The shifting distinctions between the public and private lives of northern women is analyzed in Nina Silber, *Daughters of the Union: Northern Women Fight the Civil War* (Cambridge: Harvard University Press, 2005), 87–122.

56. *Daily National Republican* (Washington, DC), June 12, 1863; *Civilian and Telegraph* (Cumberland, MD), December 21, 1865; *Plymouth (IN) Weekly Democrat,* July 24, 1862; *Rutland*

(VT) Weekly Herald, October 2, 1862. On the sexual teachings of the day, see Helen Lefkowitz Horowitz, *Attitudes toward Sex in Antebellum America: A Brief History with Documents* (New York: Palgrave Macmillan, 2006); Ronald G. Walters, ed., *Primers for Prudery: Sexual Advice to Victorian America*, updated ed. (Baltimore: Johns Hopkins University Press, 2000). See also Joseph F. Kett, *Rites of Passage: Adolescence in America, 1790 to the Present* (New York: Basic, 1977), 133–35.

57. *Mineral Point (WI) Weekly Tribune*, February 25, 1863; *Allegany County Republican* (Angelica Court House, NY), April 15, 1863; *Rockland County Journal* (Nyack, NY), September 9, 1865; *Democratic Watchman* (Bellefonte, PA), December 8, 1865; *Willimantic (CT) Journal*, December 25, 1863; *Knoxville (TN) Register*, September 27, 1860.

58. *Wood County Reporter* (Grand Rapids, WI), July 21, 1864. On evolving concepts of honor during the Civil War and the preservation of the nation, see Lorien Foote, *The Gentlemen and the Roughs: Manhood, Honor, and Violence in the Union Army* (New York: New York University Press, 2010), 171–80. Other works that analyze concepts of manhood during the Civil War and the mid-nineteenth century include Mark H. Dunkelman, *Brothers One and All: Esprit de Corps in a Civil War Regiment* (Baton Rouge: Louisiana State University Press, 2004); Amy S. Greenberg, *Manifest Manhood and the Antebellum American Empire* (New York: Cambridge University Press, 2005); Craig Thompson Friend and Lorri Glover, eds., *Southern Manhood: Perspectives on Masculinity in the Old South* (Athens: University of Georgia Press, 2004); and Mark C. Carnes and Clyde Griffin, eds., *Meanings for Manhood: Constructions of Masculinity in Victorian America* (Chicago: University of Chicago Press, 1990).

59. *Lewistown (PA) Gazette*, November 23, 1864; *Ohio Democrat* (Canal Dover), March 27, 1863; *Chicago Daily Tribune*, July 16, 1864.

60. "The Speaker of the New York Assembly upon Morals and Morality," *New York Herald*, January 15, 1862; "The Wrong Mode," *Union County Star and Chronicle* (Lewisburg, PA), January 29, 1864; "Editor's Easy Chair," *Harper's Magazine* 28, no. 168 (May 1864): 853–54. An excellent discussion is Janet Farrell Brodie, *Contraception and Abortion in Nineteenth-Century America* (Ithaca, NY: Cornell University Press, 1994). The influence of military service on Anthony Comstock and his crusade against contraceptive devices, including those in the advertisements, is detailed in Judith Giesberg, *Sex and the Civil War: Soldiers, Pornography, and the Making of American Morality* (Chapel Hill: University of North Carolina Press, 2017).

61. *Boston Post*, August 13, 1863; *Cleveland (OH) Daily Herald*, April 21, 1862; *Daily National Republican* (Washington, DC), February 6, 1863.

62. *Dayton (OH) Daily Empire*, March 2, 1865; *Marshall County (IN) Republican*, December 14, 1865. The "feminized war" is analyzed in Fahs, *The Imagined Civil War*, 120–49.

63. Linderman, *Embattled Courage*, 1.

EPILOGUE: MEMORIES

1. *Daily Picayune* (New Orleans), August 25, 1865.

2. *Farmer's Cabinet* (Amherst, NH), March 26, 1868, and June 11, 1868; *Daily National Intelligencer* (Washington, DC), February 5, 1869, and March 15, 1869.

3. *Ripley (OH) Bee*, January 29, 1868; *Farmer's Cabinet* (Amherst, NH), October 20, 1870; *Milwaukee (WI) Daily Sentinel*, January 4, 1868.

4. *Spirit of Democracy* (Woodsfield, OH), January 25, 1870; *Western Reserve Chronicle* (Warren, OH), November 17, 1869.

5. *Chicago Tribune*, May 28, 1866; *Daily Green Mountain Freeman* (Montpelier, VT), November 7, 1866; *Belmont Chronicle* (St. Clairsville, OH), November 25, 1875.

6. *New Orleans Tribune*, July 4, 1867; *Loyal Georgian* (Augusta), September 15, 1866; *Elevator* (San Francisco), December 25, 1868.

7. *Elevator* (San Francisco), January 24, 1868.

8. See Blight's *Race and Reunion*, as well as his *Beyond the Battlefield: Race, Memory, and the American Civil War* (Amherst: University of Massachusetts Press, 2002). For differing perspectives on the role of emancipation in the memory of the war, see Janney, *Remembering the Civil War*, 197–231. An analysis of the "dominant narratives" in the memory of the war through the modern day is Robert J. Cook, *Civil War Memories: Contesting the Past in the United States since 1865* (Baltimore: Johns Hopkins University Press, 2017).

9. *Chicago Tribune*, May 19, 1868; "Gen. McClernand on Gen. Grant," *Idaho Semi-Weekly World* (Idaho City), March 4, 1868; "General Adam Badeau," *Evening Telegraph* (Philadelphia), October 21, 1869.

10. *Daily Ohio Statesman* (Columbus), February 26, 1868; "The Parent of the President: An Interview with Jesse Grant," *Charleston (SC) Daily News*, September 7, 1869; *Public Ledger* (Memphis, TN), February 26, 1868.

11. *Daily National Intelligencer* (Washington, DC), March 4, 1867; *Cleveland (OH) Gazette*, June 27, 1885.

12. *Daily Richmond (VA) Examiner*, August 29, 1866; *Augusta (GA) Chronicle*, October 28, 1866, and September 26, 1874.

13. *Columbus (GA) Enquirer*, September 27, 1866.

14. *Memphis (TN) Daily Avalanche*, June 3, 1866; *Augusta (GA) Chronicle*, November 7, 1875; *Mobile (AL) Advertiser and Register*, February 14, 1866; *Richmond (VA) Whig*, November 28, 1871; *Daily Columbus (GA) Enquirer*, August 29, 1868.

15. Turner, *The Shocking History of Advertising*, 135–39; Wood, *The Story of Advertising*, 180–81.

16. *Public Ledger* (Memphis, TN), October 25, 1866; *Columbia (SC) Phoenix*, February 2, 1873; *Weekly Democratic Statesman* (Austin, TX), August 14, 1873; *Daily Picayune* (New Orleans), September 28, 1869.

17. *Daily Picayune* (New Orleans), August 3, 1877; *New Orleans Times*, December 16, 1877. The distinction between reunion and reconciliation is made in Janney, *Remembering the Civil War*.

BIBLIOGRAPHY

NEWSPAPERS

Alabama

Daily Selma Reporter
Greenville Weekly Reporter
Jacksonville Republican
Mobile Advertiser and Register
Mobile Daily Tribune
Mobile Evening News
Mobile Evening Telegraph
Montgomery Daily Mail
Montgomery Daily Post
Montgomery Sentinel
North Alabamian (Tuscumbia)
Weekly Flag and Advertiser (Montgomery)

Arizona Territory

Arizona Miner (Fort Whipple)
Mesilla Times

Arkansas

Arkansas State Gazette (Little Rock)
Daily Arkansas Gazette (Little Rock)
States-Right Democrat (Helena)
True Southron (Pine Bluff)

California

Daily Alta California (San Francisco)
Daily Evening Bulletin (San Francisco)
Elevator (San Francisco)
Marin County Journal (San Rafael)
Mendocino Herald (Ukiah City)
Mountain Democrat (Placerville)
Pacific Appeal (San Francisco)
Red Bluff Beacon
Sacramento Daily Union

Colorado Territory

Colorado Republican and Rocky Mountain Herald (Denver)
Daily Commonwealth (Denver)
Daily Miners' Register (Central City)
Daily Mining Journal (Black Hawk)
Daily Rocky Mountain News (Denver)
Tri-Weekly Miner's Register (Central City)
Western Mountaineer (Golden)

Connecticut

Collinsville Star (Canton)
Connecticut Courant (Hartford)
Connecticut Press (Hartford)
Connecticut War Record (New Haven)
Daily Advertiser and Farmer (Bridgeport)
East Haddam Journal
Elm Leaf (East Hartford)
Hartford Daily Post
Hartford Weekly Times

Housatonic Republican (Canaan)
Meriden Recorder (West Meriden)
New Haven Daily Palladium
Tolland County Herald (Rockville)
True Citizen (New Britain)
Willimantic Journal

Dakota Territory
Frontier Scout (Fort Union)
Union and Dakotian (Yankton)

Delaware
Delaware State Journal and Statesman (Wilmington)
Georgetown Union
Peninsular News and Advertiser (Milford)

District of Columbia
Daily National Intelligencer
Daily National Republican
Evening Star
National Era
National Republican

Florida
Cotton States (Gainesville)
East Floridian (Fernandina)
Family Friend (Monticello)
Florida Dispatch (Newnansville)
Florida Home Companion (Ocala)
Florida Peninsular (Tampa)
Florida Sentinel (Tallahassee)
Floridian and Journal (Tallahassee)
Jacksonville Herald
St. Augustine Examiner
Telegraph (Cedar Key)

Georgia
Albany Patriot
Augusta Chronicle
Columbus Enquirer
Confederate Union (Milledgeville)
Countryman (Turnwold)
Daily Chronicle and Sentinel (Augusta)
Daily Intelligencer (Atlanta)
Daily Morning News (Savannah)
Daily News and Herald (Savannah)
Daily Sun (Columbus)
Federal Union (Milledgeville)
Gate-City Guardian (Atlanta)
Loyal Georgian (Augusta)
Macon Telegraph
Savannah Republican
Southern Banner (Athens)
Southern Confederacy (Atlanta)
Southern Enterprise (Thomasville)
Southern Recorder (Milledgeville)
Southern Watchman (Athens)

Idaho Territory
Boise News (Bannock City)
Golden Age (Lewiston)
Idaho Semi-Weekly World (Idaho City)
North Idaho Radiator (Lewiston)

Illinois
Alton Telegraph
Centralia Sentinel
Chicago Evening Journal
Chicago Times
Chicago Tribune
Decatur Weekly Gazette
Evening Argus (Rock Island)
Freeport Weekly Journal

Illinois Farmer (Springfield)
Illinois State Chronicle (Decatur)
Louisville Republican
Madison County Courier (Edwardsville)
Ottawa Free Trader
Quincy Daily Whig and Republican
Quincy Herald
Republican and Gazette (Sterling)
Unconditional Unionist (Mt. Vernon)

Indiana

Aurora Commercial
Bedford Independent
Cambridge City Journal
Clay County Democrat (Bowling Green)
Connersville Weekly Times
Daily Wabash Express (Terre Haute)
Decatur Eagle
Evansville Daily Journal
Evansville Weekly Gazette
Fort Wayne Daily Gazette
Fort Wayne Weekly Sentinel
Franklin Democrat (Brookville)
Goshen Democrat
Indiana American (Brookville)
Indiana Reveille (Vevay)
Indiana State Guard (Indianapolis)
Indiana True Republican (Centreville)
Indianapolis Daily Journal
Indianapolis State Sentinel
Jasper Weekly Courier
Liberty Herald
Marshall County Republican (Plymouth)
National Defender (Brookville)
New Albany Daily Ledger
New Albany Daily Tribune
Plymouth Weekly Democrat
Rochester Chronicle
Rochester Sentinel
Rockport Democrat
Salem Democrat
Salem Union Advocate
Wabash Plain Dealer
White River Gazette (Worthington)

Iowa

Burlington Hawk-Eye
Cedar Falls Gazette
Cedar Valley Times (Cedar Rapids)
Daily Iowa State Register (Des Moines)
Davenport Daily Times
Dubuque Daily Times
Dubuque Democratic Herald
Glenwood Opinion
Linn County Patriot (Marion)
Linn County Register (Marion)
Marion Herald
Monticello Express
Waterloo Courier

Kansas

Big Blue Union (Marysville)
Daily Times (Leavenworth)
Emporia News
Freedom's Champion (Atchison)
Independent (Oskaloosa)
Kansas State Journal (Lawrence)
Leavenworth Daily Conservative
Smoky Hill and Republican Union (Junction City)
Western Kansas Express (Manhattan City)
White Cloud Kansas Chief

Kentucky
Covington Journal
Daily Commonwealth (Frankfort)
Daily Confederate News (Columbus)
Lexington Observer and Reporter
Louisville Courier
Louisville Daily Express
Louisville Daily Journal
Louisville Democrat
National Union (Winchester)
Sandy Valley Advocate (Catlettsburg)
Weekly Glasgow Free-Press
Weekly Kentucky Tribune (Danville)
Western Citizen (Paris)

Louisiana
Bayou Sara Ledger
Black Republican (New Orleans)
Carrollton Sun
Confederate Sates (New Iberia)
Constitutional (Alexandria)
Daily Delta (New Orleans)
Daily Gazette and Comet (Baton Rouge)
Daily Picayune (New Orleans)
Daily True Delta (New Orleans)
Gazette and Sentinel (Plaquemine)
Greensburg Imperial
Iberville Pioneer
Independent (Harrisonburg)
Louisiana Democrat (Alexandria)
Natchitoches Union
New Orleans Daily Crescent
New Orleans Times
New Orleans Tribune
New Orleans Weekly Commercial Bulletin
Opelousas Patriot
Shreveport News
South-Western (Shreveport)
Southern Sentinel (Winnfield)
Sugar Planter (West Baton Rouge)
Tensas Gazette (St. Joseph)

Maine
Aroostook Pioneer (Presque Isle)
Bangor Daily Whig and Courier
Ellsworth American
Lewiston Evening Journal
Portland Advertiser

Maryland
Alleganian (Cumberland)
American and Commercial Advertiser (Baltimore)
Baltimore Clipper
Baltimore Daily Commercial
Civilian and Telegraph (Cumberland)
Daily Exchange (Baltimore)
Democratic Advocate (Westminster)
Easton Gazette
Hagerstown Mail
Herald and Torch Light (Hagerstown)
Montgomery County Sentinel (Rockville)
South (Baltimore)
St. Mary's Beacon (Leonard Town)

Massachusetts
Barnstable Patriot
Barre Gazette
Berkshire County Eagle (Pittsfield)
Boston Daily Advertiser
Boston Daily Journal
Boston Evening Transcript
Boston Herald
Boston Investigator
Boston Post
Cambridge Chronicle
Charlestown Advertiser (Boston)
Essex Banner (Haverhill)

Fitchburg Sentinel
Gloucester Telegraph and News
Liberator (Boston)
Lowell Daily Citizen and News
Lynn Bay State
Norfolk County Journal (Roxbury)
Pine and Palm (Boston)
Quincy Herald
Quincy Patriot
Salem Gazette
South Danvers Wizard (Peabody)
Springfield Daily Republican
Worcester Palladium

Michigan
Ann Arbor Journal
Cass County Republican (Dowagiac)
Democratic Expounder (Marshall)
Detroit Advertiser and Tribune
Detroit Free Press
Grand Haven News
Grand Traverse Herald (Traverse City)
Hillsdale Standard
Marshall Statesman
Monroe Democrat
Owosso Press

Minnesota
Goodhue Volunteer (Red Wing)
Mankato Weekly Independent
Pioneer and Democrat (St. Paul)
Red Wing Sentinel
St. Cloud Democrat
St. Paul Daily Union
Winona Daily Republican

Mississippi
American Citizen (Canton)
Corinth Chanticleer
Daily Clarion (Jackson)
Daily Southern Crisis (Jackson)
Evening Gazette (Natchez)
Hinds County Gazette (Raymond)
Jackson Daily News
Macon Beacon
Mississippian (Jackson)
Natchez Daily Courier
Natchez Free Trader
Oxford Intelligencer
Southern Reveille (Port Gibson)
Vicksburg Whig
Yazoo City Whig and Political Register
Yazoo Democrat (Yazoo City)

Missouri
Cape Girardeau Weekly Argus
Daily Missouri Republican (St. Louis)
Glasgow Weekly Times
Liberty Weekly Tribune
St. Louis Missouri Democrat
Rolla Express
Weekly Border Star (Westport)

Montana Territory
Montana Post (Virginia City)

Nebraska Territory
Daily Nebraskan (Omaha)
Daily Telegraph (Omaha)
Nebraska Advertiser (Brownville)
Nebraska City Herald

Nevada
Daily Reese River Reveille (Austin)

New Hampshire
Dover Gazette
Manchester Daily Union

National Eagle (Claremont)
New Hampshire Sentinel (Keene)
New Hampshire Statesman (Concord)
New Hampshire Weekly Telegraph (Nashua)

New Jersey
Atlantic Democrat and Cape May County Register (Absecon)
New-Jersey Mirror and Burlington County Advertiser (Mount Holly)
Newark Daily Advertiser
Newark Daily Journal
South-Jersey Republican (Hammonton)

New Mexico Territory
Santa Fe Republican

New York
Albany Journal
Allegany County Republican (Angelica Court House)
Banner of Liberty (Middletown)
Brooklyn Daily Eagle
Buffalo Morning Express
Central City Daily Courier (Syracuse)
Courier and Freeman (Potsdam)
Daily Corrector (Sag-Harbor)
Geneva Gazette
Long-Islander (Huntington)
Monroe Weekly Democrat (Rochester)
Moore's Rural New-Yorker (Rochester)
National Anti-Slavery Standard (New York)
National Principia (New York)
New York Caucasian
New-York Commercial Advertiser
New York Evening Express
New York Herald
New York Times
New-York Tribune
New York World
Rochester Daily Democrat
Rochester Evening Express
Rockland County Journal (Nyack)
Rockland County Messenger (Haverstraw)
Soldier's Aid (Rochester)
Sun (New York)
Syracuse Daily Courier and Union
Weekly Anglo-African (New York)

North Carolina
Carolina Watchman (Salisbury)
Daily Bulletin (Charlotte)
Daily Confederate (Raleigh)
Daily Conservative (Raleigh)
Daily Progress (Raleigh)
Daily Rough Notes (Goldsboro)
Fayetteville Observer
Hillsborough Recorder
Iredell Express (Statesville)
Newbern Progress
North Carolina Daily Times (New Berne)
North Carolina Presbyterian (Fayetteville)
North Carolina Whig (Charlotte)
Raleigh Register
Southerner (Tarboro)
Spirit of the Age (Raleigh)
Weekly Standard (Raleigh)
Western Democrat (Charlotte)
Wilmington Journal

Ohio
Anti-Slavery Bugle (New Lisbon)
Ashtabula Weekly Telegraph
Athens Messenger

Belmont Chronicle (St. Clairsville)
Cadiz Democratic Sentinel
Carroll Free Press (Carrollton)
Cincinnati Daily Press
Cleveland Daily Herald
Cleveland Morning Leader
Daily Ohio State Journal (Columbus)
Daily Ohio Statesman (Columbus)
Dayton Daily Empire
Delaware Gazette
Democratic Press (Eaton)
Fremont Journal
Gallipolis Journal
Hancock Jeffersonian (Findlay)
Highland Weekly News (Hillsboro)
Holmes County Farmer (Millersburg)
Holmes County Republican (Millersburg)
Jeffersonian Democrat (Chardon)
M'arthur Democrat (McArthur)
Newark Advocate
Norwalk Reflector
Penny Press (Cincinnati)
Pomeroy Weekly Telegraph
Portsmouth Times
Ripley Bee
Scioto Gazette (Chillicothe)
Spirit of Democracy (Woodsfield)
Stark County Democrat (Canton)
Tiffin Weekly Tribune
Urbana Union
Weekly Lancaster Gazette
Western Reserve Chronicle (Warren)
Xenia Sentinel

Oregon Territory
Morning Oregonian (Portland)
Oregon Sentinel (Jacksonville)
State Republican (Eugene City)

Pennsylvania
Adams Sentinel (Gettysburg)
Alleghenian (Ebensburg)
Altoona Tribune
American Citizen (Butler)
Beaver Weekly Argus
Bedford Gazette
Bradford Reporter (Towanda)
Central Press (Bellefonte)
Christian Recorder (Philadelphia)
Citizen (Smethport)
Clearfield Republican
Columbia Democrat and Bloomsburg General Advertiser (Bloomsburg)
Columbia Spy
Daily Evening Bulletin (Philadelphia)
Daily Morning Post (Pittsburgh)
Daily Patriot and Union (Harrisburg)
Democrat and Sentinel (Ebensburg)
Democratic Watchman (Bellefonte)
Elk Advocate (Ridgway)
Erie Observer
Evening Telegraph (Philadelphia)
Franklin Repository (Chambersburg)
Huntingdon Globe
Indiana Messenger
Independent Republican (Montrose)
Jeffersonian (Stroudsburg)
Juniata Sentinel (Mifflintown)
Lancaster Daily Intelligencer
Lebanon Advertiser
Lewistown Gazette
McKean Democrat (Smethport)
North American and United States Gazette (Philadelphia)
North Branch Democrat (Tunkhannock)
Pennsylvania Daily Telegraph (Harrisburg)

Philadelphia Inquirer
Pittsburgh Daily Gazette and Advertiser
Press (Philadelphia)
Reading Gazette and Democrat
Republican Compiler (Gettysburg)
Sunbury American
Sunday Transcript (Philadelphia)
Tioga County Agitator (Wellsboro)
Union County Star and Lewisburg Chronicle (Lewisburg)
Valley Spirit (Chambersburg)
Waynesburg Messenger
Weekly Mariettian (Marietta)

Rhode Island

Newport Daily News
Newport Mercury
Providence Daily Post
Providence Evening Press
Woonsocket Patriot and Rhode-Island State Register

South Carolina

Anderson Intelligencer
Camden Confederate
Camden Weekly Journal
Charleston Advocate
Charleston Courier
Charleston Daily News
Charleston Mercury
Columbia Phoenix
Daily South Carolinian (Columbia)
Daily Southern Guardian (Columbia)
Darlington Southerner
Edgefield Advertiser
Independent Press (Abbeville)
Journal and Confederate (Camden)
Keowee Courier (Pickens Court House)
South Carolina Leader (Charleston)
Tri-Weekly Herald (Newberry)
Yorkville Enquirer

Tennessee

Athens Post
Chattanooga Daily Gazette
Chattanooga Daily Rebel
Clarksville Chronicle
Daily East Tennessean (Knoxville)
Daily Nashville Patriot
Daily Southern Chronicle (Knoxville)
Daily Union and American (Nashville)
Fayetteville Observer
Gazette and Advertiser (Chattanooga)
Home Journal (Winchester)
Knoxville Register
Knoxville Tri-Weekly Whig
Memphis Daily Appeal
Memphis Daily Avalanche
Memphis Morning Enquirer
Public Ledger (Memphis)
Republican Banner (Nashville)

Texas

Beaumont Banner
Belton Democrat
Clarksville Standard
Colorado Citizen (Columbus)
Confederate News (Jefferson)
Daily Ledger and Texan (San Antonio)
Dallas Herald
Democrat and Planter (Columbia)
Galveston Daily Civilian
Galveston News
Goliad Messenger
Henderson Times
Houston Telegraph

Matagorda Gazette
Navarro Express (Corsicana)
San Antonio Herald
San Antonio Ledger and Texan
Southern Intelligencer (Austin)
State Gazette (Austin)
Texas Almanac (Austin)
Tri-Weekly Alamo Express
True Issue (La Grange)
Tyler Reporter
Victoria Advocate

Utah Territory
Daily Union Vedette (Camp Douglas)
Deseret News (Salt Lake City)
Mountaineer (Salt Lake City)

Vermont
Burlington Free Press
Caledonian (St. Johnsbury)
Christian Repository (Montpelier)
Daily Green Mountain Freeman (Montpelier)
Lamoille Newsdealer (Hyde Park)
Middlebury Register
Vermont Journal (Windsor)
Vermont Patriot (Montpelier)
Vermont Phoenix (Brattleboro)
Vermont Semi-Weekly Record (Brattleboro)
Vermont Transcript (St. Albans)
Vermont Watchman and State Journal (Montpelier)

Virginia
Abingdon Virginian
Alexandria Gazette
Daily Dispatch (Richmond)
Daily News (Petersburg)
Daily Register (Petersburg)
Daily Republican (Lynchburg)
Daily Richmond Enquirer
Daily Richmond Examiner
Daily Virginia Chronicle (Alexandria)
Evening Virginia Sentinel (Alexandria)
Farmville Journal
Grant's Petersburg Progress
Local News (Alexandria)
Lynchburg Virginian
Norfolk Examiner
Norfolk Post
Petersburg Express
Richmond Times
Richmond Whig
Rockingham Register (Harrisonburg)
Sentinel (Richmond)
Staunton Spectator
Staunton Vindicator
Winchester Gazette
Winchester Republican
Winchester Virginian

Washington Territory
Pioneer Democrat (Olympia)
Seattle Gazette
Washington Gazette (Seattle)
Washington Standard (Olympia)
Washington Statesman (Walla Walla)

West Virginia
Daily Intelligencer (Wheeling)

PUBLISHED PRIMARY SOURCES

Abbott, John S. C. *The History of the Civil War in America.* 2 vols. New York: Henry Bill, 1862–64.

———. *South and North, Or, Impressions Received during a Trip to Cuba and the South.* New York: Abbey and Abbot, 1860.

Adams, Francis Colburn. *The Story of a Trooper: With Much of Interest Concerning the Campaign on the Peninsula, Not Before Written.* New York: Dick and Fitzgerald, 1865.

"Advertisement Extraordinary." *Vanity Fair* 5 (June 28, 1862): 309.

"Advertising Nuisances." *Round Table* 2, no. 17 (December 30, 1865): 273.

Armstrong, Halleck. *Letters from a Pennsylvania Chaplain at the Siege of Petersburg, 1865.* Edited by Mary M. Bronson Armstrong. N.p., 1961.

"Atonement." *Southern Literary Messenger* 38, no. 2 (February 1864): 128.

Bacon, Georgeanna Muirson Woolsey, and Eliza Woolsey Howland, eds. *Letters of a Family during the War for the Union, 1861–1865.* Vol. 1. New Haven, CT: Tuttle, Morehouse and Taylor, 1899.

Belcher, James J. "Typographical Errors." *Harper's New Monthly Magazine* 32, no. 188 (January 1866): 228–32.

Belcher, Joseph J. "Newspaper Advertisements." *Harper's New Monthly Magazine* 33, no. 198 (November 1866): 781–84.

"Bonaparte, Cromwell, and Washington." *De Bow's Review* 28, no. 2 (August 1860): 139–54.

"Books and Authors." *Appleton's Journal* 15, no. 367 (April 1, 1876): 440–42.

Bouton, John Bell. *Round the Block: An American Novel.* New York: D. Appleton and Co., 1864.

Brooks, Noah. "Lincoln." *Scribner's Monthly* 15, no. 6 (April 1887): 884–86.

Burnett, Alfred. *Incidents of the War: Humorous, Pathetic, and Descriptive.* Cincinnati, OH: Ricky and Carroll, 1863.

"Confederate Women and the War." *Southern Literary Messenger* 38, no. 2 (February 1864): 127.

Connolly, James A. *Three Years in the Army of the Cumberland: The Letters and Diary of Major James A. Connolly.* Edited by Paul Angle. Bloomington: Indiana University Press, 1996.

Conyngham, David P. *The Irish Brigades and Its Campaigns.* Edited by Lawrence Frederick Kohl. New York: Fordham University Press, 2002.

Cranch, C. P. "An Old Newspaper." *Galaxy* 6, no. 3 (September 1868): 411–16.

"Critical Notices." *Dial: A Monthly Magazine for Literature, Philosophy and Religion* 1, no. 12 (December 1860): 774–78.

"Critical Notices: Edward McPherson's Political History of the Rebellion." *North American Review* 100, no. 206 (January 1865): 241–42.

Day, Samuel Phillips. *Down South; or, An Englishman's Experience at the Seat of the American War.* Vol. 2. London: Hurst and Blackett, 1862.

Dodge, David. "Domestic Economy in the Confederacy." *Atlantic Monthly* 58, no. 346 (August 1886): 229–43.

"Editor's Drawer." *Harper's New Monthly Magazine* 28, no. 165 (February 1864): 421–31.

"Editor's Easy Chair." *Harper's New Monthly Magazine* 27, no. 159 (August 1863): 419–29.

"Editor's Easy Chair." *Harper's New Monthly Magazine* 28, no. 168 (May 1864): 850–63.

"Editor's Table." *Southern Literary Messenger* 31, no. 5 (November 1, 1860): 390–96.

"The First Century of the Republic." *Harper's New Monthly Magazine* 50, no. 297 (February 1875): 371–92.

Fitzhugh, George. "The Domain of Fashion." *De Bow's Review* 29, no. 6 (December 1860): 695–702.

Frelinghuysen, Frederick T. *Obsequies of Abraham Lincoln, in Newark, N.J., April 19, 1865.* Newark, NJ: Daily Advertiser, 1865.

Gardner, Samuel Jackson. "Style." In *Autumn Leaves.* New York: Hurd and Houghton, 1865.

Greeley, Horace. *Aunt Sally, Come Up! or, The Nigger Sale.* London: Ward and Lock, 1859.

———. *The American Conflict: A History of the Great Rebellion in the United States of America, 1860–64.* 2 vols. Hartford, CT: O. D. Case, 1864.

———. *Recollections of a Busy Life: Including Reminiscences of American Politics and Politicians.* New York: J. B. Ford, 1868.

Haco, Dion. *J. Wilkes Booth, The Assassinator of President Lincoln.* New York: T. R. Dawley, 1865.

Hale, Edward Everett. "The Man without a Country." *Atlantic Monthly* 12, no. 73 (December 1863): 665–80.

"Hannibal, a Nigger, Parts I–IV." *Southern Literary Messenger* 30, no. 6 (June 1860): 410–20.

Higginson, Thomas Wentworth. "Cheerful Yesterdays." *Atlantic Monthly* 79, no. 476 (June 1897): 780–91.

Holmes, Oliver Wendell, Sr. "Bread and Newspapers." *Atlantic Monthly* 8 (September 1861): 346–52.

———. "Doings of the Sunbeam." *Atlantic Monthly* 12, no. 69 (July 1863): 1–16.

Hopley, Catherine Cooper. *Life in the South: From the Commencement of the War.* Vol 1. London: Chapman and Hall, 1863.

Hosmer, James Kendall. *The Color-Guard: Being a Corporal's Notes of Military Service in the Nineteenth Army Corps.* Boston: Walker, Wise, 1864.

Howe, Mary A. *The Rival Volunteers; Or, The Black Plume Rifles.* New York: John Bradburn, 1864.

Humbug: A Look at Some Popular Impositions. New York: S. F. French, 1859.

Hutchinson, W. S. "In the Shadow of a Great Tragedy." *Overland Monthly* 13, no. 74 (February 1889): 123–33.

"Information Wanted." *Vanity Fair* 5 (May 17, 1862): 243.

Jacobs, Harriet A. *Incidents in the Life of a Slave Girl.* Boston: Published for the author, 1861.

Jones, John Beauchamp. *A Rebel War Clerk's Diary at the Confederate States Capital.* Vol. 2. Philadelphia: J. B. Lippincott, 1866.

"Journal of the War." *De Bow's Review* 2, no. 5 (November 1866): 537–57.

Kennedy, Joseph C. G. *Preliminary Report on the Eighth Census, 1860.* Washington, DC: Government Printing Office, 1862.

Kenny, Daniel J. *The American Newspaper Directory and Record of the Press: Containing an Accurate List of All the Newspapers, Magazines, Reviews, Periodicals, . . .* New York: Watson and Co., 1861.

LeGrand, Julia. *The Journal of Julia LeGrand, New Orleans 1861–1863.* Edited by Kate Mason Rowland. Richmond, VA: Everett Waddey, 1911.

"Letter from a Country Editor." *Vanity Fair* 5 (May 24, 1862): 253–54.

Life and Letters of Wilder Dwight: Lieut.-Col. Second Mass. Inf. Vols. Edited by Elizabeth Amelia Dwight. Boston: Ticknor and Fields, 1868.

"Literary Notices: Popular Edition. Results of Emancipation. By Augustin Cochin." *Continental Monthly* 6, no. 2 (August 1864): 232–33.

"Matrimonial." *Vanity Fair* 2 (November 24, 1860): 257.

"Matrimonial Advertising." *Vanity Fair* 4, no. 100 (November 16, 1861): 228.

Mearns, David C., ed. *The Lincoln Papers.* Vol. 1. Garden City, NY: Doubleday, 1948.

Miller, Alonzo. *Diaries and Letters, 1864–1865.* Prescott, WI: n.p., 1958.

"Million Dollars for Assassination." In *The Assassination of President Lincoln and the Trial of the Conspirators*, edited by Benn Pitman. Cincinnati, OH: Moore, Wilstach and Baldwin, 1865.

Mitchell, David W. *Ten Years in the United States: Being an Englishman's View of Men and Things in the North and South.* London: Smith, Elder and Co., 1862.

"The Molly O'Malley Papers." *Continental Monthly: Devoted to Literature and National Policy* 2, no. 2 (August 1862): 202–5.

Moulton, Louise Chandler. "Out of Nazareth." *Harper's New Monthly Magazine* 28, no. 164 (January 1864): 202–13.

Mount, Joseph. "Recollections of a Deaf and Dumb Teacher." *Ladies' Repository: A*

Monthly Periodical, Devoted to Literature, Arts, and Religion 21, no. 8 (August 1861): 457–59.

"The Napoleon of Advertising." *Cyclopaedia of Commercial and Business Anecdotes.* Vol. 1. Edited by Richard Miller Devens. New York: Appleton, 1864.

Newell, Robert Henry. *The Orpheus C. Kerr Papers.* 2 vols. New York: Carleton, 1863–65.

"Newspaper Advertising versus Advertising Schemes." *Advertisers Gazette: A Monthly Journal Devoted to the Interests of Advertisers and Newspaper Publishers* 7, no. 1 (April 1873): 47.

"Notes and Queries." *Ladies' Repository: A Monthly Periodical, Devoted to Literature, Arts, and Religion* 22, no. 8 (August 1862): 501–2.

"Our Book Review." *Vanity Fair* 4 (August 10, 1861): 70.

"A Page of History." *Papers from the Society for the Diffusion of Political Knowledge.* New York: Society for the Diffusion of Political Knowledge, 1863–64.

"Patent-Medicine Makers—Morrison, Brandreth, Townsend, etc." In *Cyclopaedia of Commercial and Business Anecdotes,* edited by Richard Miller Devens, vol. 2. New York: D. Appleton, 1864.

"Peremptory Sale." *Vanity Fair* 5 (January 18, 1862): 40.

"The Philosophy of Advertising." *Merchants' Magazine and Commercial Review* 23, no. 5 (November 1, 1850): 580–81.

Pittenger, William. *Daring and Suffering: A History of the Great Railroad Adventure.* Philadelphia: J. W. Daughaday, 1863.

Prescott, Harriet E. "Yet's Christmas Box." *Harper's New Monthly Magazine* 20, no. 119 (April 1860): 644–59.

"Proposals for a New Dictionary of the English Language." *Vanity Fair* 5 (May 10, 1862): 229.

"Pugilistic Piety." *Vanity Fair* 2 (October 18, 1860): 191.

"Recent Publications." *Christian Review* 26 (October 1861): 654–86.

Redpath, James. *The Public Life of Capt. John Brown.* Boston: Thayer and Eldridge, 1860.

Redwood, Allen C. "A Boy in Gray." *Scribner's Monthly* 22, no. 5 (September 1881): 641–50.

"Reform Needed," *Vanity Fair* 1 (April 14, 1860): 254.

"Relations of the Negro Race to Civilization." *De Bow's Review* 28, no. 6 (December 1860): 638–47.

"Revenue of the Commonwealth of Pennsylvania." *Report of the Auditor General, on the Finances of the Commonwealth of Pennsylvania, For the Year Ending November 30, 1862.* Harrisburg: Singerly and Myers, 1863.

"Reviews and Literary Notices: Cochin's Results of Emancipation." *Atlantic Monthly* 11, no. 65 (March 1863): 395–97.

Richardson, Albert. *The Secret Service, the Field, the Dungeon, and the Escape.* Hartford, CT: American Publishing Co., 1865.

Ringwalt, John Luther. "Advertisement." *American Enyclopaedia of Printing.* Philadelphia: Menamin and Ringwalt, 1871.

Russell, William Howard. *My Diary North and South.* Boston: T. O. H. P. Burnham, 1863.

"Sad Case of Pictorial Paralysis." *Vanity Fair* 5 (May 24, 1862): 250.

Sala, George Augustus. *My Diary in America in the Midst of War.* London: Tinsley Brothers, 1865.

Smucker, Samuel Mosheim. *The Yankee Slave Driver, or, the Black and White Rivals.* New York: H. Dayton, 1860.

Soldiers' Letters from Camp, Battle-field and Prison. Edited by Lydia Minturn Post. New York: Bunce and Huntington, 1865.

Sumner, Charles. *"The Barbarism of Slavery": Speech of Hon. Charles Sumner on the Bill for the Admission of Kansas as a Free State.* Washington, DC: Buell and Blanchard, 1860.

Tennant, Charles. *The American Question and How to Settle It.* London: S. Low, Son, and Co., 1863.

"To Owners of Sharp Sticks," *Vanity Fair* 4 (August 31, 1861): 100.

Trent, W. P. "Gleanings from an Old Southern Newspaper." *Atlantic Monthly* 86, no. 515 (September 1900): 356–64.

"Two Immense Treats." *Vanity Fair* 4 (November 23, 1861): 237.

U.S. War Department. *The War of the Rebellion: A Compilation of the Official Records of the Union and Confederate Armies* (cited as "O.R."). 128 parts in 70 vols. Washington, DC: Government Printing Office, 1880–1901.

Wakeman, George. "Advertising." *Galaxy* 3, no. 2 (January 1867): 202–12.

———. "Verbal Anomalies," *Galaxy* 2, no. 1 (September 1866): 29–39.

"The War—How It Began and What Keeps It Up." *Old Guard* 2, no. 1 (January 1864): 1–7.

"A Well-Digested Plan for the Relief of Richmond." *Southern Literary Messenger* 37, no. 12 (December 1863): 726–32.

"What Is a Square?" *Advertisers Gazette: A Monthly Journal Devoted to the Interests of Advertisers and Newspaper Publishers* 2, no. 6 (April 1868): 4.

"Wooden School Slates." *Scientific American* 1003, no. 19 (November 3, 1860): 298.

SECONDARY SOURCES

Aaron, Daniel. *The Unwritten War: American Writers and the Civil War.* Madison: University of Wisconsin Press, 1987.

Abel, E. Lawrence. *Confederate Sheet Music.* Jefferson, NC: McFarland, 2004.

Altschuler, Glenn C., and Stuart M. Blumin. *Rude Republic: Americans and Their Politics in the Nineteenth Century.* Princeton, NJ: Princeton University Press, 2000.

Anderson, Paul Christopher. *Blood Image: Turner Ashby in the Civil War and the Southern Mind.* Baton Rouge: Louisiana State University Press, 2006.

Andrews, J. Cutler. *The North Reports the Civil War.* Pittsburgh: University of Pittsburgh Press, 1955.

———. *The South Reports the Civil War.* Princeton, NJ: Princeton University Press, 1970.

Baker, Jean H. *Affairs of Party: The Political Culture of Northern Democrats in the Mid-Nineteenth Century.* Ithaca, NY: Cornell University Press, 1983.

Baldasty, Gerald J. *The Commercialization of News in the Nineteenth Century.* Madison: University of Wisconsin Press, 1992.

Ball, Douglas B. *Financial Failure and Confederate Defeat.* Urbana: University of Illinois Press, 1991.

Berlin, Ira, Joseph P. Reidy, and Leslie S. Rowland, eds. *Freedom's Soldiers: The Black Military Experience in the Civil War.* New York: Cambridge University Press, 1998.

Bernstein, Iver. *The New York City Draft Riots: Their Significance for American Society and Politics in the Age of the Civil War.* New York: Oxford University Press, 1990.

Berry, Stephen William. *All That Makes a Man: Love and Ambition in the Civil War South.* New York: Oxford University Press, 2003.

Bezanson, Randall P. *Taxes on Knowledge in America: Exactions on the Press from Colonial Times to the Present.* Philadelphia: University of Pennsylvania Press, 1994.

Blight, David W. *Beyond the Battlefield: Race, Memory, and the American Civil War.* Amherst: University of Massachusetts Press, 2002.

———. *Race and Reunion: The Civil War in American Memory.* Cambridge: Harvard University Press, 2001.

Blondheim, Menahem. *News over the Wires: The Telegraph and the Flow of Public Information in America, 1844–1897.* Cambridge: Harvard University Press, 1994.

Boorstin, Daniel J. *The Americans: The Democratic Experience.* New York: Random House, 1973.

Bosse, David C. *Civil War Newspaper Maps: A Historical Atlas.* Baltimore: Johns Hopkins University Press, 1993.

Brodie, Janet Farrell. *Contraception and Abortion in Nineteenth-Century America.* Ithaca, NY: Cornell University Press, 1994.

Bruce, Susannah Ural. *The Harp and the Eagle: Irish-American Volunteers and the Union Army, 1861–1865.* New York: New York University Press, 2006.

Burton, William L. *Melting Pot Soldiers: The Union's Ethnic Regiments.* New York: Fordham University Press, 1998.

Carnes, Mark C., and Clyde Griffin, eds. *Meanings for Manhood: Constructions of Masculinity in Victorian America*. Chicago: University of Chicago Press, 1990.

Cohen, Lizabeth. *A Consumer's Republic: The Politics of Mass Consumption in Postwar America*. New York: Knopf, 2003.

Cook, Robert J. *Civil War Memories: Contesting the Past in the United States since 1865*. Baltimore: Johns Hopkins University Press, 2017.

Cook, Robert J., William L. Barney, and Elizabeth R. Varon. *Secession Winter: When the Union Fell Apart*. Baltimore: Johns Hopkins University Press, 2013.

Coopersmith, Andrew Seth. *Fighting Words: An Illustrated History of Newspaper Accounts of the Civil War*. New York: Norton, 2004.

Cornish, Dudley Taylor. *The Sable Arm: Black Troops in the Union Army, 1861–1865*. Reprint, Lawrence: University Press of Kansas, 1987.

Cozzens, Peter. *This Terrible Sound: The Battle of Chickamauga*. Urbana: University of Illinois Press, 1992.

Cushman, Stephen. *Bloody Promenade: Reflections on a Civil War Battle*. Charlottesville: University of Virginia Press, 1999.

Dean, Eric T. *Shook over Hell: Post-Traumatic Stress, Vietnam, and the Civil War*. Cambridge: Harvard University Press, 1997.

Devine, Shauna. *Learning from the Wounded: The Civil War and the Rise of American Medical Science*. Chapel Hill: University of North Carolina Press, 2014.

Dew, Charles B. *Ironmaker to the Confederacy: Joseph R. Anderson and the Tredegar Iron Works*. New Haven: Yale University Press, 1966.

Deyle, Steven. *Carry Me Back: The Domestic Slave Trade in American Life*. New York: Oxford University Press, 2005.

Dunkelman, Mark H. *Brothers One and All: Esprit de Corps in a Civil War Regiment*. Baton Rouge: Louisiana State University Press, 2004.

Egerton, Douglas R. *Year of the Meteors: Stephen Douglas, Abraham Lincoln, and the Election That Brought on the Civil War*. New York: Bloomsbury, 2010.

Escott, Paul D. *After Secession: Jefferson Davis and the Failure of Confederate Nationalism*. Baton Rouge: Louisiana State University Press, 1978.

Fahs, Alice. *The Imagined Civil War: Popular Literature of the North and South, 1861–1865*. Chapel Hill: University of North Carolina Press, 2001.

Faust, Drew Gilpin. *The Creation of Confederate Nationalism: Ideology and Identity in the Civil War South*. Baton Rouge: Louisiana State University Press, 1988.

———. *This Republic of Suffering: Death and the American Civil War*. New York: Knopf, 2008.

Flannery, Michael A. *Civil War Pharmacy: A History of Drugs, Drug Supply and Provision, and Therapeutics for the Union and Confederacy*. New York: Pharmaceutical Products Press, 2004.

Foner, Eric. *Free Soil, Free Labor, Free Men: The Ideology of the Republican Party before the Civil War.* New York: Oxford University Press, 1970.

Foote, Lorien. *The Gentlemen and the Roughs: Manhood, Honor, and Violence in the Union Army.* New York: New York University Press, 2010.

Fox, Stephen. *The Mirror Makers: A History of American Advertising and Its Creators.* New York: William Morrow, 1984.

Franklin, John Hope, and Loren Schweninger. *Runaway Slaves: Rebels on the Plantation.* New York: Oxford University Press, 1999.

Frassanito, William A. *Antietam: The Photographic Legacy of America's Bloodiest Day.* New York: Scribner, 1978.

Freemon, Frank R. *Gangrene and Glory: Medical Care during the American Civil War.* Urbana: University of Illinois Press, 2001.

Friend, Craig Thompson, and Lorri Glover, eds. *Southern Manhood: Perspectives on Masculinity in the Old South.* Athens: University of Georgia Press, 2004.

Gallagher, Gary W. *The Confederate War: How Popular Will, Nationalism, and Military Strategy Could Not Stave Off Defeat.* Cambridge: Harvard University Press, 1997.

———. *The Union War.* Cambridge: Harvard University Press, 2011.

Gallman, J. Matthew. *Defining Duty in the Civil War: Personal Choice, Popular Culture, and the Union Home Front.* Chapel Hill: University of North Carolina Press, 2015.

Gienapp, William E. "'Politics Seem to Enter into Everything': Political Culture in the North." In *Essays on Antebellum American Politics, 1840–1860,* edited by Stephen E. Maizlish and John J. Kushma. College Station: Texas A&M University Press, 1982.

Giesberg, Judith Ann. *Army at Home: Women and the Civil War on the Northern Home Front.* Chapel Hill: University of North Carolina Press, 2009.

———. *Civil War Sisterhood: The U.S. Sanitary Commission and Women's Politics in Transition.* Boston: Northeastern University Press, 2000.

———. *Sex and the Civil War: Soldiers, Pornography, and the Making of American Morality.* Chapel Hill: University of North Carolina Press, 2017.

Glatthaar, Joseph T. *Forged in Battle: The Civil War Alliance of Black Soldiers and White Officers.* New York: Free Press, 1990.

Greenberg, Amy S. *Manifest Manhood and the Antebellum American Empire.* New York: Cambridge University Press, 2005.

Grimsley, Mark. *The Hard Hand of War: Union Military Policy toward Southern Civilians, 1861–1865.* New York: Cambridge University Press, 1995.

Grinspan, Jon. "'Young Men for War': The Wide Awakes and Lincoln's 1860 Presidential Campaign." *Journal of American History* 96 (September 2009): 357–78.

Gudmestad, Robert H. *A Troublesome Commerce: The Transformation of the Interstate Slave Trade.* Baton Rouge: Louisiana State University Press, 2003.

Halttunen, Karen. *Confidence Men and Painted Women: A Study of Middle-Class Culture in America, 1830–1870*. New Haven: Yale University Press, 1982.

Harris, Brayton. *Blue and Gray in Black and White: Newspapers in the Civil War*. Washington, DC: Brassey's 1999.

Heller, Dana, ed. *The Selling of 9/11: How a National Tragedy Became a Commodity*. New York: Palgrave Macmillan, 2005.

Henkin, David M. *City Reading: Written Words and Public Spaces in Antebellum New York*. New York: Columbia University Press, 1998.

Hodes, Martha Elizabeth. *Mourning Lincoln*. New Haven: Yale University Press, 2015.

Holzer, Harold. *Lincoln and the Power of the Press: The War for Public Opinion*. New York: Simon and Schuster, 2014.

Holzer, Harold, Gabor S. Borrit, and Mark E. Neely Jr. *The Lincoln Image: Abraham Lincoln and the Popular Print*. Urbana: University of Illinois Press, 1984.

Horowitz, Helen Lefkowitz. *Attitudes toward Sex in Antebellum America: A Brief History with Documents*. New York: Palgrave Macmillan, 2006.

Horrocks, Thomas A. *Lincoln's Campaign Biographies*. Carbondale: Southern Illinois University Press, 2014.

Houze, Herbert G., Carolyn C. Cooper, and Elizabeth M. Kornhauser. *Samuel Colt: Arms, Art, and Invention*. New Haven: Yale University Press, 2006.

Howe, Daniel Walker. *The Political Culture of the American Whigs*. Chicago: University of Chicago Press, 1979.

Hudson, Frederic. *Journalism in the United States from 1690 to 1872*. New York: Harper and Brothers, 1872.

Humphreys, Margaret. *Marrow of Tragedy: The Health Crisis of the American Civil War*. Baltimore: Johns Hopkins University Press, 2013.

Huntzicker, William. *The Popular Press, 1833–1865*. Westport, CT: Greenwood, 1999.

Janney, Caroline E. *Remembering the Civil War: Reunion and the Limits of Reconciliation*. Chapel Hill: University of North Carolina Press, 2013.

Jordan, Brian M. *Marching Home: Union Veterans and Their Unending Civil War*. New York: Liveright, 2014.

Kelley, Mary. *Private Women, Public Stage: Literary Domesticity in Nineteenth-Century America*. New York: Oxford University Press, 1984.

Kett, Joseph F. *Rites of Passage: Adolescence in America, 1790 to the Present*. New York: Basic, 1977.

Kreidberg, Marvin A., and Merton G. Henry. *History of Military Mobilization in the United States Army, 1775–1945*. Reprint, Westport, CT: Greenwood, 1975.

Laird, Pamela Walker. *Advertising Progress: American Business and the Rise of Consumer Marketing*. Baltimore: Johns Hopkins University Press, 1998.

Larson, Harriet M. *Jay Cooke: Private Banker.* Cambridge: Harvard University Press, 1936.

Lawson, Melinda. *Patriot Fires: Forging a New American Nationalism in the Civil War North.* Lawrence: University Press of Kansas, 2002.

Lears, Jackson. *Fables of Abundance: A Cultural History of Advertising in America.* New York: Basic, 1994.

Lee, Alfred McClung. *The Daily Newspaper in America: The Evolution of a Social Instrument.* New York: Macmillan, 1937.

Lehuu, Isabelle. *Carnival on the Page: Popular Print Media in Antebellum America.* Chapel Hill: University of North Carolina Press, 2000.

Lewin, J. G., and P. J. Huff. *Lines of Contention: Political Cartoons of the Civil War.* New York: Collins, 2007.

Long, David E. *The Jewel of Liberty: Abraham Lincoln's Reelection and the End of Slavery.* Mechanicsburg, PA: Stackpole, 1994.

Lonn, Ella. *Desertion during the Civil War.* Reprint, Lincoln: University of Nebraska Press, 1998.

———. *Foreigners in the Union Army and Navy.* Baton Rouge: Louisiana State University Press, 1951.

Lystra, Karen. *Searching the Heart: Women, Men, and Romantic Love in Nineteenth-Century America.* New York: Oxford University Press, 1989.

Manning, Chandra. *What This Cruel War Was Over: Soldiers, Slavery, and the Civil War.* New York: Knopf, 2007.

Marten, James A., ed. *Children and Youth during the Civil War Era.* New York: New York University Press, 2012.

———. *Children for the Union: The War Spirit on the Northern Home Front.* Chicago: Ivan R. Dee, 2004.

Martinez, Jaime Amanda. *Confederate Slave Impressment in the Upper South.* Chapel Hill: University of North Carolina Press, 2013.

McCaffrey, James M. *Army of Manifest Destiny: The American Soldier in the Mexican War, 1846–1848.* New York: New York University Press, 1992.

McCardell, John. *The Idea of a Southern Nation: Southern Nationalists and Southern Nationalism, 1830—1860.* New York: Norton, 1979.

McClintock, Russell. *Lincoln and the Decision for War: The Northern Response to Secession.* Chapel Hill: University of North Carolina Press, 2008.

McCurry, Stephanie. *Confederate Reckoning: Power and Politics in the Civil War South.* Cambridge: Harvard University Press, 2010.

McGovern, Charles. *Sold American: Consumption and Citizenship, 1890–1945.* Chapel Hill: University of North Carolina Press, 2006.

McKivigan, John R. *Forgotten Firebrand: James Redpath and the Making of Nineteenth-Century America*. Ithaca, NY: Cornell University Press, 2008.

McPherson, James M. *Crossroads of Freedom: Antietam*. New York: Oxford University Press, 2002.

———. *For Cause and Comrades: Why Men Fought in the Civil War*. New York: Oxford University Press, 1997.

———. *War on the Waters: The Union and Confederate Navies, 1861–1865*. Chapel Hill: University of North Carolina Press, 2012.

Meier, Kathryn Shively. *Nature's Civil War: Common Soldiers and the Environment in 1862 Virginia*. Chapel Hill: University of North Carolina Press, 2013.

Miller, Brian Craig. *Empty Sleeves: Amputation in the Civil War South*. Athens: University of Georgia Press, 2015.

Mitchell, Reid. *Civil War Soldiers: Their Expectations and Their Experiences*. New York: Viking, 1988.

Moore, Albert Burton. *Conscription and Conflict in the Confederacy*. Reprint, Columbia: University of South Carolina Press, 1996.

Murdock, Eugene C. *One Million Men: The Civil War Draft in the North*. Madison: State Historical Society of Wisconsin, 1971.

———. *Patriotism Limited, 1862–1865: The Civil War Draft and the Bounty System*. Kent, OH: Kent State University Press, 1971.

Neely, Mark E, Jr. *The Boundaries of American Political Culture in the Civil War Era*. Chapel Hill: University of North Carolina Press, 2005.

Noe, Kenneth W. *Reluctant Rebels: The Confederates Who Joined the Army after 1861*. Chapel Hill: University of North Carolina Press, 2010.

Oakes, James. *Freedom National: The Destruction of Slavery in the United States, 1861–1865*. New York: Norton, 2013.

Oberholtzer, Ellis P. *Jay Cooke: Financier of the Civil War*. Vol. 1. Philadelphia: G. W. Jacobs, 1907.

Pope, Daniel. *The Making of Modern Advertising*. New York: Basic, 1983.

Presbrey, Frank. *The History and Development of Advertising*. Garden City, NY: Doubleday, 1929.

Quigley, Paul. *Shifting Grounds: Nationalism and the American South, 1848–1865*. New York: Oxford University Press, 2012.

Rable, George C. *Civil Wars: Women and the Crisis of Southern Nationalism*. Urbana: University of Illinois Press, 1989.

———. *Damn Yankees! Demonization and Defiance in the Confederate South*. Baton Rouge: Louisiana State University Press, 2015.

Ramold, Steven J. *Across the Divide: Union Soldiers View the Northern Homefront*. New York: New York University Press, 2013.

Risley, Ford. *Abolition and the Press: The Moral Struggle against Slavery.* Evanston, IL: Northwestern University Press, 2008.

———. *Civil War Journalism.* Santa Barbara, CA: Praeger, 2012.

Robertson, James I., Jr. *Soldiers Blue and Gray.* Columbia: University of South Carolina Press, 1998.

Rothman, Ellen K. *Hands and Hearts: A History of Courtship in America.* New York: Basic, 1984.

Rubin, Anne Sarah. *A Shattered Nation: The Rise and Fall of the Confederacy, 1861–1868.* Chapel Hill: University of North Carolina Press, 2005.

Rutkow, Ira M. *Bleeding Blue and Gray: Civil War Surgery and the Evolution of American Medicine.* New York: Random House, 2005.

Sachsman, David B., S. Kittrell Rushing, and Roy Morris, Jr., eds. *Words at War: The Civil War and American Journalism.* West Lafayette, IN: Purdue University Press, 2008.

Sampson, Henry. *A History of Advertising from the Earliest Times.* London: Chatto and Windus, 1874.

Samuels, Shirley. *Facing America: Iconography and the Civil War.* New York: Oxford University Press, 2004.

Sauers, Richard A., and Peter Tomasak. *The Fishing Creek Confederacy: A Story of Civil War Draft Resistance.* Columbia: University of Missouri Press, 2012.

Schantz, Mark S. *Awaiting the Heavenly Country: The Civil War and America's Culture of Death.* Ithaca, NY: Cornell University Press, 2008.

Schermerhorn, Calvin. *The Business of Slavery and the Rise of American Capitalism, 1815–1860.* New Haven, CT: Yale University Press, 2015.

Sears, Stephen W. *Landscape Turned Red: The Battle of Antietam.* New Haven, CT: Ticknor and Fields, 1983.

Silber, Nina. *Daughters of the Union: Northern Women Fight the Civil War.* Cambridge: Harvard University Press, 2005.

Simpson, Brooks D. *Let Us Have Peace: Ulysses S. Grant and the Politics of War and Reconstruction, 1861–1868.* Chapel Hill: University of North Carolina Press, 1991.

Smith, Culver H. *The Press, Politics and Patronage: The American Government's Use of Newspapers, 1789–1875.* Athens: University of Georgia Press, 1977.

Smith, Jean Edward. *Grant.* New York: Simon and Schuster, 2001.

Smith, Kristen M., ed. *The Lines Are Drawn: Political Cartoons of the Civil War.* Athens, GA: Hill Street, 1999.

Smith, Michael Thomas. *The Enemy Within: Fears of Corruption in the Civil War North.* Charlottesville: University of Virginia Press, 2011.

Stampp, Kenneth M. *And the War Came: The North and the Secession Crisis, 1860–1861.* Baton Rouge: Louisiana State University Press, 1950.

Starr, Louis M. *Bohemian Brigade, Civil War Newsmen in Action.* New York: Knopf, 1954.

Steigerwald, David. "All Hail the Republic of Choice: Consumer History as Contemporary Thought." *Journal of American History* 93, no. 2 (September 2006): 385–403.

Sutton, Albert A. *Design and Makeup of the Newspaper.* New York: Prentice-Hall, 1948.

Tadman, Michael. *Speculators and Slaves: Masters, Traders, and Slaves in the Old South.* Madison: University of Wisconsin Press, 1989.

Thomas, Emory. *The Confederate Nation: 1861–1865.* New York: Harper Torchbooks, 1979.

Toll, Robert C. *Blacking Up: The Minstrel Show in Nineteenth-Century America.* New York: Oxford University Press, 1974.

Turner, E. S. *The Shocking History of Advertising!* New York: Dutton, 1953.

van Tuyll, Debra Reddin. *The Confederate Press in the Crucible of the American Civil War.* New York: Peter Lang, 2013.

Walters, Ronald G., ed. *Primers for Prudery: Sexual Advice to Victorian America.* Updated ed. Baltimore: Johns Hopkins University Press, 2000.

Warshauer, Matthew. *Connecticut in the American Civil War: Slavery, Sacrifice, and Survival.* Middletown, CT: Wesleyan University Press, 2012.

Waugh, Joan. *U.S. Grant: American Hero, American Myth.* Chapel Hill: University of North Carolina Press, 2009.

Waugh, John C. *Reelecting Lincoln: The Battle for the 1864 Presidency.* New York: Crown, 1997.

Weitz, Mark A. *More Damning Than Slaughter: Desertion in the Confederate Army.* Lincoln: University of Nebraska Press, 2005.

White, Jonathan W. *Emancipation, the Union Army, and the Reelection of Abraham Lincoln.* Baton Rouge: Louisiana State University Press, 2014.

Wiley, Bell I. *The Life of Billy Yank: The Common Soldier of the Union.* Indianapolis: Bobbs-Merrill, 1952.

———. *The Life of Johnny Reb: The Common Soldier of the Confederacy.* Indianapolis: Bobbs-Merrill, 1943.

Wilson, Edmund. *Patriotic Gore: Studies in Literature of the American Civil War.* New York: Oxford University Press, 1962.

Winders, Richard B. *Mr. Polk's Army: The American Military Experience in the Mexican War.* College Station: Texas A&M University Press, 1997.

Windley, Lathan A. *Runaway Slave Advertisements: A Documentary History from the 1730s to 1790.* 4 vols. Westport, CT: Greenwood, 1983.

Wood, James P. *The Story of Advertising.* New York: Ronald, 1958.

Young, James Harvey. *American Self-Dosage Medicines: An Historical Perspective.* Lawrence, KS: Coronado, 1974.

———. *The Toadstool Millionaires: A Social History of Patent Medicines in America before Federal Regulation.* Princeton, NJ: Princeton University Press, 1961.

WEBSITES

Davis, William C. "American Civil War Newspapers." Virginia Center for Civil War Studies, Virginia Polytechnic Institute and State University. https://dcr.emd.vt.edu/vital/access/manager/Index?site_name=American%20Civil%20War%20Newspaper.

Edwards, Jim. "The 10 Best Subliminal Ads Ever Made." CBS Moneywatch. October 20, 2011. www.cbsnews.com/news/the-10-best-subliminal-ads-ever-made/.

Frazier, Ian. "All Consuming Patriotism." *Mother Jones.* March/April 2002. www.motherjones.com/politics/2002/03/all-consuming-patriotism.

Love, Dylan. "The Shocking Drink and Incredible Coke History of Subliminal Advertising." Business Insider, May 26, 2011. www.businessinsider.com/subliminal-ads-2011-5 (2017).

"Political Cartoons, 1860–1870." Library of Congress. www.loc.gov/pictures/related/?fi=format&q=Political%20cartoons—1860–1870.

Rieck, Dean. "9 Proven Headline Formulas That Sell Like Crazy." Copyblogger Media. 2014. www.copyblogger.com/proven-headline-formulas/.

INDEX